THE PREACHER'S LIBRARY

The aim of this small collection of new books is to help preachers with the basic problems of their task of proclaiming the Christian Gospel under modern conditions. Titles already published are *The Living Word* by Gustaf Wingren; *A Gospel Without Myth?* by David Cairns; *The Theology of Dietrich Bonhoeffer* by John D. Godsey; *The Interpretation of Scripture* by James D. Smart; and *Theology and Church* by Karl Barth.

❖

GOD LOVES LIKE THAT!
The Theology of James Denney

GOD LOVES LIKE THAT!

THE THEOLOGY OF JAMES DENNEY

❖

JOHN RANDOLPH TAYLOR

with a Foreword by
A. M. HUNTER

SCM PRESS LTD
BLOOMSBURY STREET LONDON

FIRST PUBLISHED 1962
© JOHN RANDOLPH TAYLOR 1962
PRINTED IN GREAT BRITAIN BY
ROBERT CUNNINGHAM AND SONS LTD
ALVA, SCOTLAND

To
H. KERR TAYLOR
my father
in the faith
as well as in the flesh

CONTENTS

FOREWORD

'THE whirligig of time brings in his revenges.' Those of us who have lived through the first half of this century have witnessed a remarkable swing-back of the theological pendulum and the rediscovery of some almost forgotten men. P. T. Forsyth is a shining example. But there was a contemporary of Forsyth's—like himself a Scotsman—of whom he once wrote: 'He has more important things to say than anyone at present writing on theology.' The man was James Denney; and it is his theology which is the theme of this book by John Randolph Taylor, the distinguished minister of the Church of the Pilgrims, Washington.

The book has long been needed. Denney died in 1917; but, though two volumes of his letters were published after his death, for one reason or another—perhaps it was the aftermath of World War I, with all its weariness and confusion—no adequate *critique* of this theology ever appeared. Accordingly, half a dozen years ago, when Dr Taylor was in Scotland doing some post-graduate work, I told him of the gap and invited him to fill it. So, for two years, Dr Taylor not only read all that Dr Denney had written but talked with many who had known him. The result is this fine book, and I may add that the substance of it received the admiring *imprimatur* of Denney's best pupil, Professor William Manson, before he died.

That Denney was, in A. B. Macaulay's phrase, 'an alpha plus scholar' goes without saying—at Glasgow University he took 'a double first'. But he was also a tremendous moral force and a great person. Like his favourite Dr Johnson, he held strong opinions on men and movements, as he had the same enviable gift of clothing his judgments in epigrammatic and trenchant speech. If I resist the temptation to quote some of his *obiter dicta* here—and every Scots minister worthy of his salt knows some—it is because Dr Taylor has sprinkled his pages with the choicest of them.

Yet, after all, it is Denney's theology which is our main concern, and at the risk of trespassing on Dr Taylor's preserves I must say just enough about it to whet the reader's appetite for what is to follow.

What was it that distinguished Denney's work from that of other fine scholars in the Biblical field? It was, said Dr Hastings Rashdall, 'his *passionate* scholarship'. To scholarship of the first rank he brought a burning conviction of the truth and adequacy of the Gospel, and he would have no truck with those who, desiring to be in tune with the Zeitgeist, would have watered it down. In all his writing about the Christian faith he sought, as Dr Taylor shows, to be Biblical, real, whole and clear, and he often declared that he had not the faintest interest in a theology which would not preach. 'If kings were philosophers or philosophers kings, we should have the ideal state, according to Plato. If evangelists were our theologians or theologians our evangelists, we should be nearer the ideal Church.'

Denney could write with power and insight on all the chief Christian doctrines, but it was the Atonement which was the centre of his theological thinking. 'Not Bethlehem but Calvary', he said, 'is the focus of revelation in the New Testament.' And, stout Protestant though he was, he used to say that he envied the Roman Catholic priest his crucifix. 'I would like to go into every church in the land', he said, 'and, holding up the crucifix, cry to the congregation "God loves like that".' For Denney, then, the Cross was 'the hiding-place of God's power and the inspiration of all Christian praise'. And that is why in this book Dr Taylor, while not neglecting Denney on the other doctrines, devotes two chapters to his thought about the Atonement.

There are just two more things that I want to say briefly to the reader. Though forty years have passed since he died, Denney's work has not lost its relevancy and force. His writing, like Forsyth's, has 'dated' very little. (When I read him, it is only in the matter of New Testament eschatology—a subject which in our day, thanks to Dodd and others, has made immense advances—that I find him a little outmoded.) If you doubt this, read his *Studies in Theology* given, in lecture-form, to students in Chicago as long ago as 1895.

The other thing is this. In Denney you find what you do not always find in our modern theologians—be it Barth or Tillich—what is in fact one of the first virtues of great theological writing—perfect lucidity of thought and expression. He had drilled himself on Burke, and he always wrote with pellucid precision.

Here, then, in this book, is the theology of a great Scotsman penetratingly expounded by an able young American minister. Theological passion and power married to complete clarity of exposition is not a common combination. But there is God's plenty of it in Denney, as Dr Taylor will show you. Over now to him!

                                                      A. M. HUNTER

Christ's College,
Aberdeen

PREFACE

At dawn of a September day in 1954, my wife and I looked over the starboard rail of an ocean liner at a seaport nestled near the base of a green hill which dipped abruptly to touch the water on the south shore of the Firth of Clyde. It was our first view of Scotland. The town was Greenock, the community where James Denney grew up as a child. For the next two years we saw his country through his eyes, although he himself had been dead for over three decades. His name still carries magic in the minds of many men who knew him, and the legend of the man lingers in the life and literature of the scholars, the pastors and the members of the Church of Scotland. From the professor's study in Aberdeen, to the rock garden in Bearsden, to the vestry in Glasgow, the discovery and discussion of James Denney moved on until one came to feel that the insights of this man and his works are too good to keep, and must be shared with the oncoming generations of churchmen, who more often than not are coming to think like him but who do not realize the relationship.

To study theology through the mind of Denney and to read the Scripture and the world through his eyes is to enter into an intensely interesting and intriguing experience. Denney cast his spell upon those who sat under him in his day; he casts it still. It is possible to be considerably more objective about his contributions to Biblical theology than it would have been during his lifetime, but even from this distance it is possible to feel the force of his personality and his mind and to be drawn into a personal loyalty to him. I confess to this sense of loyalty. It was not there when I began; it has asserted itself in the course of the study. The fact that theology in the twentieth century has taken such a course that Denney is more than just a figure of the past, but a man who serves as a bridge to our understanding of contemporary theology and who speaks with prophetic voice to our own day, has given this personal interest a remarkable relevancy.

I owe a debt of gratitude to a great many persons who have given me assistance along the course of this inquiry into Denney's theological contribution. Above all my thanks are due to Professor A. M. Hunter, of the University of Aberdeen, who introduced me to Denney and to the challenge of this study in a hotel lobby in Richmond, Virginia, and who in hundreds of conversations—in his study, at the fireside, over steaming cups of tea, camping under the Cuillins or tramping alongside the River Dee—gave guidance and criticism and inspiration. I am also indebted to Professor John Macleod and the late Professor G. D. Henderson, both of Aberdeen University, and the late Professor William Manson, of New College, Edinburgh, for their helpful counsel.

There have been a number of men who have personal memories of Principal Denney, some of them having sat in his classroom, which they have kindly shared with me either in correspondence or in personal conference. I am indebted for this service to the following: the Rev. Alexander Borland, Barrhead, Renfrewshire; the Rev. J. Christian Brown, Glasgow; the Rev. Dr John W. Coutts, Kinross; the Rev. Dr W. H. Hamilton, Insch, Aberdeenshire; the Rev. Dr George Johnstone Jeffrey, Glasgow; the Rev. Philip W. Lilley, Helensburgh, Dunbartonshire; the Rev. Graham Park, Aberdeen; Mr R. Buchanan Reith, Newcastle-upon-Tyne; the Rev. Dr Alexander Ross, Burghead, Morayshire; the Rev. David B. Smith, Saltcoats, Ayrshire; the Rev. James Wishart, Cults, Aberdeenshire.

Several institutions have been generous in making available to me their library facilities; especially, Kings' College, Aberdeen; Christ's College, Aberdeen; Trinity College, Glasgow; the Mitchell Library, Glasgow; and New College, Edinburgh.

I am particularly grateful to Lady C. Robertson Nicoll, who received me hospitably in her home in Lumsden, Aberdeenshire, under the shadow of the Correen Hills, where we talked together with her late husband's library towering around us on all sides, and where she gave me access to a collector's volume in which her husband, Sir William Robertson Nicoll, had kept letters and clippings from many sources, all of them having to do with Denney and most of them concerning the volume of his letters which Nicoll published in 1920.

On this side of the water, I am indebted to the faculty of the Union Theological Seminary, Richmond, Virginia, whose Walter W. Moore Fellowship enabled me to undertake the study in Scotland, and to Mrs Thell C. Williams and a gracious company of other friends whose generosity enabled me to remain long enough to complete the work. As the manuscript has been made ready for the printer, I have been thankful for the assistance of the Union Theological Seminary in Virginia and for the cool and quiet of their library during the hot summer of 1960, and to the John Knox Press, as well as to my father, for their helpful advice. To Mrs Robert C. Kuehling and Mrs Eric R. Radhe I am indebted for their assistance in typing the manuscript.

And to the fine and patient people of the Church of the Pilgrims, who not only bore with me but encouraged me during the time of revision, is due my enduring gratitude for this and for all their many kindnesses.

It is not enough to read about Denney. He himself must be read to be appreciated. Any book about him must recognize before it begins that at the very best it could only be a sign post offering in shadowed outline an invitation to meet this man and his thought. I shall feel a genuine sense of fulfillment if the reader puts down this volume with an intense desire to take up the works of Denney himself and to become acquainted with the Principal from Glasgow.

JOHN RANDOLPH TAYLOR

Washington, D.C.

I

THE THEOLOGICAL PROPHET

As theologian and as man, there was no one like him.
H. R. Mackintosh[1]

WE are living in the midst of a theological revolution. The faith of men and women, young and old, has felt the force of the changes which have shaken our society within the twentieth century and people are asking new questions, and asking the old questions with new meaning. A world conditioned by scientific inquiry, disciplined by the tragedies of history and threatened by the possibility of racial suicide will not be satisfied by rigidly patterned answers of traditionalism. Consequently, we are experiencing a new birth of theological interest, and the whole range of theology has come alive in a day of revaluation and reformation. Because faith is so serious, men search desperately for guidance in such a shifting sea of change. All of us—ministers and laymen, students and teachers—know something of this search for a voice of stability and assurance.

An American professor—young and well-informed—testified recently that when his students reached that point of desperation he had found no man who was better able to give stability and guidance than James Denney. What a surprise to discover that this man, Denney, was born a hundred years ago! Yet, what is even more startling is the discovery that his writings ring with the contemporaneous notes of current interest. Here was a man who was writing at the beginning of this century and who was raising then many of the questions which currently concern us; a man whose works carry such contemporary concepts as the emphasis upon the revelation of the Word, the insistence upon faith existentially held, the understanding of realized eschatology, the appreciation and use of the insights of higher criticism, the insistence upon the primary place in the New Testament of the primitive *kerygma*, and the importance of the ecumenical church. Such a man speaks from another age with insights into our own. He gives an historical perspective to the shifting concerns of the present hour and provides a prophetic voice in theology for our time.

Denney helps us also to bridge the period of development which has led up to our contemporary theological world. Born at the height of the period of firm orthodoxy in Britain and America, he grew up in the midst of the shift toward liberalism, and out of the discipline of that dialogue he began to search for clearer answers to the deepest longings within men. He gives guidance along a course in balance between rigid patterns of thought on the one hand and the sacrifice of the core of Christianity on the other, and thus he helps us to span a whole century of theology and leads us beyond both orthodoxy and liberalism into a new day of reformation in theology.

In all of this, he gives us a good insight into what is lasting. The value of Denney's work is that he was grappling with fundamental problems of faith and did not concern himself with details along the periphery. The themes of his theology are the basic doctrines of Christian belief and experience, the themes of reconciliation and of revelation as they are found in the life and death and resurrection of Jesus Christ. Denney anticipated many of the interesting aspects of today's thought, but his commitment to the essentials of Christianity made him deal with fascinating fads and phases of theology only as they stood in relationship to the central realities of the gospel. Seeing the lasting quality of his emphasis in the past helps us to see more clearly our opportunities and obligations along the path which lies ahead.

In his own right, apart from his relationship to his age and ours, Denney stands as a man this generation should know because of the remarkable capacity of his mind and the prophetic insight of his theology. In his own day he cast his spell upon men as few are able to do; he casts it still. James Moffatt once remarked, 'No one can be said even to put you in mind of Denney.'[2] He was expressing what many of his contemporaries felt about the man, what most of his students knew and respected, and what those of us of succeeding generations can sense through his works—the unique quality of his mind and personality, the exceptional and original nature of the man. H. R. Mackintosh, of Edinburgh, said of him:

> As theologian and as man, there was no one like him. I have known many theologians both scholarly and devout; but I have never known his equal for making the New Testament intelligible as the record and deposit of an overwhelming experience of redemption, and for generating in those who listened to him the conviction that the gospel incarnate in Jesus is the only thing that matters.[3]

His Life

James Denney was born on 5 February 1856 in the town of Paisley—

near Glasgow—in Scotland, and grew up in the seaport of Greenock, on the Firth of Clyde. His family were loyal members of the Reformed Presbyterian Church, the small denomination known as the Cameronians which had its origin in the courageous controversies which gripped Scotland toward the end of the seventeenth century. Early in his life, under the influence of his devout parents, he came into an earnest faith.

The year in which Denney was born marked the nineteenth year of the reign of Queen Victoria. The Crimean War had stumbled to its close, while Big Ben was striking for the first time and the historic castle at Balmoral was rebuilt and made ready for the royal family. In America the dark cloud of civil strife hung on the horizon and the Republican Party had just been formed. From the Orient came news that, following Commodore Perry's mission, Japan's ports were open for trade with the rest of the world.

Scotland, as all of Britain, was experiencing new wealth and confidence as the empire was being built and international trade was beginning to expand to the limits of imagination, while the new industrial processes were producing a different world with new prosperity and new problems. The railroad was just beginning its revolution in transportation and isolated Scottish communities were suddenly being brought into contact with the outside world and with new ideas.

The situation among the churches in Scotland was characterized by rivalry and formalism. The villages of Scotland were marked by opposing church steeples and ministers and congregations, most of them Presbyterian but each of them committed firmly not only to what they held in common but also to the policies and principles which divided them one from the other. In addition to the three major denominations —the Established Church, the Free Church and the United Presbyterian Church—there were a number of independent bodies and splinter groups, such as the Cameronians, each small in size and holding tenaciously to its importantly distinctive dogmas. The attention of religious thinking in Scotland was focused by and large, upon the past. There was a dependence upon the conservative evangelicalism of the sixteenth and seventeenth centuries with resolute reliance upon the formulas of Calvinistic doctrine rigidly interpreted. It was a day of theological formalism and of austere orthodoxy.

Within the year of Denney's birth, however, there were signs that it could not always be so. It was in 1856 that Macleod Campbell published his book *The Nature of the Atonement*, which placed its emphasis upon the universal love revealed in Christ; and it serves as a landmark—

B

along with the controversy which surrounded it—to indicate the point which had been reached in the process of change in theology. The Church's social concern found expression in the establishment of the Wynd Mission in Glasgow, and a new interest in world missions was developing with the opening of the Punjab Mission and the beginning of work in the New Hebrides. It was in 1856 that a congregation in Glasgow dared to install an organ in its sanctuary, while another in Edinburgh ventured warily upon a new order of worship. In many ways the world in the year of Denney's birth was standing on the brink of a departure from the old traditionalism. Scotland and its churches, as indeed the whole world, stood poised for change.

As a Student

Following a strictly disciplined basic education at the Highlanders' Academy in Greenock, Denney entered the University of Glasgow in 1874 and established a record of scholarship which has seldom been rivaled. By the time he had entered upon his college course the changes which could have been anticipated earlier were absorbing the major interest of the thought of his country. The first breaths of fresh ideas were coming across from the continent, and, while the majority looked askance upon German philosophy and theology, the younger scholars were embracing the developmental dialectic of Hegel with his 'Ja', 'Nein', 'Doch'; it seemed to promise release from the staid, traditional structures of belief and thought. Some few were beginning to feel at home in the thought forms of Schleiermacher's *Gefühl*, the emphasis upon religious experience and feeling. Scientific study was moving to the center of the stage following the release of Darwin's bombshell into the whole world of thought in the publication—three years after Denney's birth—of *On the Origin of Species*. In the universities of Scotland, confessional tests for professors had been abolished and there was a feeling of new freedom and approaching change in the intellectual atmosphere. Denney graduated from the University in 1879 with First Class Honors in both classics and philosophy, a rare academic achievement and one which marked him out among his contemporaries.

It was said of him at the time of his graduation that he could have occupied with distinction more than one of the chairs in the faculty of Arts. However, he had already made his decision to enter the ministry and therefore gave himself to the study of theology. He seldom spoke of the factors which went into the making of this decision, though his home life and his early interest in the New Testament were significant influences which clearly played upon his mind and soul. The deepest currents in a man's life run quietly. His Reformed Presbyterian Church had united with the Free Church of Scotland while he was at the University, and so it was at the Free Church College in Glasgow that he entered upon the study of theology.

Theology in that day was feeling the disturbance of the dialogue between confessionalism and the new forms of Biblical and historical criticism. Two years after Denney entered the Free Church College, that Church was shaken by the trial of Professor William Robertson Smith, who was removed from his chair of theology in Aberdeen because of his introduction of the Wellhausen school of higher criticism into the English-speaking world. The striking defense by the brilliant scholar, even in defeat, secured for the Church—not only in Scotland but beyond—the right to bring to the study of the Bible all of the means and findings of textual and historical criticism. Denney's record at the College was equal to that which he had made at the University, and W. M. Macgregor recalls the impression which he made upon his fellow students:

> He was then a shy, austere, rather formidable figure, a little older than many of us, and by no means easy of approach. In the Theological Society, where others splashed in the shallows, theorizing and talking at large, he was able to push out into deep waters as one who knew his way. He had been by far the most distinguished student of his time in the University, and to us he appeared already a master in classics and philosophy, in literature and the history of opinion within the Church. He had also the most admirable gift of pregnant and witty and often demolishing utterance. And to this rich intellectual equipment he added an overawing sense of the religious realities in their dogmatic form.[4]

Following his graduation, in 1883, he served for three years in the East Hill Street mission of the Free St John's Church in Glasgow, bringing his theological capacities into contact with the crying needs of men and women in the tragic area of a large industrial city.[5]

As a Pastor

In 1886, at the age of thirty, he was ordained to the ministry of the East Free Church in Broughty Ferry, an interesting church in a community four miles outside the city of Dundee and a pulpit notable for its succession of preachers: A. B. Bruce had served the church earlier and James Moffatt was to be among those who would succeed him. A few months after taking the church at Broughty Ferry he was married to Miss Mary Carmichael Brown, of Glasgow. Intelligent, devout, loving and gay, she gave him much which he himself would have lacked and drew out of him the kindness and tenderness which within him were always seeking expression. He was minister in Broughty Ferry for eleven years, and the letters which he wrote during that time give indication of his joy in the pastorate, of his many interests, his warm affection for the people of his congregation and his conscientious concern to fulfill the responsibilities of his ministry. His congregation was not long in realizing that their young minister was a Biblical scholar of unusual capacity whose expositions had the force of keen argument coupled with deep earnestness and a striking clarity of style. It was while he was a pastor that he published his two contributions to *The Expositor's Bible*—the commentaries on I and II Thessalonians and on II Corinthians. Both volumes represent work which was given first of all to the Broughty Ferry congregation and they indicate clearly the quality of his preaching during those years. It is strong Biblical preaching, the work of a scholar filled with moral intensity.

As a Professor

In 1897 the General Assembly of the Free Church of Scotland elected him Professor of Systematic and Pastoral Theology in its Glasgow College. He returned to Glasgow recognized and respected as a man of exceptional ability whose capacity in the field of theological scholarship was matched by the promise of his contribution in the future. In addition to his commentaries, the series of lectures which he had delivered at the Chicago Theological Seminary in 1894 had been published under the title *Studies in Theology* and drew wide attention to this new voice in theology. After three years in the Chair of Systematics he was transferred, upon the death of A. B. Bruce, to the Chair of New Testament Language, Literature and Theology, which he held to the time of his death. The two decades of Denney's service as a professor marked the golden age of the theological College in Glasgow; it was looked to for leadership throughout the theological world and it is fair to say that no divinity school of the time stood higher, certainly none in the English-speaking world. With him on the faculty were Thomas M. Lindsay, the Church historian, whose *History of the Reformation* is still regarded as the classic in its field; James Orr, who followed Denney in the Chair of Systematic Theology and who has left us, among many other works, his *International Standard Bible Encyclopedia*; George Adam Smith, in Old Testament studies, who is even today recognized as one of the most constructive Old Testament exegetes and expositors, and whose commentaries on Isaiah and on the Minor Prophets are still widely read. It was during the opening years of this century that this team of scholars brought the College to the zenith of its power and influence.

At the Turn of the Century

The division of history into centuries is sometimes criticized as being artificial, but the beginning of the twentieth century serves as a genuine turning point which marks the end of one epoch and the beginning of another. This was particularly true for the British people. The death of Queen Victoria (1901) signified in many ways the death of an age, and the Boer War (1899-1902)—with its overtones of the clash between nationalism and imperialism—along with such other indications as the rise of the Labor Party and the violent movement for Irish independence, were the sure markings of a time of transition. The changes which at the time of Denney's birth had been barely visible on the horizon were now filling the whole landscape and were introducing a new way of life, of science and communications and industry, in the progressing patterns of which we are still living. America was rising rapidly in wealth and world influence following the days of the Spanish-American War, but was still leaning rather heavily upon the writers and philosophers and theologians of England and Scotland. Events upon the continent of Europe and in the Far East began to foreshadow the dark days which were to come.

Scotland, particularly in the relationship of its churches, was representative of this time of transition. It was just at the turn of the century, in 1900, that Denney and others led two of the three major denominations in coming together to form the United Free Church of Scotland, and the nation's thought began to rise to a still broader union than that. It was expressive of the change from sectarianism toward cooperation and union, and a foretaste of the ecumenical temper of our own times. It was just ten years later, in Edinburgh, that the International Missionary Conference launched the new day of ecumenical experience and organization.

Behind these external facts of the period lay the atmosphere of thought in which Denney lived and to which he addressed himself. It is important to see him in the context of the theological climate of those days when he was making his major contributions. Theology at the turn of the century was in a state of flux. Where in Denney's earlier life there had been visible the first signs of a breaking in the rigid formalism, now that break was more or less complete and the flood of new thought seemed to carry away with it all fixed forms. Some, of course, faced with such a situation, retreated into a hard-shelled fundamentalism, but for most there was general rejoicing at the throwing off of shackles and the free acceptance of a constantly changing world of thought. Nathaniel Micklem has given us a first-hand description of the theological times:

> I was brought up in the fine tradition of intellectual freedom and liberal theology. When I was a boy, the Churches of the Congregational and Presbyterian order in England and Scotland were the pioneers in unfettered theological reflection. The bonds of rigid dogmatism were being thrown off; Seeley in his *Ecce Homo* had enabled thousands to realize for the first time the true humanity of our Lord, while Harnack from Germany was demonstrating, as we supposed, that Church history between the apostolic age and the Reformation was the sad story of a Hellenizing and paganizing of the Gospel, and was offering us a version of the essence of Christianity which accorded well with the liberalism of the period . . . The older and wiser amongst us, like Fairbairn and Denney and Forsyth, were, of course, delivered from this kind of crudity, but I am representing the atmosphere which we young men breathed when I was first a student of theology. I remember that for many years I thought that a Faculty of Divinity at a university was a sheer anachronism; Church history, I supposed, was just history distorted by a bias; dogmatics should be subsumed under philosophy of religion, and the Holy Scriptures should be treated by Christians precisely as any other literature.[6]

There were many factors of the age which served both as causes and as characteristics of this theological climate. There was, first of all, the tremendous impact made by the astonishing advances in physical science, as the whole world seemed to be coming to life with strange new evolutionary capacities. There was also the influence of the popular philosophy of the day which was moving toward a vague humanism, based upon Spinoza, implemented with the metaphysics of Hegel and inspired with the dreams of universal progress. At the same time, there was the undermining effect of the growing field of the comparative study of religions, which sought to discredit the uniqueness of Christ and of Christianity. In addition, the rising interest in the social sciences reflected itself in a popular utilitarian pragmatism. And playing upon this unsettled scene of British thought was the aura of authority which surrounded the extreme exponents of German scholarship; the mantle of Schleiermacher, Hegel and Ritschl had fallen upon Harnack, and his *What Is Christianity?* (1900)[7] gives a good picture of the liberal climate of the time.

Within these aspects of the scene and in a sense riding upon the crest of them all was the dominant fact of the changed and changing attitude toward the Bible. A key to an understanding of the period lies in the realization of the breakdown of faith in the authoritative formulas concerning the infallibility of the Scripture, and the widespread abandonment of Biblical theology which followed. The great nineteenth century advance in Biblical criticism had taken place and a new day of freedom of investigation and interpretation had dawned. We are indebted to such men as Strauss and Baur, Wellhausen and Gunkel, for the questions which they began to ask, however much we may not be satisfied with many of the answers which they themselves offered. We are still facing many of their questions today and are calling them modern. The course of thought seemed to move in those days—and there are current indications that this course has not greatly changed—from the germinal centers of the continent, across the channel to Great Britain and thence across the ocean to America and to the rest of the world. Thus it was that the impact of extreme Biblical criticism, which had served to establish theological liberalism on the continent in the last half of the nineteenth century, was felt in Britain in the early years of the twentieth century and, in turn, moved across the Atlantic to capture the attention of America in the second and third decades. As the radical results of criticism came wave upon wave they seemed to engulf the faith itself and to carry away certainty and stability, and men looked in desperation for some ark of safety.

This was the common texture of the thought of the day and its influence was broad and deep, even where men were not professing liberals. This was the context in which Denney's work was done and toward the creative correction of which he set himself. It was his constant contact with this general pattern of thinking which sharpened his keen mind and gave to his lectures in the Glasgow College and to his major contributions to the theological dialogue of his day the piercing note of battle.

As a Theologian

Denney had the characteristics and qualities of a great religious teacher—profound piety, strong spiritual insight, broad background of culture, deep and penetrating scholarship which was at once as exact and critical as it was far-seeing and constructive, and a unique

gift of clear and effective speech. Professor H. R. Mackintosh said of him:
He towered above the general body of theological teachers in this
country. Some years since, an American student of divinity who had
taken a protracted course of study in Europe singled out three men
as having made upon him the deepest impression of power: Herrmann
of Marburg, Wernle of Basel, Denney of Glasgow. He belonged
emphatically to the very small class of great lecturers. Men went
into his auditorium expecting something to happen, and came out
awed and thrilled.[8]

What every man can sense in his writings was a living experience of
forceful reality for the men who sat in his classroom, and to this day
they recall in intimate detail the spiritual intensity of their study under
his guidance.

It was during these years as a professor that he was making his
greatest contributions to theological literature. Major books in Biblical
theology (*The Death of Christ, The Atonement and the Modern Mind,
Jesus and the Gospel, The Christian Doctrine of Reconciliation*—published
posthumously), his commentary on the Epistle to the Romans, volumes
of sermons (*The Way Everlasting, Gospel Questions and Answers*),
smaller theological works (*The Church and the Kingdom, The Sermon on
the Mount, Factors of Faith in Immortality*), significant contributions
to many of the important dictionaries and encyclopedias which were
then being published, frequent articles in several of the magazines of
the time, and regular reviews and articles in the most vital religious
newspaper of the day—all these flowed from his pen with remarkable
proficiency and power during these years when he was at his peak. In
addition, he kept up a large volume of correspondence with other theologians and personal friends, much of which was saved and has been
printed in the two volumes of letters which were published after his
death. We are fortunate to have this diversity of material from such a
man, for it provides us with an exceptional opportunity of seeing many
facets of his personality and of understanding his thought through the
variety of his work.

During his active life at the Glasgow College he spent six years
editing, along with Orr, a theological publication which was known as
The Union Magazine.[9] He was in demand as a lecturer far beyond the
limits of his own city and nation, and his travels included a second and
third crossing of the Atlantic in order to give lectures in America and
Canada. His greatest interest outside the work of the College was in
preaching. He felt that this was a necessary part of his life which kept

him in touch with the active ministry of the Church and helped him in preparing others to preach. It was to him the most important single task of the Church and therefore a responsibility which he could not shirk, and so he preached constantly. Strangely enough, he added to his capacity as a scholar and teacher and preacher of first rank the additional talents of an exceedingly effective and able administrator and Church leader. For several years he took charge of the Central Fund of the United Free Church. This fund was basic to the support of the work of the denomination, for upon it many of the churches of the General Assembly were dependent. He served as well on the committee which worked on negotiations to bring together into one united Church the various divisions of Presbyterianism in Scotland. In his later years he was caught up in the fight over pressing social issues and gave himself unstintedly to problems which confronted the nation at the time of the First World War.

As the Principal

At the meeting of the General Assembly in May of 1915, he was unanimously elected Principal of the Glasgow College, succeeding T. M. Lindsay. The Principalship was the highest permanent position which the Church could give and it was the crowning honor of Denney's life. It came to him just two years before his death. The stress of the critical times of the war, the loneliness after the loss of his wife and his most intimate friends, the pressure of expanding work and the responsibility of increasing leadership all weighed upon him more heavily than anyone realized, including himself. He became ill in February, 1917, having caught a fever while returning home from a preaching engagement. He was never able to regain his strength and died on June the eleventh of that year.

In his College, as indeed in his Church, his passing marked the end of an era which neither has since really equalled. In the theological world his death was a serious shock, for he was taken at the height of his powers and many around the world were looking to him for particular leadership in the progress from an age of liberalism, through the agony of war, into a more realistic and more meaningful atmosphere of faith and thought. Sir William Robertson Nicoll expressed the feeling of a large body of thoughtful men concerning his stature and the meaning of his death:

He was taken away at a time when he had reached the highest point of his influence. He would have gone much higher if he had been spared to us, through the sheer strength and beauty and wisdom of his nature. He never sought power. He was one of the most unworldly, unselfish, retiring of men, and was in a manner forced to the front. In his own Church, he was the chief leader. In his beloved city of Glasgow he had come to be one of the most influential of public men. All over the world he had his readers and followers. That he was in many respects the first man in Scotland was coming to be acknowledged. It is my own deliberate opinion that hardly any greater loss could have befallen the Christian Church, for he seemed destined to guide thought and action in the difficult years to come as hardly anyone could but himself.[10]

P. T. Forsyth wrote some years after Denney's death, 'Denney became a court of reference in my silent thought. No man was so needful for the conscience of the Church and the public . . . There is nobody left now to be the *theological prophet* and lead in the moral reconstruction of belief.'[11]

The World of Theology Today

Since the time of Denney's death we have passed through two world wars, a major economic depression, the fall of great nations and the rise of weak ones; we have witnessed the birth of an atomic age and have entered upon a seemingly limitless ideological warfare which has divided the world in two and has been inadequately characterized as cold. The inventions of Marconi and Ford and the Wrights which were being announced in the early days of the century have been developed into the necessary means of our communication and the common conveniences of our lives. Our horizons of discovery have exploded into outer space, and changes surround us in almost every area of experience.

In the world of theology the process of transition has been just as thorough and the changes involved have been just as remarkable. A little over a year after Denney's death the First World War ground to its close. The war had carried with it a collapse of understanding of life and of civilization as it had been known, and the liberal thought of the earlier years found that the very props on which it had been built were now knocked from under its assumptions. Men turned with a helpless feeling to the Bible. As Thurneysen said,

We read it with the eyes of shipwrecked men, for whom everything has gone overboard. And we did so, as it turned out, not wholly in vain. The Bible gained a new meaning for us. Beyond all interpretations, its real word again began to speak: the word of forgiveness of sins, the proclamation of the, not humanly, but divinely coming kingdom.[12]

The collapse had been most nearly complete on the battleground itself, the continent, and it was on the continent that the movements of a new day had their origin. Denney died in 1917; in 1918 Karl Barth published his commentary on the Epistle to the Romans, and the theological world leapt into new life and moved into the age of revival in Biblical theology which is such a vital part of the context of our thinking today.

The series of interests and movements, the advance and the growth, which have occurred in their turn since that time is fraught with excitement and with life and is well known, at least in outline, to most men today. We are living in a day of fresh Biblical introductions and dynamic presentations of Biblical theology. Systematic reconstructions of thought today are thoroughly rooted in firm exegesis and experience and we are encountering new discoveries and rediscoveries of truths about the Bible and within the Bible. The current application of the gospel to the needs of men is paralleled by the reinterpretation of history and of life itself in the light of God's living Word to men.

The inherent authority of the Bible is being reasserted; the depth of man's need is being profoundly assessed and the nature of sin shown as being as serious as it is; a new vision is being gained of what the creative truth of revelation means in life; a new appreciation and appropriation of the New Testament faith in Christ is coming to men and an exalted view of His person and work is following in consequence; a worthier and richer conception of the Church is emerging and its force is being felt in the experience of the ecumenical movement; the dynamic interpretation of eternity breaking into time is giving the whole structure of theology a renewed significance in terms of eschatology.

This change in theology has been so thorough and so vital that one might wonder if anything that Denney said in his time could have real relevance for ours. It is easy to see and to say that so much water has flowed under many theological bridges. But the intriguing fact is that all that has taken place has pointed directly to the revaluation and the reassertion of the importance of what Denney was saying some fifty years ago. Here is one who is a pioneer and veteran in the theological struggles which have passed before us and have brought us to our present day. Under the pressures of theological conflict he was charting the course that we were to follow, employing many of the modern methods to substantiate those ancient answers which are crucial.

As Kierkegaard has come from an even earlier age to speak to our own, and as Forsyth—Denney's contemporary and companion in theology—has risen to a prominence beyond his own lifetime, just so, and perhaps for directive even more, does Denney deserve a reappraisal and a new appreciation in our day, for he has an amazing way of speaking to the context of our thought. He serves in many ways as 'the theological prophet' for our age.

II

THEOLOGY AT WHITE HEAT

I haven't the faintest interest in any theology which doesn't help us to evangelize.[1]

THE intensity with which Denney approached the task of theology is a challenge to the commitment of everyone who would think seriously about faith. He helps us come to the study of sacred realities with a creative and vital understanding of what we are seeking to do. When we enter into an interpretive encounter with this man and with his mind, we find that his approach to theology sets a direction and a purpose for our own work and that the devotion of his life to the task stands as a continuing call upward to us. He lets us see what theology is, or—what is more important—raises our sights to what it should be.

Out of the books and papers which he has left as his legacy to the world of theological endeavor, there are certain themes of commitment and interest which define and describe his dynamic approach to theology. For Denney, theology, to be true and strong, must be characterized by certain indispensable qualities.

It Must Be Evangelistic

'If evangelists were our theologians or theologians our evangelists', said Denney, 'we should be nearer the ideal.'[2] The keen quality of his mind which ranged widely through the world of knowledge was always pointed and sharpened by his devotion to the task of making the truth as he knew it relevant to the needs of men as he found them. His books and sermons, his lectures and letters, all serve as a composite illustration of the way in which a theologian can be at the same time an evangelist.

The characteristics which we currently associate with the term 'evangelist' were not his, but the passion which underlies the evangelist's mission was his in such a high degree as to show by its very intensity the superficial nature of those characteristics. He once wrote, 'I haven't the faintest interest in any theology which doesn't help us to evangelize.'[3] So much of theology, now as then, has about it an air of unreality, with

distinctions and definitions, philosophical fads and proof texts, which
have little or no contact with the life and work of the Church in the
world and are practically useless when men stand as God's messengers
in the presence of living people. Denney eschewed all such approaches
to theology. Said he, 'The evangelist is in the last resort the judge of
theology. If it does not serve his purpose it is not true.'[4] On one occasion he poured out his scorn upon the head of an unfortunate minister
who had complained that he was too busy to prepare a proper address
and had asked to be excused for delivering a simple evangelistic
sermon. 'As if', retorted Denney, 'there was any task that could so tax
the strength of the Christian preacher as to preach the love of God, and
so to preach it that men should commit themselves to it.'[5]

This evangelistic zeal was grounded upon his deep Christian commitment which was so basic to everything that he did and said that it
would be impossible to understand him apart from this central element
in his mind and spirit, for his Christian faith was the foundation stone
of his experience and he built his life on that. As a young man he
wrote to a close friend, 'I have committed myself in the most absurd
way to the Christian religion, even in its New Testament form'.[6]
Carnegie Simpson of Cambridge said after Denney's death that he was
'intense and passionate in his Christianity. He was one of the very few
men I have ever seen at white heat over what Christ has done for the
world'.[7]

This quality of his mind found its primary expression in his preaching, and it was this commitment within him which kept him preaching
all his life. He did not have the marks of a 'popular preacher', nor had
he any desire for them. It was his theology that he preached, born of
his own experience and faith and strengthened by the discipline of his
vocation, and as it made him the man and the teacher that he was so it
lifted him to a leading place among the preachers of his time. One
minister said that while he 'loved to sit at the feet of James Denney, he
made one afraid to preach. He revealed not the preacher's art but his
heart—a tremendous earnestness, a burning passion for Christ, an
intense belief in the power of the Cross'.[8]

His theology reflects the dialogue going on within himself between
the scholar and the evangelist, and in the life of the Church he continually pressed for a closer working relationship between the pro-
fessional theologian and the parish minister. His thought has this
evangelical stamp upon it everywhere and there are many places in his
written works where it bursts forth and finds eager expression.

The propagation of Christianity and its interpretation by the intelligence—in other words, preaching and theology—should never be divorced. At the vital point they coincide. The simplest truth of the Gospel and the profoundest truth of theology must be put in the same words—He bore our sins. If our Gospel does not inspire thought, and if our theology does not inspire preaching, there is no Christianity in either.[9]

It Must Be Biblical

Denney was a Biblical theologian. All of his work is rooted in the scriptures as the essential source of theology and it is his insistence upon their primary place which gives much of the force of contemporaneity to his work. The years since his death have been years of rediscovery of the Bible and its message, so that theology has come to a position where we are able to hear with more understanding the prophetic words of Biblical truth which Denney speaks.

We feel in his books, as men felt in his classroom, that it is as he opens the Bible—and particularly the New Testament—and makes its message and its meaning come alive that his mind grips us with power. It was the field of New Testament studies which drew from him what has been called his 'passionate scholarship'.[10] W. M. Clow wrote of him:

> He was essentially a man of one book. That book was the New Testament. Its history, its sources, its authors, and especially the Gospel writers, and Paul as their interpreter, called forth from him all his powers, with a deep joy in their exercise. To state the problem of a great passage, to trace and lay bare the writer's thought, to expound the doctrines and apply the message to the lives of men, was a visible delight to him, as it was a devout fascination to his students . . . He lived in and loved the world and personalities disclosed in the New Testament.[11]

His understanding of the New Testament began with a thorough and detailed knowledge of the original language. He could quote the New Testament with as much ease in Greek as in English. In translation and exegesis he was an authority, meticulous as to details, intimately familiar with Biblical usage, careful in his appreciation of the exact value of both the Greek and the English.

To the knowledge of the Biblical language he added a thorough understanding of the field of Biblical criticism of his day. George Jackson said of him, 'He knew all that modern scholarship had to say about the New Testament, but he neither feared the one nor feared for the other.'[12] He was considered by many to be liberal in his view of inspiration and he believed strongly in the scientific methods of textual and historical criticism. He could meet the advances of critical scholarship, understand them thoroughly, accept them when they made positive contributions, correct them when they seemed to go astray and reject them with deadly effectiveness when they sought to destroy the bed-rock of the Christian faith. This was what the Church needed in his day, and continues to need in ours. His theology was in the most thoroughgoing sense Biblical theology, coming naturally out of his study of the scriptures. While it is sometimes difficult to categorize his theories on particular points of doctrine, and at time unprofitable to attempt to establish his 'orthodoxy' in certain areas of theology, nevertheless his work unfailingly serves to remind one of the thought of the New Testament, and that at all points is much more significant.

In Denney's approach, the theologian must come to the Bible as his authoritative source, and this authority is not legally imposed but is inherent in the Bible itself. He discovered this in the light of his own religious experience. 'It is the only book in the world', he wrote, 'to which God sets His seal in our hearts when we read in search of an answer to the question, How shall a sinful man be righteous with God?'[13] He was concerned that our understanding of Christianity should be built upon the historical origins found in the faith of the New Testament Church.

> The authority of the New Testament for the theologian depends on its being an authentic testimony to the faith of the primitive Church. It depends upon its Apostolic character; and it is to the Apostolic writing that, as a theologian, I go back . . . The truth enshrined in the faith of the Apostles is the inmost truth with which theology has to deal.[14]

Thus, the Bible is the authority which establishes the standard by which Christian experience and faith and doctrine are tested and judged. Said Denney:

> Primitive historical Christianity must always be essentially normative, and if later types of religion so diverge from the primitive type as to find the New Testament rather an embarrassment than an inspiration, the question they raise is whether they can any longer be recognized as Christian.[15]

There were two opposing opinions concerning theology which were exciting attention in Denney's day, and their influence is still with us today. On the one hand, there were those who sought to move theology out of the historical realm and to 'elevate' it to the level of a purely speculative, spiritually apprehended system of thought; on the other, there were those who would make of it an historical science, arguing that the one thing necessary was a return to the historical Christ and a study, apart from any apostolic theologizing, of His life and the truths which He taught. Denney answered both by his commitment to the Bible. To the one he said that Christianity must be understood as an *historical* religion. To strike out in search of religious certainty in the speculations of philosophy, with little regard for the historical origin of Christianity seen in the Scriptures, is to cut ourselves off from the very means by which we can understand the Christian religion, and while its intent may be admirable its result can never be other than unreal because it has closed its eyes to its source and has ignored the facts on which it rests. Said he:

> Christianity does not mean the recognition of necessary truths of reason, but an attitude of the soul to God, determined by Christ; and history is not to the religious man a chapter of accidents, but the stage on which a Divine purpose is achieved which could not be more ineptly described than by calling it accidental. Religion can no more be simplified by making it independent of history than respiration would be simplified by soaring beyond the atmosphere.[16]

To the other approach Denney replied that Christianity must be understood as an historical *religion*. To limit theology to the dimensions of an historical science is to ignore the spiritual content of the Bible and of life which it is its very task to explain. Those who insist upon following this course, said Denney, 'shut up Jesus of Nazareth into a past growing continually more remote, and while they admit His posthumous influence do not distinguish Him otherwise from all who have lived and died upon the earth'.[17] Such a person could never serve as the explanation for the historical fact of Christianity. The first century Christians found that in their experience with the historical reality of Jesus they encountered the eternal and divine. Denney put it this way:

> Unless we have renewed the experience of the first Christians— unless in the exercise of faith we have come into contact, in Christ Jesus, with divine eternal truth—all that is called Christian doctrine must remain unreal to us. We do not know on what it rests; we cannot see what it is about.[18]

It is this vital commitment to the Bible and his spiritual understanding of its validity which hold him in a purposeful balance between opposing extremes and give him a positive and dynamic approach to the task of theology.

C

There was in Denney an eager yearning for reality. His search for the truth—for that which is ultimate and vital, essential to faith and authentic to life—was so significant for him that it permeated his mind and personality and gave a distinctiveness and directness to his theological work. 'Reality'—his students remembered as 'his favourite or most characteristic word'.[19]

In theology he was insistent that for doctrine to be true it must be real. It must have about it the note of personal faith born of religious experience. 'No dogmatic', he said, 'is worth reading or thinking about in which one cannot feel at all the critical places the pulse of vital religion.'[20] The truth with which theology deals is a truth which asserts a personal claim upon the theologian, so that one is challenged by it not only to be convinced of its validity but to be personally committed to its authority. This means that personal experience is of crucial importance if theology is to be true and real. Denney asserted that, 'The material with which the theologian deals can only be certified to him through religious experience; in other words, only a living Christian is competent to look at the subject.'[21] An illustration of this essential note of personal involvement in theology came to his hand as he pointed out the difference between the medical and pastoral vocations: 'You can study other people's diseases in hospitals, whether they like it or not, but in the last resort the only soul you can study is your own.'[22]

This does not mean that theology is simply a personal and private affair. Denney conceives of experience in the broadest terms. It includes the experience of the Christian fellowship as it has been expressed in the history of the Church, most pointedly in the historic creeds. Denney sees these as testimonies of the experience of faith within the life of the Christian community, not as permanent statutory restrictions upon that experience. 'The creeds and confessions are sources, not laws, for theology. Faith comes to us, no doubt, as an inheritance, yet it is a new birth in every man; and he who lives by faith does not live under law.'[23] It is the experience of faith lying behind the historic confessions which leads the theologian to rely upon them as a part of his experiential source. And in all of Christian history, the basic and normative expression of experience is in the scriptures. Denney said in this connection, 'There is no proper contrast between Scripture and experience. Scripture . . . is a record of experience or an interpretation of it.'[24] The New Testament is the original testimony of what faith in Christ is and, as such, it is in a unique sense authoritative in experience.

We can readily see that this provides a vital and vibrant ground for theological study. Theology is as alive for Denney as experience itself, and as real. Much of our present interest in an existential approach to theology has about it this same liveliness and this same demand for reality. Denney was insisting upon the positive implications of this theological emphasis decades ago. Modern existentialists should feel at home, for example, in his treatment of man's understanding of God: 'The important thing in religion is not the belief that God is omniscient, but the experience that God knows me; . . . not the idea that God is everywhere, but the experience that wherever I am God is with me.'[25] He points to the 139th Psalm as the pure expression of this very note in theology:

A man is incapable of judging anything if he does not feel that this expresses the most real experience of which human nature is capable: *Thou* has searched *me*, and known me—and if he does not feel that the *thou* is just as real and as personal as the *me*. Only God can prove His being and His personality and His character to man, and He proves all three, in the first instance, by experiences like this.[26]

One can recognize in this a foretaste of Martin Buber and of some of the principal contributions to theology in our present day. The distinctive task of Christian theology comes out of this same relationship in experience; for, said Denney:

The specifically Christian consciousness which has to be scientifically developed by the theologian is not the consciousness of Jesus, it is the consciousness of reconciliation to God through Jesus. It is not the consciousness of the Saviour, but the consciousness of the saved, and the confession of it is not the confession of the Lord, but of the Church.[27]

This rooting of theology in the realm of experience gives a realistic ring to Denney's work and marks his theology with certain qualities. It is characterized by a *dynamic creativeness* which is felt in terms of change, for theology based on experience cannot be static. It has its norm in its original—the New Testament—and it has the testimony of Christian experience in the past, but it has as well all of the force of the present experience which Christ inspires. Denney observed, 'In grace there is infinite variety;' and then he went on to say, 'The only thing to be trusted is experience, and we must take care not to distrust it on the ground that we have the measure of all true Christian experience already in our hands, and can now impose that measure as a law.'[28] The theologian must work with and within his own present experience and he cannot stop the process and stand aside as a spectator. Denney once wrote in this connection, 'The fault of Calvin is that he is too apt to arrest the world at a given moment, and to find in the distinctions then existing the eternal and unchanging will of God.'[29] Denney's theology was in process of development every day of his life. It was that much a part of him, and he was that much a part of it. One man who knew him commented, 'Had he lived to be a hundred years of age he could never have become a "fossil". What he gave to his students and readers was his latest thought at the time.'[30] He continually rewrote his class lectures and there was a briskness and newness about them that stimulated interest, challenging and captivating the minds of his students. When he left his pastorate he burned the manuscripts of all of his sermons, although he never stopped preaching, and he said more than once that 'if every scrap of sermon under this roof at this moment were to go up in a blaze, I would not singe the tip of a finger to save the best of them.'[31] And, as W. M. Macgregor remarked, 'Why should he, when he always had himself to draw upon?'[32]

Coming directly from this dynamic and creative quality in his theology, and inextricably bound up with it, is another characteristic of his thought: *freedom*. His faith was anchored in his experience of reconciliation in Christ, and the firmness of his grasp on that allowed him to let out his line and range freely. He was fond of saying, 'The New Testament is the most free-thinking book in the world.'[33] And he would go on to say,

> Paul and John were the most daring free-thinkers who ever lived. They had no creed or catechism to follow; they do not quote anyone, hardly even Jesus Himself; they were not 'sound' in any traditional sense, but original; they were not orthodox, but inspired.[34]

The present tendency is to look back upon Denney as being rather conservative, and so he would appear to be in some of his conclusions. But in his own day he was regarded by many as being too free in his theology, too ready to accept the latest conclusions of the higher critics. If deeply conservative and traditionally oriented theologians are finding in Denney a fellow traveler, it presents us with a hopeful situation. There is enough freedom in Denney's thought to break almost any narrowness, and it may be that speaking out of the past he presents a means of uniting us in the present. He actually held firmly to only a few things, and these were at the center, and they freed him from anxiety as to what was taking place along the circumference. His attitude toward legal requirements and restrictions in theology is made clear in his telling words:

It does not matter whether it issues from Nicea or Augsburg, from Trent or Westminster; the mind that has been fascinated by Christ Himself, and that has begun to know that He is by its own experience of what He does, must never barter that original quickening and emancipation, and what it learns by them, for any doctrine defined by man.[35]

He had the mind and attitude of an explorer, and the fearlessness with which he pursued new ways of understanding and interpreting the facts of Christian experience still have the power to draw men to him as they are only drawn by an honest and unfettered search for truth. He once commented:

It is better to trust too much to the truth than too little; it puts more honour on the truth, it does more to commend it to fair treatment from ingenious minds, and, as far as we can judge by results, it issues in a larger and more wholesome acceptance of Christianity than we find in societies where it is more scrupulously guarded.[36]

It was H. R. Mackintosh who said of him:

Very few men, indeed, have reflected on the Gospel with such utter fearlessness . . . His mind was always breaking out at a new place. You could not travel over his intelligence and map it out once for all, for a creative evolution went on uninterruptedly. But so deep and strong was his faith that, so far as one could see, these transitions were accomplished without friction.[37]

Reality was of such importance to Denney that he insisted on brushing past everything else in his pursuit of it. It was this which oftentimes made him seem sternly serious, hard and austere. He was merciless to himself, putting himself under a rigorous discipline in order that his powers might not be scattered over superficial matters and he might give himself to the purpose of his life which were most significant and most real. He could be merciless to others, as well; for—wisely or unwisely—what he demanded of himself he expected of them. He had no patience with people who would not take life and thought seriously and who lived on meaningless and undigested words. Whenever he sensed insincerity or unreality in any man's work, the telling lash of his tongue left its mark on the memory of all who heard him. Needless to say, his students remember this quality in him particularly. One of them wrote recently, 'There could only be one James Denney. Severe on himself, he despised the slothful.'[38] Another recalls, 'We soon learned that what we presented to Denney had to be done with our whole might. He could pencil a brief, blighting sentence at the end of an essay that was not so much mere words written on paper as marks seared and branded on our shoulders.'[39] Who could forget how he peered out through his glasses and characterized a certain loquacious student as 'not having the ghost of a glimmering of an idea of what he is talking about'?[40] As he returned one man's expanded exegesis on a New Testament passage, he commented, 'This does not increase in *weight* as it grows in *bulk*!'[41] His students bear him testimony that his caustic remarks were not simply for his pleasure, but that he knew his men and knew what was needed to spur them along the same road to reality on which he was moving, and this became for them their very life. A visitor once asked a group of the students what they thought of Dr Denney. One answered promptly, 'Sir, we would die for him.' And then another added slyly, 'Yes, rather than live with him.'[42] Twenty years after leaving the College, one of his former students asked another how diligently he was working on a particular piece of study; 'He flashed out, "Sir, I am getting it up *as for Denney*." There was no more to be said.'[43]

Outside of the College he was known for this same sort of abrupt and impatient insistence upon that which is true and real. Men remember that often in private and in public 'some sharp, piercing remark, like a rapier thrust, flashed from his lips—usually aimed at superficialities, pretensions, insincerities'.[44] One of many examples comes from a debate on the floor of the General Assembly, in which he said, 'I would not give a square inch of history with flesh and blood and memories and passion behind it, for a whole wilderness of propositions like some that have been submitted here.'[45] To read his letters and reviews is to encounter scores of his clear and telling *obiter dicta* which disclose the procession of theologians and of theology under the surgical insight of a mind fiercely impatient with work which seemed loose or slovenly, tangled or confused, irrelevant or unreal. He was suspicious of the sentimentalist and of the ritualist because of the extremes of unreality to which they so often carried people. He was not fully appreciative of the mystical element in religion and would warn his students against 'mystery-mongering in the ministry'.[46] He was not set against all mystical approaches to theology, for he was certainly not blind to the truth of union with Christ, but he feared the unintelligibility of mysticism and its tendency to draw men away from the moral and the 'real'. His trenchant comment on mysticism was, 'I would rather be saved in Christ than lost in God.'[47]

It is well to point out that while his passion for reality was one of his greatest sources of power it was one of his weaknesses as well. It is perhaps true of all men that underneath their loftiest virtues lie their deepest disabilities. He was probably too quick to brush aside things which he did not fully appreciate, and even as wide as his vision and understanding were, it is a perilous enterprise for any man to make himself the measure of what is real. There is some justice in Peake's remark concerning him: 'What he could see he saw with unusual sharpness and expressed with great force. What he didn't see didn't exist.'[48]

It Must Be Whole

Denney had a feeling for wholeness under God and he was continually calling theology to strive to draw together the disciplines of thought and study into an ever-increasing and challenging unity. 'Theology', he wrote, 'must contain the ideas and the principles which enable us to look at our life and our world as a whole, and to take them into our religion, instead of leaving them out.'[49] If we are to deal with theology we must treat seriously the reality of Who God is, for to know Him is to be compelled to think in consistent terms about Him and to be forced to know all that is His—the world about us, the personalities in the world, including ourselves. 'We must know God;' he said, 'and our task, when we theologize, is to define our knowledge; to put it in scientific and systematic form, and to show, at least in outline, that general view of the world which it involves.'[50]

He was impatient with those who would divide their understanding of life and nature into separate and unrelated compartments, and he sought to think in cohesive terms about philosophy and science, about the supernatural and the natural.

The mind cannot have two *unrelated* explanations of the same thing; it cannot interpret it, in the first place religiously, and in the second scientifically, without being compelled to define the connection of the two interpretations with each other. If they are both true, it will not be impossible to do so; but if we cannot do so, the impression will be irresistible that one or other of them is not true.[51]

He recognized the difficulty which is presented by such a challenge to harmony of thought, but insisted that to seek to discharge the theologian's task on any easier terms is to renounce his responsibility and so to be pushed off the scene of serious thought. As he put it, 'All knowledge is one, all intelligence is one; and it belongs to theology, above every science, not to dissolve, but in the very name of God, to maintain and interpret that unity.'[52]

He did not, of course, think that all knowledge could be bound together into a unity which would be perfect and permanent, without any inconsistencies within it. To suggest that he did would be to imply that he had left his basis of experience, and it was precisely on that basis that for him theology had any wholeness at all. As a matter of fact, there was a strong assertion in Denney of Christian agnosticism, which for him was not so much opposed to faith as it was a part of it. He felt the sense of magnitude and immensity in the truths of revealed religion with which the theologian deals, but he went on to say:

> Religion does not depend on the things we are ignorant of, but on the things we know. Its basis is revelation, not mystery; and it is not affected by the fact that mysteries abound. Little as we know, and much as we are ignorant of, our responsibility for what we know is unqualified.[53]

Thus he put his own spacious, yet incisive, mind upon the wide range of knowledge, seeking always to keep before himself the ideal of wholeness, and he became recognized as a scholar of unusual stature and versatility. Men differed from him on many different points but no one looked down on him; there was disagreement but never disrespect. In the theological controversies which agitated his age, P. T. Forsyth said of him, 'Denney is the greatest thinker we have upon our side.'[54] His scholarship had the twin virtues of breadth and depth. He ranged widely in his interests, yet in each area he pursued a subject in which he was concerned until his grasp of it was firm, both in its details and in its larger implications. He had a thorough knowledge of seven languages, and this linguistic ability served as an expansive background for all of his scholarship. The breadth of his interest in literature was extraordinary, and his letters are punctuated with comments which cover the whole sweep of ancient and modern writers and which sparkle with first-hand familiarity, caustic criticism and honest appreciation. Perhaps it is enough to say that a friend once drew from him the shy admission that if Shakespeare's tragedies were lost, he could reproduce them from his memory.[55] He had a deep interest in history and was actively engaged in the social and political life of his own day. He gave himself to a study of science and of philosophy, recognizing that while neither had his first loyalty both were essential to truth in thought and to relevance in communication.

The catholicity of his tastes in reading and study can be seen most clearly in the rich element of humanism which gave savor and spice to all his work. As Denney himself put it, using Amiel's word of Vinet, 'It is a real want in a man when his mind is always at church.'[56] He enjoyed lecturing on Benvenuto Cellini and on Edward Gibbon, a rather strange pair for Free Church public meetings, but Denney readily confessed that 'they are more interesting than Fathers, Reformation theologians, or modern divines'.[57] Commenting on the 119th Psalm, he said, 'I should always lift *Punch* after it with expectation'. And then he continued:

> Does it ever occur to you that we read our Bibles too much, and that it might do us good to read none for a twelve-month, just as it would do some people good if for as long they read nothing else? I have sometimes felt weary of the very look and sound of the New Testament; the words are so familiar that I can read without catching any meaning, and have to read again, far oftener than in another book, because I have slid a good bit unconsciously.[58]

He once observed that 'A man whose calling is to interpret the New Testament needs to make a special effort to appreciate all that God has given to man in nature—in human nature, that is, and its native tendencies and productions.'[59] Such was the unusual combination of Christian faith and humanistic understanding which was within his mind.

It was to the field of theology that he drew all of this variety and intensity of insight, and it is the striking together of these various interests in the unity of his thought which bring forth many of the sparks which enliven all of his work. In the area of theology his mind found its natural ground of highest interest and his scholarship reached its full powers. He was at home in every department of theology and in the course of his years at the Glasgow College he served in three of the five divisions of the Divinity Faculty. As he studied, his mind readily assimilated what was good in a man's work, and as readily discarded what seemed unworthy. Thus, Ritschl could be castigated heavily on occasion, and yet one cannot fail to see that he was influenced himself by Ritschlian thought. The breadth of his scholarship was increased by his facility in reading German and he was familiar with the German works in theology and Biblical criticism long before their translations made them known to most English-speaking theologians. A striking expression of Denney's up-to-dateness with our times is his early familiarity with the writings of Kierkegaard, from the German translations. He quotes Kierkegaard at some length in *The Death of Christ*, and a telling example of the danger of counting Denney out too early can be seen in a review of the 1952 reprint of that work, where the reviewer states, 'Tasker (the editor of the reprint) has once or twice

introduced something from Kierkegaard, as well as from several other authors more recent than Denney.'[60] The remarkable thing is that while Professor Tasker—unfortunately—edited out some things, he did not add anything. Everything that the reviewer recognized as being more or less contemporary was in Denney's original work. He has a remarkable way of being in step with the beat of our times.

Carnegie Simpson said of him, 'What a combination he was: Horace and St Paul—severity and charity—the life of men and the Gospel of God. He was everywhere *rich*.'[61] He studied all of his life, bringing together in a growing and expanding unity the wide insights of the various fields of his interest. He had said many years earlier of another that he 'died learning', and had added, 'No one could wish to have his days linked each to each by a nobler aspiration than that which breathes in these two words.'[62] This was the nature of his continuing commitment to all knowledge under the wholeness of God.

> 'The greatest part of our perfection is to thirst for perfection,' and to keep the goal of Christian theology—which is the goal of the human spirit admitted to fellowship with the true God in Jesus Christ—perpetually before our eyes, though well aware that we can only greet it afar off, is the one hope of theological progress. To divide the mind, or to divide truth, is in the long run to renounce God. It is with no arrogance I speak emphatically of this, under no illusion that the theologian, any more than the speculative philosopher, can find out God to perfection; but in the strong conviction that in Jesus Christ we are in contact with the ultimate truth and reality of the world, and that we must labour, in thought as in practice, to gather together in one all things in Him.[63]

It Must Be Clear

To these aspects of his approach to theology Denney added a final quality of his mind that stamped his work with a distinctive mark which helped to make the others effective: the gift of a style which was the epitome of clarity. 'Gentlemen', he would say to his class, 'the first thing in a sermon is lucidity; the second is lucidity; and the third is lucidity.'[64] What was true for preaching was true for theology and for life, so that in everything he did he was constantly striving to express his thought in the most concise, direct and penetrating manner. His informal conversation and letters, his lectures and sermons, his articles and his books all show a style, at once clear and convincing, which almost invariably complied with Swift's definition of good writing: 'The proper words in the proper places.' His clarity of style originated in his grasp upon reality, and what he saw with the keenness of his mind he said with the sharpness of his tongue and of his pen. Everything extraneous was stripped away till nothing was left but the naked truth which he wished to communicate, and that in its epigrammatic and most forceful form. He gave himself with such fervour to the development of a style of perfect clarity that during his own lifetime and since his name has become associated in the minds of many with the accurate and crisp word and the succinct and forceful phrase which became the hallmark of all his work. Mackintosh spoke of his 'confident and incisive mastery of expression which bites upon the mind like a diamond'.[65]

His style was a rather remarkable combination of hard labor and seemingly perfect ease and freedom. While he was concerned about his style and worked to get his ideas formed and expressed with clarity, there was nevertheless a spontaneity and a freshness about what he said and wrote which was the natural overflow of his own personality. 'It is the things a man says without thinking', Denney once observed, 'that have the sap of nature in them.'[66] And it was this same insight which prompted him to say, 'The worst of speaking without thinking is that you say what you think.'[67] It was this spontaneous quality of mind that he looked for in other men, feeling that the stamp of original personality should be upon their work. Thus he commented with a frown on Thomas Aquinas, 'His *Summa Theologica* is a lake into which many streams have flowed, and from which many have drawn, but it is not a spring.'[68]

There is no question that his influence in his own day was greatly increased by his style, and that his interest for ours lies in part in the same thing. He left no doubt as to his meaning, and while one might not always agree with him one could always know whether one did or not, and that cannot be said of many writers in his age and in ours. Theologians seem at times to be gifted in the art of making things unclear and, while we are much more fortunate now in this respect than in Denney's generation—and certainly than in the generation which immediately preceded his—we still find his transparent and trenchant style unusual and gratifying and it is not difficult for us to imagine that Denney stood out like a beacon of clarity in his own day of cloudy expression.

His fierce love for clearness brought him into tension with a good bit of the thought and writing of his day and some of his sharpest thrusts were directed at the confusion in ideas and communication which he encountered. After listening to an involved paper on the

thought of an abstruse writer, he was heard to mutter, 'It is bad
enough to be at sea, but to be at sea in a fog!'[69] A typical comment is
included in one of his letters to Nicoll: '. . . seems to reverence a man
provided he cannot understand him, but I never feel inclined to be
humble because a fellow-creature contrives to be unintelligible.'[70] 'The
worst of being erudite', he once said, 'is that a man forgets there are
things which are better forgotten.'[71] With regard to the dependence
upon esoteric terms in much of philosophical writing, he asked:

> Who has not groaned over the technical jargon to which philosophy
> has been degraded by its modern interpreters—a jargon which is not
> the necessary instrument of precision, but the sure sign that the
> mind has lost its freedom; and that philosophy itself, which ought
> to be the most universal of human interests, has sunk into a mere
> professionalism?[72]

Of a prominent religious figure of the day he said, 'He has a really
notable gift for the clamorous presentation of the obvious.'[73] It pained
him to see anyone for whose ideas he had real respect dissipating his
influence through an obscure style. The chief example of this was in
his close relationship with P. T. Forsyth. Most of their generation that
knew them well grouped them together, thinking of them as the
English Nonconformist and the Scottish counterparts, and it is still
quite natural and common to associate them closely.[74] Because of this
association and also because of the renewed influence of Forsyth and
the recognized importance of his contribution to the theology of today,
it is interesting to see Denney concentrating upon the problem of
Forsyth's style and thus revealing the regard which he had for what
Forsyth was trying to say:

> The peculiarity of his style is such that only people who agree with
> him strongly are likely to read him through. (He) is immensely
> clever at some points at which it is not enough to be clever. It is like
> hitting Goliath between the eyes with a pebble which does not sink
> into his skull, but only makes him see clearer.[75]
> I found his book very difficult to read. If this is how one feels who
> is heartily at one with the writer, how must it strike an unsympa-
> thetic reader? . . . If these papers were preached, as most of them
> seem to have been, I am sure most of the audiences, while willing
> enough to take hold of them, must have been sadly perplexed to
> find the handle.[76]

It is probable that Denney wanted everything around him just a
little clearer than things can ever be, that just as in his passion for
reality he became a little unrealistic so also he pressed too hard in his

love for clarity. His directness of speech, his forceful use of the cutting edge of his tongue, made him seem—as indeed at times he was—brusque and abrupt. If there is justice in this criticism it points again to a vice which is hidden within his strong virtue, for it was his ringing clarity which helped to draw men to him and which gives him all the more effectiveness as he speaks to us today. As Professor A. M. Hunter has said:

> In Denney you find what you do not find in many of our modern theologians, . . . what is in theological writing perhaps the first of all the virtues—perfect lucidity of thought and expression. In a time when theological unclarity is sometimes hailed as profundity and the method of the expositor is often *obscurum obscurius*, many of us thank God for Denney's clarity.[77]

Denney's approach to theology is the expression of himself. His life, revealed in his work, has about it the challenge to a high and holy calling, and claims from men the best that they can offer to the task of theology. All of his work has upon it his personal seal of Christian commitment coupled with Biblical insight, of a dynamic realism wedded to a search for wholeness, channelled through a style of limpid clarity. His words are like the sparks which fly up from the anvil of his experience and they catch and burn into the mind because of the reality of the truth that is within them and the disciplined precision with which they are expressed. In all we find 'that rare distinction and touch of grace that Principal Denney could somehow give to the most casual of his most commonplace communications . . . the Denney touch'.[78]

III

THE DIAMOND PIVOT
The Cross in the New Testament

*It is in passages like these that the Christian consciousness
in all ages has found the very core of the Gospel, . . . the
diamond pivot on which the whole system of Christian
truth revolves.*[1]

THE cross of Christ, for Denney, is the center of all Christian theology.
Here before the cross faith finds the heart of its experience and theology
finds the loadstone of its wholeness. Except for the cross, Denney
would have had nothing to say; all that he says draws its ultimate
significance from the cross. The remainder of the field of theology has
its roots here, and Denney's interpretation of each additional area is
marked primarily by the lengthened shadow of the cross. He made this
the particular province of his thought and work, for he felt that this
was the key to all of the rest, and in outlining the themes of his theology
this is the point at which we must begin.

On this he himself would insist:

> If the atonement, quite apart from precise definitions of it, is any-
> thing to the mind, it is everything. It is the most profound of all
> truths, and the most recreative. It determines more than anything
> else our conceptions of God, of man, of history, and even of nature;
> it determines them, for we must bring them all in some way into
> accord with it. It is the inspiration of all thought, the impulse and
> law of all action, the key, in the last resort, to all suffering. Whether
> we call it a fact or a truth, a power or a doctrine, it is that in which
> the *differentia* of Christianity, its peculiar and exclusive character is
> specifically shown; it is the focus of revelation, the point at which
> we see deepest into the truth of God, and come most completely
> under its power. For those who recognise it at all it is Christianity
> in brief; it concentrates in itself, as a germ of infinite potency, all
> that the wisdom, power and love of God mean in relation to sinful
> men.[2]

The force of these words sets the tone for all of Denney's discussion of
the cross. It puts in bold letters the significance of that which we do
when we deal with the death of Christ, and heightens our awareness

that here is the focal point of faith and theology, the heart of the experience of reconciliation to God in Christ.

This becomes clear to us, first of all, as we study the New Testament. In Denney's thought, we turn to the New Testament because here the experience and the truth of the cross are disclosed to us historically, and apart from that historical basis it is impossible to understand the cross of Christ—either that it is or what it is. It is in the New Testament that we meet the cross, and as we are confronted by it we are confronted as well by the original and normative expression of its importance and its meaning. So Denney would direct our attention to the crucial passages which are at the heart of the Biblical proclamation.

> It is in passages like these that the Christian consciousness in all ages has found the very core of the Gospel, the inmost heart of God's redeeming love; they have been the refuge of despairing sinners from generation to generation; they are not 'faults', as a geologist would say, in the structure of Christian thought; they are not erratic boulders that have been carried over somehow from a pre-Christian—i.e. a Jewish or pagan—condition of mind, to a Christian one; they are themselves the most profoundly, purely and completely Christian of all Scripture thoughts. The idea they contain . . . is the diamond pivot on which the whole system of Christian truth revolves.

The Cross in the Life of Jesus

Denney turns our attention initially to the life of Jesus as it is presented in the synoptic gospels. He sees the theme of the cross running through the record of Christ's life from beginning to end. His presentation of the materials of the documents themselves leaves little room for the picture of the pale Galilean, meek and mild, whose popular ministry was dashed to the ground in disappointment and death. Denney had little patience with this sort of misreading of the record which was widespread in his day and which still clings to the sentiment of some. Denney's advice was: read the New Testament; see what the gospels themselves say.

HIS BAPTISM

All of the gospels begin the account of Jesus' ministry with a record of His baptism (Mark 1.9-11; Matt. 3.13-17; Luke 3.21-22), and Denney felt there was no way to understand that spiritual experience apart from His own account of the fusion in His consciousness of the two strains of Old Testament prophecy (Ps. 2 and Isa. 42) into the declaration of the voice from God: 'Thou art my Son, the Beloved, in Thee I am well pleased.' This was the service of ordination of the Servant of the Lord, and Jesus understood it as such. The evidence leads to no other alternative than that from the opening of His public ministry Jesus saw foreshadowed 'the sense of something tragic in His destiny ... It had a necessary relation to his consciousness from the beginning, just as surely as His consciousness from the beginning had a necessary relation to the prophetic conception of the Servant of the Lord'.[4]

HIS TEMPTATION

Confirmation of this is found in the connected narratives of the temptation (Mark 1.12-13; Matt. 4.1-11; Luke 4.1-13). The meaning of the temptation story, standing where it does, is that from the outset of His ministry Jesus saw the alternative paths lying before Him and chose the path of the Servant. These opening narratives have about them the note of identification with mankind, as Jesus, who knew no sin, submits to the anomaly of a baptism of repentance with a view to forgiveness of sins and as he undergoes the tempting trials which come out of that baptism. Denney commented that it would not have been surprising if Jesus had taken His stand by John the Baptist, confronting the people. But the atonishing thing is that He took His stand beside the people. He identified Himself with them and with their need. 'It is as though He had looked on them under the oppression of their sin, and said: On Me let all that burden, all that responsibility descend.'[5] The key to this experience lies in the Servant Psalm of Isa. 53: 'Here in the Baptism we see not the word but the thing: *Jesus numbering Himself with the transgressors* ... It was "a great act of loving communion with our misery", and in that hour, in the will and act of Jesus, the work of atonement was begun.'[6]

HIS TEACHING

Turning from this opening drama, Denney would call our attention to the Lord's teaching in which He gives indication, even in the early days, of His impending death. The opposition which was mounting against Him was not the only indication of the future events, for there was within Him the presentiment of sorrow which occasionally flashes out in His words.[7] It is with the experience in Caesarea Philippi, following the disciples' confession of Him as the Messiah, that His understanding of His death became the open subject of His teaching: 'And he began to teach them that the Son of man must suffer many things ...' (Mark 8.31; cf. Matt. 16.21; Luke 9.22). In the face of the disciples' admitted failure to comprehend what His Messiahship meant, He continued to teach them out of His own awareness of His task, seeking to initiate them into an understanding of the fact that He *must* suffer. Denney insists that the important question throughout this teaching has to do with what is meant by the Greek word *dei* (δεῖ), the 'must', the sense of necessity. There are two possible meanings, that of outward constraint—its being 'inevitable', and that of inward constraint —its being 'indispensable'. While he recognizes the importance of the first, Denney nevertheless feels that the deeper significance of Jesus' thought lies in the second.

> The divine necessity for a career of suffering and death is primary; it belongs, in however vague and undefined a form, to our Lord's consciousness of what He is and what He is called to do; it is not deduced from the malignant necessities by which He is encompassed; it rises up within Him, in divine power, to encounter these outward necessities and subdue them.[8]

The fact that He began at the moment of the disciples' confession to emphasize His vocation as Messiah, serves to strengthen our acceptance of this truth. As Denney put it, 'When He unfolds Messiahship it contains death. This was the first and last thing He taught about it, the first and last thing He wishes His disciples to learn.'[9] There can be little doubt that the disciples' later presentation of Him as the fulfill-ment of the prophetic picture of Isaiah fifty-three had its basis here in the divine necessity which Jesus saw in His death, that it was as the Servant of the Lord that He must suffer.

In the later stages of His ministry, there are more pointed references to His death, and Denney focuses attention upon two of the most important of these. The first is contained in Jesus' answer to the ambi-tious request of James and John (Mark 10.32 f.). This entire passage is significant in this connection and Denney argues that its arrangement is important. It begins with the disciples' amazement that He should press forward toward Jerusalem, carries through one of His three explicit teachings about His death, issues into His reply to the sons of Zebedee and culminates in the great 'ransom' saying in the company of them all. Much of His meaning is found in His use of metaphors, such as 'the cup' and 'the baptism' and 'the ransom'. This last forms a climax in Christ's revelation of Himself and of His task: 'The Son of man came not to be ministered unto, but to minister, and to give His life a ransom for many' (v. 45). Jesus describes the life of men as being under forfeit and declares that the object of His coming into the world was to offer

His life that these lives might be set free. 'This was the supreme service the Son of Man was to render to mankind; it demanded the supreme sacrifice, and was the path to supreme greatness.'[10] Denney points out that this is the equivalent—in a figure—of Paul's statements concerning His bearing of our sins. 'If we find the same thought in St Paul', he said, 'we shall not say that the evangelist has Paulinised, but that St Paul has sat at the feet of Jesus.' And going on to acclaim this 'ransom' word of Jesus, he wrote:

> If we feel that such a thought carries us suddenly out of our depth —that as the words fall on our minds we seem to hear the plunge of lead into fathomless waters—we shall not for that imagine that we have lost our way. By these things men live, and wholly therein is the life of our spirit. We cast ourselves on them, because they outgo us; in their very immensity, we are assured that God is in them.[11]

Denney calls special attention to a second experience of Jesus and the disciples which took place prior to His death and which helps us to understand the meaning for Him and for them which lay within His death. This concerns the supper in the upper room in Jerusalem on the night of betrayal and particular importance is placed upon Jesus' reference to the covenant blood (Mark 14.24; Matt. 26.28; Luke 22.20). After dealing with the critical details, Denney builds his discussion on the background which the Old Testament provides for the passage, concluding that covenant blood is sacrificial blood, and that it was associated with propitiatory power. Carrying this insight further, he builds upon the prophecy of the 'new covenant' found in Jer. 31.34, and feels that we can best appreciate what was in Jesus' thought on that night by bringing these references together. 'He is establishing, at the cost of His life, the new covenant, the new religious relation between God and man, which has the forgiveness of sins as its fundamental blessing.'[12] Seeing these themes united in the one grand word, 'This is my blood of the covenant,' Denney commented. 'It is a word which gathers up into it the whole promise of prophecy and the whole testimony of the apostles; it is the focus of revelation, in which the Old Testament and the New are one. The power that is in it is the power of the passion in which the Lamb of God bears the sin of the world.'[13]

HIS PASSION

From Jesus' teaching about His death it is important to turn to the story of the death itself, and significant that the story of the passion takes prominence—in space and in meaning—in each of the gospels.

The narratives substantiate the impressions already drawn from His life and teaching concerning the importance of the cross and its growing significance. The expression of agony in Gethsemane and the experience of being forsaken on the cross do not refute Jesus' conception of His vocation or His commitment to it, but rather represent its victorious assertion in the face of the darkness of the hour itself. Denney holds this aloft as the reality of the sacrifice; it was as real as *this*. He sees this as the actual fulfillment of Christ's calling and the acceptance of the burden of the sin of the world.

> It was the condemnation in the Cross which made Him cry, 'O My Father, if it be possible, let this cup pass from me;' it was the anticipation of that experience in which, all sinless as He was, the Father would put into His hand the cup our sins had mingled. It was not possible that this cup should pass. There was no other way in which sin could pass from us than by being laid on Him; and it was the final proof of His obedience to the Father, the full measure of His love to us, when He said to God, 'Not my will, but Thine, be done'.[14]

HIS POST-RESURRECTION MINISTRY

Coming to the post-ressurection encounter with the Risen Lord and His further revelation of the disciples' task, Denney points to 'the great commission' as the disciples' combined summary of Jesus' final teaching. He compares the gospel accounts of that concluding command, noting that all of them have to do either with baptism (as in Matt. and Mark) or with the remission of sins (as in Luke and also in John). These two thought forms are recognized as being inseparably associated in the New Testament and are also tied fundamentally to the death of Christ. When the risen Lord sends out His disciples, He makes forgiveness of sins the burden of their gospel, and that can have meaning only in the light of the cross. According to Denney:

> Here, where the final revelation is made by our Lord of all that His presence in the world means and involves, we find Him dealing with ideas—baptism and forgiveness—which alike in His own earlier teaching, and in the subsequent teaching of the apostles, can only be defined by relation to His death.[15]

Such is the paramount place of the cross in the life and the thought of Jesus. It dominates the scene from the ordination to the conclusion of His earthly ministry. We now turn to see the impact which it made upon the minds of His disciples.

The Cross in the Earliest Christian Preaching

Denney calls our attention to the *kerygma*, the earliest Christian preaching, found in the Book of Acts. In so doing, he gives us another indication of his capacity and tendency to speak in terms of the current interests of our time, for this has become one of the most fruitful areas of research in recent New Testament studies. Years ago Denney was asserting its importance. He does not outline the *kerygma* thoroughly but emphasizes the pre-eminent and fundamental place of the cross within it.

The apostles proclaimed it as a fact, but they clothed this fact with a meaning and sought to communicate it in intelligible terms to men. They preached 'the word of the cross', placing their experience of His death into relationship with the realities which surrounded it. They presented the cross, first of all, in connection with a divine purpose and in the light of a divine necessity. It took place, they declared, 'by the determined counsel and foreknowledge of God' (2.23).[16] 'A divine necessity', Denney commented, 'is not a blind but a seeing one . . . Not blank but intelligible and moral necessity is meant here.'[17]

The second relationship, coming directly from that sense of purpose, concerns the fulfillment which they found in the fact of the suffering Christ.[18] When Christ sought to lead them to understand that He must suffer they could not fathom His meaning. But now they saw what then they could not see.

> When the meaning of His words broke on them, it was with that overwhelming power which made the thing that had once baffled them the sum and substance of their Gospel. The center of gravity in their world changed, and their whole being swung round into equilibrium in a new position. Their inspiration came from what had once alarmed, grieved, discomfited them. The word they preached was the very thing which had once made them afraid to speak.[19]

The third relationship within which the cross is seen in the early *kerygma* has to do with the reality of sin and its forgiveness. This is the refrain of every apostolic sermon and its prominence is not accidental.[20] In the light of the context of the experience of the primitive church, it is natural and necessary to see these references to forgiveness as pointing to the saving significance of the death of Christ.

The fourth relationship which Denney indicates has reference to the continuing life of the believers, specifically seen in the early Church's expression of its experience through the symbols of the sacraments.

They were basic to the life of the Church and were witnesses to the connection between the death of Christ and the forgiveness of sins. As Denney put it, 'There is nothing in Christianity more primitive than the sacraments. They were celebrated universally in the Church before any part of the New Testament was written, and they still bear un-equivocal witness to Him Who came in the water and in the blood.'[21]

Thus the atonement is presented in the primitive preaching in its relationships, and it is important to note at this point that each of these relationships in meaning and interpretation has its root in that of which Jesus Himself had been conscious and to the understanding of which He had been seeking to lead His disciples. What they now proclaimed was not a gospel which was original with them, but the gospel which they had seen fulfilled in Christ.

The Cross in the First Epistle of Peter

From the early *kerygma* Denney goes on to consider the First Epistle of Peter, feeling that the apostle who preached the initial sermons in Acts also stands behind this New Testament letter. He finds 'Pauline' elements in many of the passages, but this is taken not so much as an indication of Peter's dependence upon Paul as an indica-tion of the one common tradition of Christian faith which they shared. Peter writes about the cross of Christ with the realistic touch of an eye-witness, and it is central to his epistle. We tend to idealize the death of Christ, but when he writes about it, as in 2.20 f., 'the Passion is set before us as a spectacle of human pain which the writer had watched with his own eyes as it moved to its goal at the cross.'[22] Even with the detailed account, however, there is still the interpretive meaning which lies at the heart of his vivid words (e.g., 'Who His own self bore our sins'—2.24). This understanding of Christ bearing our sins is an experiential doctrine for the apostle, not a speculative idea. To put it in Denney's strong language: 'This is not a theorem he is prepared to defend; it is the Gospel he has to preach. It is not a precarious or a felicitous solution of an embarrassing difficulty—the death of the Messiah; it is the foundation of the Christian religion, the one hope of sinful men.'[23]

Symbols of thought which by now are becoming familiar to us are used to describe this meaning of the cross. The author of the letter pictures it in terms of sacrifice and in the relationship of covenant. These two symbols are intimately associated in Denney's interpreta-tion: 'As sacrificial, it is sin-covering; it is that which annuls sin as the obstacle to union with God. Within the covenant, God and men have, so to speak, a common life . . . But the covenant is made by sacrifice; its basis and being are in the blood.'[24] The apostle also uses the symbol of ransom in picturing the significance of the cross (1.18 f.), and seems to strengthen its meaning in the continuing terms of substitution (3.18 f.). With this imagery before him, Denney wrote:

> Once we understand what Christ's death means—once we receive the apostolic testimony that in that death He was taking all our responsibilities upon Him—no explanation may be needed. The love which is the motive of it acts immediately upon the sinful; gratitude exerts an irresistible constraint; His responsibility means our emancipation; His death our life; His bleeding wound our heal- ing. Whoever says 'He bore our sins' says substitution; and to say substitution is to say something which involves an immeasurable obligation to Christ, and has therefore in it an incalculable motive power.[25]

In addition, there are in First Peter two new ideas of interpretation which deserve attention from this point on. The first is the moral influence of that which was done upon the cross. This recognition of the moral quality within the sufferings of Christ is not independently conceived but rests for its inspiration upon the deeper interpretation of His death. The other additional note is the statement of the aim or intention in the atonement, expressed in the words, 'that He might bring (conduct) us to God' (3.18). This is the highest privilege con- ceivable, that we should have access to God, and it completes that which has already been said about the cross in its relationship to the Father.

Denney's drawing together of the symbols in the apostle's preaching and epistle has helped us to bridge the gap which might loom large in the minds of some between the accounts recorded in the synoptic gospels and the theology which we find in Paul.

The Cross in the Epistles of Paul

When we pass to the epistles of Paul, we find ourselves at the feet of the great preacher of the cross, and his letters contain the most explicit interpretations of the death of Christ. It is impossible to understand the Pauline epistles apart from an appreciation of the central and funda- mental place which the cross occupies within them. Denney was a theologian after the order of Paul, and with detailed exegesis he enters, in one work or another, into almost all of the Pauline passages dealing with the atonement. We can do no more than draw some basic con- clusions from this wealth of material.

It is well from the beginning to understand some of the inherent characteristics of Paul's presentation of the cross. First, there is the *assurance* with which Paul expresses himself on the subject of the cross. There is an absoluteness about his presentation which is not short of intolerance; and, said Denney, 'Intolerance like this is an essential element in true religion.'[26] Secondly, there is his *dependence* upon the cross. From the first to the last of his ministry, to touch his teaching at the point of the atonement is to feel its heart. 'The doctrine of the death of Christ and its significance was not St Paul's theology, it was his gospel. It was all he had to preach.'[27] In the third place, he stands *related to the common Christian tradition*. His gospel was not original with him, but came out of the experience of the wider fellowship of the primitive Church. Paul said, 'I delivered unto you first of all that which I also received, that Christ died for our sins' (I Cor. 15.3). Fourthly, there is variety in his treatment of the cross. Denney would caution us against drawing a firm distinction between Paul's arguments in the midst of controversy and his exaltations of sheer joy. Both are necessary to give us the full pattern of Paul's thinking on this theme. One final preliminary point is the relationship in Paul's mind between the cross and *the resurrection*.

> There can be no salvation from sin unless there is a living Saviour: this explains the emphasis laid by the apostle on the resurrection. But the Living One can only be a Saviour because he has died: this explains the emphasis laid on the Cross. The Christian believes in a living Lord, or he could not believe at all; but he believes in a living Lord Who died an atoning death, for no other can hold the faith of a soul under the doom of sin.[28]

Against this background, Denney helps us to see Paul's presentation of the cross in the light of the realities with which it is related, so that in these relationships it becomes an intelligible fact. The cross stands, to begin with, *in relation to God*. The love of God is the first quality which is revealed in the cross, and the apostle comes to this ground of understanding about God's nature because of the atoning death of Christ. 'But for this', said Denney, 'the apostles would never have known that God is love; apart from this, they could never have found meaning for the phrase, God is love.'[29]

In addition to the love of God, Paul interprets the cross in the light of the righteousness of God. ἡ δικαιοσύνη τοῦ θεοῦ is one of the primary conceptions in Paul's theology. It is clear to Denney that the phrase is more than a passive attribute of God, and he goes into the interpretation of its meaning in several different places in his works.[30] He was insistent that the righteousness of God is the foundation of Paul's gospel of salvation. 'There can be no Gospel unless there is such a thing as a righteousness of God for the ungodly. But just as little can there be a Gospel unless the integrity of God's character be maintained.'[31] He justifies because He Himself is just.

There is a third factor in this relationship which is important for Paul: the wrath of God. This is Paul's word for God's reaction to sin and Denney feels that it cannot be eliminated from the apostle's interpretation of the gospel.

> Both the righteousness of God which constitutes the gospel, and the wrath of God to which men are exposed apart from the gospel, are spoken of as revelations.[32] God is behind both and present in both. Both have a divine reality and objectivity. It is because the wrath of God is divinely real that those who are exposed to it need to have a real divine righteousness; while the divine righteousness must have such a character as to meet the situation created by the divine wrath.[33]

This leads us into the second area of relationship, in which Paul sees the cross *in relation to the sin of men*. It is human sin which made the cross necessary, the sin which had involved us in death and which required for Him, in taking our responsibility upon Himself, to die. Denney feels that there were two things with regard to sin which Paul was emphasizing: its universality and its hopelessness. In order to express both these aspects of sin the apostle makes particular use of three words. The first is 'the flesh'. Concerning this Denney comments, 'All the passion of which his nature is capable comes out when he speaks of the flesh—a passionate loathing and repulsion, a passionate sense of bondage, a passion of ignominy and despair.' And then he goes on to add that Paul's use of the word 'describes human nature as it is, and the man who has not in himself the key to Paul's doctrine is a man who does not know himself'.[34] The second term which the apostle uses is 'the law'. His is a universal conception of the law which makes morality relevant for all men, but which also carries with it the sense of condemnation because we have broken the law. This is 'the curse of the law' (Gal. 3.13). The third word which Paul uses to describe the universality and hopelessness of sin is the word 'death'. Paul speaks of death in its total sense and is not concerned to divide the world into various spheres and interpret the term in the light of each. It is death, conceived of as coming from God and realized in the life of man. It is for him the very 'wages of sin' (Rom. 6.23). As such it cannot be separated from sin, nor can sin be taken away apart from it. Said Denney, 'He Who came to bear our sin must also die our death. Death is the word which sums up the whole liability of man in relation to sin, and therefore when Christ came to give Himself for our sins He did it by dying.'[35]

Within these two relationships Paul sees the cross *in relation to Christ*. It is, above all, the cross of the Christ. In His cross, He reveals the nature of God and thus discloses who He Himself is. As Denney looked at this, he observed:

> It is in the obedience of Christ to the Father that the great demonstration of *His* love to men is given. 'He loved me', as the apostle says, 'and gave Himself for me.'[36] In His obedience, in which He makes His great sacrifice, Christ is fulfilling the will of God; and the response which He evokes by His death is a response toward God. It is at this point, in the last resort, that we become convinced of the deity of Christ. It is a work of God which He is working, and the soul that is won for it is won for God in Him.[37]

It is necessary, also, to see the cross in relation to Christ as it is brought to bear upon the situation created by sin. This is what sin cost; this is what God in Christ was willing to pay. Denney saw this in Paul's declaration, 'Ye were bought with a price' (I Cor. 6.20; 7.23).

> The work of man's salvation was a costly work, and the cost, however we are to construe it, is represented by the death of Christ. Ye were bought with a price, means, Ye were not bought for nothing. Salvation is not a thing which can be assumed, or taken for granted; it is not an easy thing, about which no difficulty can possibly be raised by any one who has any idea of the goodness of God. The point of view of the New Testament is the very opposite. Salvation is a difficult thing, an incredible thing, an impossible thing; it is the miracle of miracles that such a thing should be; the wonder of it never ceases, and it nowhere finds a more thrilling expression than in St Paul's words, Ye were bought with a price.[38]

Again and again Paul stands and marvels at this, continually coming back to it and rephrasing it. At the *locus classicus*, in II Cor. 5.14 f., he puts it into the words that 'one died for all', on which Denney wrote, 'There, on the Cross, while we stand and gaze at Him, He is not simply a person doing us a service; He is a person doing us a service *by filling our place and dying our death*.'[39] The description of this relationship of Christ's cross to the fact of God and to the fact of sin finds its decisive word, for Denney, in Paul's presentation of Christ as ἱλαστήριον, 'a propitiation'.

> Paul is not preaching to men, but to sinners, to men who know what a bad conscience is, and who have a witness within them from which there is no appeal that the wages of sin is death . . . Death is part of the total reality which sin is for the conscience; and as nothing can be of any use to the sinner in which the reality of sin, or any part of it, is ignored, so, it may be said, to a ἱλαστήριον death is vital.[40]

And this which Christ has done is a finished work, according to Paul. This is the sense of the word καταλλαγή, 'reconciliation' (cf. esp. II Cor. 5.18 f.), as Paul used it to describe the work of Christ. 'Reconciliation is not something which is doing; it is something which is done,' said Denney; and then he continued.

> Unless we can preach a finished work of Christ in relation to sin, a καταλλαγή or reconciliation or peace which has been achieved independently of us, at an infinite cost, and to which we are called in a word or ministry of reconciliation, we have no real gospel for sinful men at all. It is not in something Christ would fain do that we see His love, it is in something He has already done; nay, it is only through what He has already done that we can form any idea, or come to any conviction, of what He would fain do. He has died for us all, and by that death He has so demonstrated the reality and infinity of the love of God to the sinful, as to make it possible for apostles and evangelists to preach peace to all men through Him.[41]

Finally, Paul sees the cross *in relation to the believer*. The key word in this connection is the word 'faith'. Paul felt that as a man stands before the cross, realizing its meaning in history and in his life, there is no adequate response for him other than the response of faith. 'He must trust himself to such love,' wrote Denney, 'instantly, unreservedly, for ever . . . The only right thing to do is to trust it, to let go, to abandon ourselves to it, keeping nothing back. This is what Paul means by faith.'[42] Faith, understood in this Pauline sense, is the saving response which the cross of Christ calls forth from the soul of man and represents the whole of the gospel as it is personally or subjectively approached. This faith in Christ Who died includes in it a death on the part of the believer—a death to sin, and to the flesh and to the law. Denney put it this way:

> The man who plants his whole hope in the revelation of God made in Christ, the propitiation, is a man who in the act and for the time is taking sin, death, the law, and the judgment of God, as all that they are to Christ; that is, he is owning sin, and disowning it utterly;

acknowledging it as unreservedly in all its responsibility, and separating himself as entirely from it, as Christ did when He died.[43]

Two other aspects of this relationship were important to Paul. The
first is the place of the Spirit in the experience of the believer, always
present in the commitment of faith. The other is the importance of the
sacraments in the life of the fellowship of believers. They are the
symbols of the gospel, and the gospel for Paul was the word of the
cross.

> Both the sacraments are forms into which we may put as much of
> the gospel as they will carry; and St Paul, for his part, practically
> puts the whole of his gospel into each . . . In both the sacraments,
> the Christ to Whom we enter into relations is Christ who died; we
> are baptized into His death in the one, we proclaim His death till
> the end of time in the other.[44]

The Cross in the Epistle to the Hebrews

When we turn to the Epistle to the Hebrews we find ourselves in a
field of thought somewhat remote from Paul. But when we concentrate
on the importance and the meaning of the cross, we find the same basic
emphasis which we have seen before.

Denney feels that the first thing we should note here is that the cross
is understood in relation to God, to His love and His grace (cf., e.g.,
2.9). This is emphasized by two ideas in the epistle. The first is the
place and honor of the priesthood, founded not upon the priest but
upon the call of God. The second is the concept of obedience to the
will of God revealed in the cross. In this connection, Denney said,

> There is nothing in Christ's life and death of irresponsibility or
> adventure. It is all obedience, and therefore it is all revelation . . .
> Atonement is not something contrived, as it were, behind the Father's
> back; it is the Father's way of making it possible for the sinful to
> have fellowship with Him.[45]

The author of the epistle also views the cross in relation to sin. Here
the emphasis is upon sacrifice, and Denney considers the numerous
cases in point (cf. esp. chapters 9 and 10), and then concludes: 'The
death of Christ is defined as a sacrificial death, or as a death having
relation to sin: the two things are one.'[46] The concept of the priesthood
is an additional mode of thought, closely related to sacrifice, which
serves as a further connection between the cross and sin and depicts
the importance of a mediator between God and man in his predicament
of sin.

The writer to the Hebrews sees, in the third place, the close relationship between the cross and the Christ. He is the eternal High Priest, the mediator. Denney finds this in the author's presentation of Christ as He is revealed in His atoning work, and Recognizes that this work is an accomplished and an eternal fact.

> The blood of Christ is the blood of an 'eternal covenant', i.e. in the death of Christ a religious relation is constituted between God and men which has the character of finality. God, if it may be so expressed, has spoken His last word; He has nothing in reserve; the foundation has been laid of the kingdom which can never be removed.[47]

The nature and quality of the personality of Christ are hereby disclosed. He is sinless (cf. 9.14): 'The sinlessness of Jesus entered into the Atonement: only one who knew no sin could take any responsibility in regard to it which would create a new situation for sinners.'[48] But He is more than that, for His work reveals Him to be One whose obedience was not merely that which is demanded of men, but that which is required of the redeemer, the mediator (cf. 10.10). Denney insisted on this. 'Christ did not come into the world to be a good man: it was not for this that a body was prepared for Him. He came to be a great High Priest, and the body was prepared for Him that by the offering of it He might put sinful men for ever into the perfect religious relation to God.'[49] However, the author of the epistle also asserts the note of Christ's identification with men in the representative role of the High Priest. 'It is a great concern with the author', Denney wrote, 'to bring out the extent to which Christ identifies Himself with men. He does not save us, so to speak, from afar off . . . He not only enters into our nature, He enters into our experience. He suffers what we suffer, and because we suffer.'[50]

The final area of relationship is that between the cross and the believer. Here again the appropriation of the eternal covenant lies in the reality of faith. Denney calls attention to the familiar chapter on faith (Heb. 11), saying, 'Faith is to the invisible world what sight is to the visible; it is the means of realizing it, so that its powers and motives enter into the life of men, and enable them after patient endurance and fulfilment of God's will to inherit the promises.'[51] The center of the unseen world revealed to faith is Christ, filled with the virtue of His death, and it is in this same concentration upon grace and faith that the writer to the Hebrews finds himself at one with Paul and with the remainder of the New Testament writers.

The Cross in the Johannine Writings

Taking up the Johannine literature—the Book of Revelation, the Fourth Gospel and at least the First Epistle—we find ourselves in yet another area of ideas and expression. In face of all of the critical problems involved, it seemed well to Denney to group these writings together, primarily because of the similarity of thought within them concerning the significance of the cross.

Turning, first of all, to the Book of Revelation, we find that the opening doxology carries us into the center of our subject: 'To Him that loveth us, and loosed us from our sins in His blood . . .' (1.5). Said Denney, 'Redemption springs from love, yet love is only a word of which we do not know the meaning till it is interpreted for us by redemption.'[52] The predominant reference in the Apocalypse is found in the person of 'the Lamb'—'the Lamb as it had been slain' (5.6 f.)—depicting Christ's finished work in the cross, His sovereignty and His continuing call to faithful witness, even to death (12.11). The image of the Lamb is new, but the relationships found here are familiar.

Proceeding to the Fourth Gospel, we find that while the tone is different the message about the cross is much the same. The life is re-counted in such a way as to point up from the opening moments at the baptism the place of the death of Christ in His life. The references are everywhere throughout the gospel and demonstrate clearly that, as Denney said, 'Christ's death is not an incident of His life, it is the aim of it. The laying down of His life is not an accident in His career, it is His vocation; it is that in which the divine purpose of His life is revealed.'[53] The throbbing emphasis throughout is on the relationship between the cross and the love of God—'God so loved the world that He gave . . .' (3.16). In line with this, the cross is also seen in relation to the love of Christ Himself—'greater love hath no man than this . . .' (15.13); 'I lay down my life of myself . . .' (10.18). The recurring 'must' concerning His death is here as well. Life is only realized through death, and death is bound up with sin. This is the pattern of thought of this author.

In the First Epistle, we find the relationship to sin stated more explicitly. 'The blood of Jesus His Son cleanseth us from all sin . . .' (1.7; cf. 2.1 f., 2.12, 3.5, 4.10) says the writer, and the significance of this becomes apparent when we realize that the author has used to describe the relation of Christ to sin a word akin to Paul's ἱλαστήριον, the word ἱλασμός. This note of propitiation is emphasized by Denney as essential to an understanding of the emphasis upon the cross.

If the propitiatory death of Jesus is eliminated from the love of God, it might be unfair to say that the love of God is robbed of all meaning, but it is certainly robbed of its apostolic meaning. It has no longer that meaning which goes deeper than sin, sorrow, and death, and which recreates life in the adoring joy, wonder, and purity of the first Epistle of St John.[54]

Thus, we are on the point of propitiation once more and the unity of the apostolic teaching on the death of Christ is clearly demonstrated.

The remainder of the books of the New Testament—the Pastoral Epistles, James, II Peter, II and III John, Jude—Denney passes by because of critical questions concerning them and because they do not add anything to our understanding of the cross, but rather assume the background of understanding which has been outlined. Out of this recognition of the place of the cross in New Testament thought—in its full relationship to God, to Christ, to the sin of man and to the life of believers—Denney draws his doctrine of the meaning of the cross. This development of doctrine must be done in terms of experience, and to that we turn. But as we turn, let us note that Denney's primary effort was to identify himself with the New Testament way of looking at life and truth, so that in his exegesis he has sketched the outlines of what remains to be said of his theology of the cross. The cross, he has asserted, is the central reality throughout the New Testament; it is, as well, the central reality for Denney's soul.

> You cannot get the Cross nor its meaning out of the New Testament by going behind it: you must stand in front of it to see what the gospel is; and if you do so, with the New Testament in your hand, the meaning will not be obscure. The Cross is the place at which the sinless One dies the death of the sinful: the place at which God's condemnation is borne by the Innocent, that for those who commit themselves to Him there may be condemnation no more. I cannot read the New Testament in any other sense. I cannot see at the very heart of it anything but this—grace establishing the law, not in a 'forensic' sense, but in a spiritual sense; mercy revealed, not over judgment, but through it; justification disclosing not only the goodness but the severity of God; the Cross inscribed 'God is love', only because it is inscribed also, 'The wages of sin is death'.[55]

IV

THE CUP IS DRAINED
The Cross in Experience

*Sin is exhausted in His experience on the cross; the cup
is not tasted but drained.*[1]

IT was said of Denney that when he wrote of the death of Christ he
seemed to be writing 'with blood from his own arm'.[2] There is an
urgency and an intensity about everything that he said concerning the
cross. It held sway over his life. James Moffatt wrote of him, on the day
Denney died: 'The atoning death of the Lord Jesus Christ was all and
all to him. He spent and was spent in making it everything to the
Church.'[3]

His faith in the cross of Christ, and the theology which he built
upon that faith, were born out of his own life, and he was insistent that
belief in the cross should never be regarded as a matter of formula but
should spring out of the basic reality of the Christian experience of
atonement and reconciliation. On the ground of its place in experience,
he held that the doctrine of reconciliation was 'the most urgent, in a
religious sense, of all doctrines; it is the one in which most is revealed
of God, and the one of which man has most need to hear. It is the
doctrine in which the offence of the Gospel is concentrated, as well as
its divine power to save.'[4] Elsewhere he commented, 'Because the
experience of reconciliation is the central and fundamental experience
of the Christian religion, the doctrine of reconciliation is not so much
one doctrine as the inspiration and focus of all.'[5] Therefore, for an
understanding of Christian faith and theology it is necessary above all
that our vision at this point be clear.

The place of the cross in experience can only be understood, in
Denney's thought, in the light of its place and interpretation in the
New Testament. The texture of relationships which we have considered in the New Testament must be verified in life. It has become
popular to speak of certain ways of thinking about the cross as being
'orthodox'. Denney was not greatly concerned that he be orthodox in
the matter; what concerned him was that he should be true to the New

Testament interpretation, as that interpretation is confirmed in experience. And this is the source of his power in his chosen field of presenting the atonement: he reminds one of the New Testament.

The Fact of the Cross

Denney begins his doctrine of the atonement with the fact of the cross. It is an historical reality. It actually took place. 'Christianity is as real as the blood of Christ: it is as real as the agony in the garden and the death on the cross. It is not less real than this, nor more real; it has no reality whatever which is separable from these historical things.'[6] Reconciliation is not simply a subjective matter; it is based on this historical fact. But this fact is mediated and verified in experience and it is this combination of fact and experience which gives meaning to the atonement. The simplest expression which can be given to the experiential fact of the atonement is this: 'Christ died for our sins.' By itself, Denney feels, this is too brief to be fully intelligible and it implies many things which must be made explicit concerning the relations between God and Christ, man and sin, death and life. But all of this must come on the basis of our grasp of this fact.

> The important thing, to begin with, is not to define relations, but to look through the words to the broad reality which is interpreted in them. What they tell us, and tell us on the basis of an incontrovertible experience, is that the forgiveness of sins is for the Christian mediated through the death of Christ.[7]

The Fact and the Theory

There are some who would stop at this point and say that theology has done all that it can do and should do in recognizing the fact of the atonement and in appreciating the truth which experience reveals there. It is enough, for them, to say that Christ died and that He died for our sins. To say any more is to force an interpretation upon the fact. There were those at the turn of the century—and their intellectual heirs are still with us today—who carefully drew the distinction between 'fact' and 'theory'. They professed belief in the fact of the atonement apart from any theory of it. Because the atonement transcends any interpretation of it, they felt it impossible to do more than hold to the fact and regard it as a mystery which cannot be resolved by any theory. Such disunity in our understanding did not appeal to Denney.

> A fact of which there is absolutely no theory is a fact which stands out of relation to everything in the universe, a fact which has no

connection with any part of our experience; it is a blank unintelligibility, a rock in the sky, a mere irrelevance in the mind of man. An absolutely unintelligible fact, to an intelligent being, is exactly equivalent to zero.[8]

He felt that this was the testimony of the New Testament as well as of experience; that the apostles were declaring this when they insisted not only on the fact but on the interpretation of the fact, not just 'the cross' but 'the word of the cross'. The Church, since New Testament times, has always proclaimed a fact that had meaning, that was intelligible, that involved in it a theory. The cross has been the great source of motive for spiritual life throughout the centuries of the Church. But, said Denney, 'Nothing can be a motive unless it has a meaning.'[9] Everything combines then to make it clear that if we are to know the power of the cross in life, we must seek to know the meaning—the theory, the gospel—of the cross.

The Relationship Between God and Man

'The Gospel', Denney said, 'is the revelation of God's redeeming love, made in view of a certain situation existing between God and man.'[10] We cannot understand it as revelation apart from the situation to which it speaks. The atonement is determined by the actual circumstances in which men are, by the relations which are present between God and men. It is important for us to see clearly this relationship.

The relations between God and men are, first of all, *personal*. The personal pronouns are required to express the situation in which we live, according to Denney. Our experience of God is within an 'I-Thou' relationship. It is important for us, in company with the Biblical writers, to 'regard man as a being in nature akin to God, capable of fellowship with Him and designed for it, conscious of moral freedom and responsibility, and therefore morally responsible and free'.[11] In order to establish this we do not need to go back and try to establish the ideal relationship which could have originally existed between God and a first man, Adam. It is assured for us by what we know of ourselves and by what we know of God and of man in the person of Jesus. 'Man's nature is revealed by what he is, interpreted by the course of God's dealings with him; it is revealed above all, and his destiny along with it, in Jesus Christ our Lord; and it is as gratuitous as it is futile to seek to discover it in all its integrity in a first man.'[12] Our personal experience and our knowledge of Christ bear witness to the fact that

E

we were made for fellowship with God. The atonement can only be
understood against the background of this personal relationship.

The relations between God and man are not only personal, they are
moral. 'The relations of God to man are not capricious though they are
personal: they are reflected or expressed in a moral constitution of
eternal and universal validity, which neither God nor man can ultimately treat as anything else than what it is.'[13] Denney insisted that this
does not imply a formally 'forensic' or 'legal' conception of the universe,
and that man is not to be regarded as before God like a criminal at the
bar. But if the relationship is to be at all intelligible it must be understood in the light of the moral context in which it exists. 'If the sinner
is not a criminal before his judge, neither is he a naughty child before
a parent whose own weakness or affinity to evil introduces an incalcul-
able element into his dealing with his child's fault.'[14] This is not
'judicial', it is moral; and if we are to think in experiential terms then
it is necessary to think in terms of such moral law. 'Without the recognition of that law—that moral order or constitution in which we have
our life in relation to God and each other—righteousness and sin,
atonement and forgiveness, would all alike be words without meaning.'[15]
God's very nature is felt in the universe in such a way as to establish
this moral law, and His relationship to men has about it this ethical
quality.

The Reality of Sin

These relations between God and men are *disordered by sin*. On the
basis of what Denney has already said, we can recognize that sin is not
seen as the natural state of man. 'Sin creates what for us can never be
anything but an unanticipated situation, the dealing with which must
always have something exceptional about it.'[16] Sin is not a neat part of
God's order; it is a breaking into the personal relationship between
God and man and a violation of the constitution of God's moral universe.
We do not know its origin, we only know that it is here, and that is
enough.

> We know immediately and at first hand the only things which are of
> any consequence: that sin is rooted in our nature so deeply, is so
> congenital and powerful, that we cannot save ourselves; and on the
> other hand, that God has made us for Himself, and never left
> Himself without a witness in our consciences, so that the possibility
> and hope of reconciliation are not precluded. This is far surer and
> far more important than anything we can find out about Adam, and
> it is quite independent of it.[17]

The sense of sin, the consciousness of being wrong with God, emerges in connection with some definite act. It is *a* sin which is seen by man to affect his relation to God. This is the aspect of the sense of sin which places upon us the responsibility: it is our own act. However, nothing in life is of a purely incidental character, and the cumulative effect of all of our choices is a part of the total unity of our lives. Underlying all our acts is the will which draws them together, which takes an active part in shaping them and which continues in the experience of sin along its own rebellious path. It is this fuller consciousness of sin which leads us past the view of sin as an incident to regard it as a state.

At a primitive stage of advancement, just as in childhood, men repent of what they have done; but at a more mature stage they repent of what they are. At first they feel that they must make amends; but when they come to know themselves, they feel that they must be born again.[18]

Sin and Guilt

This consciousness of sin carries with it a sense of guilt. The reality of sin comes home to man in an instantaneous and yet abiding experience of a bad conscience. 'The bad conscience means definitely the sense of being wrong with God—of being estranged from Him by what we have done, yet unable to escape from Him, at once alienated and answerable.'[19] Denney goes further into the paralyzing nature of this sense of guilt. It blunts moral intelligence, so that we come to know Paul's meaning of 'a reprobate mind'[20]; it weakens the power to repent, taking from us healing sorrow when we need it most; it impairs and finally destroys moral effort, causing us to seek good not through God—the only source of goodness—but in hiding from Him.

This sense of being wrong with God, under His displeasure, excluded from His fellowship, afraid to meet Him yet bound to meet Him, is the sense of guilt. Conscience confesses in it its liability to God, a liability which in the very nature of the case it can do nothing to meet, and which therefore is nearly akin to despair.[21]

Denney quotes in this connection the lines from the hymn 'Rock of Ages',

> *Be of sin the double cure*
> *Cleanse me from its guilt and power.*

And then he comments, 'But its guilt and power are not co-ordinate. It is its guilt which gives it power. Its guilt alienates us from God and it is in virtue of this alienation that sin reigns in us. Hence to be reconciled to God is the sinner's primary need. He overcomes the power of sin through having its guilt annulled, and his bad conscience stilled.'[22]

A Kingdom of Sin

It is in this disordered relationship between God and the individual man that our understanding of sin must begin. But it cannot end there, for there is no ultimate reality in the conception of an absolutely individual man who is in an independent relationship with God. Life is not so known to us and sin cannot be so understood. We speak in these terms because we have experience in these terms, but at the same time we are fully aware that all men are members of a society in which we have a moral relationship and in which we both affect and are affected by the social body to which we belong. When Denney reviews the whole matter of corporate will and the interrelatedness of sin, he is willing to speak of 'a kingdom of sin upon earth'.[23] At the same time, he does not feel that this structure of conditions around us and within us can remove from us the sense of obligation and responsibility which sin places upon us. To excuse our sin on the basis of natural environment or heredity is unrealistic and immoral. To a certain extent our natural inheritance determines the particular mode of our temptation to sin—whether it is to be anger or lust or greed or something else—but the outcome of the temptation depends upon the individual himself. As Denney observed, 'What we inherit, strictly speaking, may be said to fix our trial, but not our fate.'[24] To argue that sin is beyond the responsibility of the individual man seemed to Denney to rule out conscience, which continuously brings the soul face to face with the living God and there makes him realize his own accountability. Every man must reckon with that.

> The saintliest man has the sap of nature in his veins. His roots strike down into its deepest and what will sometimes seem its darkest places, and he has in his own bosom the key to all that can ever appal him in the world . . . When the moral consciousness has come to any maturity, it is not only a consciousness that a given act is wrong, or that in virtue of some particular act I have incurred an abiding responsibility; it is a consciousness that what I call my nature is in some kind of antagonism to the laws of the moral world, and that sin in me is as deep as being.[25]

This understanding of the organic quality of sin leads Denney to a larger conclusion: that sin is not only involved in the whole of human nature but that it is also involved in the interrelatedness between the human and the material, the spiritual and the natural, in the world. Sin involves the whole human being, and the divine reaction to the disorder which it brings is manifested in terms of wholeness as well. It comes home to the conscience in such a way as to reveal the unity of God's universe, for everything—moral and physical—seems to share in the disarrangement which sin brings. 'When a man sins he does something in which his whole being participates, and the reaction of God against his sin is a reaction in which he is conscious, or might be conscious, that the whole system of things is in arms against him.'[26] What this means in experience is that we cannot escape punishment, that the whole world stands as the witness which inevitably detects our wrong. Denney had learned from penologists that 'what represses crime is not the severity with which it is punished but the inevitableness with which it is found out'.[27] He applied this to God's government of the world which leaves no doubt that our sin is seen and stands under judgment, and the world itself under God is in movement against us.

The reality of sin has been stated so firmly by Denney that one may be tempted to feel that he was too pessimistic about man, and that there is scarcely a foothold in human nature where God may begin His redemptive work. But this is to forget the point of origin that man's nature is such that he can have dealings—personal relations—with God. It is also to forget Denney's experiential approach to theological formulas, for the very fact that we can make some description of the depth of sin in ourselves is a proof that there is something within us which is beyond that sin. Thus Denney felt that the task of theology is to make clear the effect of spiritual inability which sin brings about in human nature—to make it obvious that man needs a redeemer—and at the same time to show that there is that in man to which God can call—to make it clear that man is susceptible of redemption. 'It is only when we fully recognise what men have, even while they disregard the gospel, that we can hopefully call their attention to what they have not.'[28] He sought to call theology to the proclamation of both the need and the possibility of redemption: 'We must hold such a doctrine of sin as makes it evident that we cannot save ourselves, but not such a doctrine as implies that not even God can save us.'[29]

The Result of Sin

The reality of sin is such that we have found in it a reaction within ourselves and within our world which is a part of the pain we bear, and

which points us to the punishment to which sin ultimately leads us.
The Biblical way of speaking of that punishment is summed up in
familiar and frightening words: 'the wages of sin is death'. There are
many explanations for the phenomenon of death, but Denney holds
that until we have seen it in its relation to sin then we have not seen it
aright, and we are not on proper ground for understanding the cross
of Christ.

The difficulty in interpretation here lies in the fact that men insist
on a distinction between the physical and the spiritual. For Denney,
all such divisions are ultimately unrealistic, because the wholeness of
our experience transcends the distinctions which they describe. It is
futile to speak of sin and death, or of spiritual as over against physical
death, as though they dwelt on separate planes, for the conscience bears
testimony that their planes intersect and interpenetrate and our experience of the whole constitution of the world reacting against evil
culminates in this one reality. 'There is nothing whatever, in human
experience, which is merely physical; death is not merely physical; it
is human; one, awful, indivisible experience, which cannot be analysed,
and which is profaned when it is identified with anything that could
befall a lower than human nature.'[30]

Denney finds this interpretation throughout the Bible, and comments on the particular reference to it in the Genesis story of the first
man:

> That the third chapter of Genesis is mythological in form, no one
> who knows what mythology is will deny; but even mythology is not
> made out of nothing, and in this chapter every atom is 'stuff o' the
> conscience'. What we see in it is conscience, projecting as it were in
> a picture on a screen its own invincible, dear-bought, despairing
> conviction that sin and death are indissolubly united—that from
> death the sinful race can never get away—that it is part of the in-
> divisible reality of sin that the shadow of death darkens the path of
> the sinner, and at last swallows him up.[31]

Sin serves as the explanation for death, not simply in the sense of
natural science nor simply in the sense of mythology, but in the one
unified knowledge of death which conscience mediates to us all. We
may call sin a spiritual thing, but unless we feel the shadow of death
upon it we do not know what it means; we may call death a natural
thing, but unless we feel its roots in our own sense of sin we do not
know its significance. In the presence of God our distinctions in thought
vanish and we are confronted by His final reaction to sin. Denney

speaks of this in a somber image: 'Death is a kind of sacrament of sin. It is in death, ultimately, that the whole meaning of sin comes home to the sinner; he has not sounded it to its depths till he has discovered that this comes into it at last.'[32]

God's Reaction to Sin

The most important aspect of this understanding of death as the result of sin is the revelation which it gives of God's reaction to our sin. The serious element in the situation lies not in the sense of sin but in the reaction of God; it is God's reaction which has created the very sense of sin. Into the personal, moral relations between God and man the reality of sin has entered, and we have seen what this means in the experience of man. But every step in our understanding of its meaning to man has been drawn from its prior and ultimate meaning to God. This is seen finally in death, where the basic significance is the fact that sin lies under the condemnation of God. The Biblical writers speak of this as 'the wrath of God', and Denney makes it clear that whether we use that word or not we cannot escape the reality for which it stands.

> It is as real as a bad conscience, as real as the difference between right and wrong, as real as the consciousness of guilt which is but the echo of it, as real as the spiritual impotence and despair, which are the effects of its paralyzing touch. The thing that has to be dealt with, that has to be overcome, in the work of reconciliation, is not man's distrust of God, but God's condemnation of man.[33]

'Evil shall not dwell with Thee', the Psalmist says,[34] and Denney feels that in that simple word lies the root of the matter: 'The wrath of God is the instinct of self-preservation in the Divine nature; it is the eternal repulsion, by the Holy One, of all evil.'[35] The reaction of God to sin is as real for us as sin's result in death. It is as real for Him as His own character, and so He cannot cheaply do away with it.

The Redemption from Sin

Against this background of the relationship between God and man, the reality of sin and its result, it is possible for us now to see what God in Christ did in redeeming us from sin, restoring the relationship and reconciling the world to Himself. Denney asserted that we must understand the need for redemption before we can adequately understand what God has done to redeem.

The ultimate fact which stands over against the fact of our sin is the love of God. If our sin has given us the need for reconciliation, His love has given us the basis for it. Apart from His love we would have no relations with Him, and apart from it we can have no restoration of the relationship. 'The source of reconciliation', wrote Denney, 'as Scripture and experience combine to teach, is to be found purely in the love of God.'[36] The final reality of life is not our sin, nor guilt, nor death; it is our experience of the love of God. That is what ultimately conquers the realities of the situation in which we are caught. The work of Christ is His obedient expression of the Father's will and, as such, His conclusive demonstration of God's love.

It is not enough, however, to say that God is love and therefore He forgives and reconciliation is made possible. God's love is manifested in moral terms. His love is righteous because He Himself is righteous. In the work of Christ, God is not seeking simply to impress men with His love. He is seeking to impress them to a certain purpose, to move them to view sin as He sees it and to identify themselves with Him. Denney insists that the work of Christ does not and cannot accomplish this simply as an exhibition of unconditioned love. It can only do it as an exhibition of a love which is righteous in character and which is focused upon moral truth. The only love of this description is love which acknowledges the reality of sin and accepts the divine reaction against it, which recognizes and humbly submits to the divine necessity not simply to forgive, but to forgive in such a way as to show that God is irreconcilable to sin, and that He can never treat it as other than it is. 'His pardoning love rushes out to welcome the penitent', says Denney. And then he goes on to add,

> But no one who speaks of the atonement ever dreams of questioning this. The atonement is concerned with a different point—not the freeness of pardon, about which all are agreed, but the cost of it; not the spontaneity of God's love, which no one questions, but the necessity under which it lay to manifest itself in a particular way if God was to be true to Himself, and to win the heart of sinners for the holiness which they had offended. The atonement is not the denial that God's love is free; it is that specific manifestation or demonstration of God's free love which is demanded by the situation of men.[37]

God cannot ignore sin or forgive as though it were not there. If He did so, He would not thereby prove Himself a loving God, He would—so far as we could recognize Him—cease to be God.

The Cross of Christ

It is in the cross that our sin and His love meet face to face and both are revealed in their ultimate forms. This ultimate character of the cross lies in the fundamental fact that it is the cross of *Christ*. It can never be understood or appreciated apart from who He is. Denney was eager to make this point clear, and would speak at times of 'Jesus in His death rather than of the death of Jesus.'[38] At the same time, he insisted that we must not fall into 'the opposite error, and think that we can appreciate Jesus fully, even in His character of reconciler, though we do not think of Him in His Cross and Passion.'[39] Wherever we meet Jesus, in His life and in ours, we find reconciling virtue coming from Him, but all of this power of reconciliation is concentrated in His death. It is His death which gives final meaning to His life.

This helps us to see the extraordinary nature of the cross. It was not simply *a* death, it was *His* death. And, said Denney, 'Death was not *His* due; it was something alien to One Who had nothing amiss; but it was our due, and because it was ours He made it His. It was thus that He made atonement. *He* bore *our* sins.'[40] The condemnation of God upon sin eventuates in the experience of death and it is this which Christ takes upon Himself. In dying He plumbs the meaning of sin; in taking responsibility for our sin He gives Himself unto death.

> Sin is exhausted in His experience on the cross; the cup is not tasted but drained. The forgiveness which comes through Him will carry deep into the heart of man the same sense of sin's reality in the divine order, and in doing so it will be the basis of man's reconciliation to God.[41]

What Christ came to do, and what the New Testament and Christian experience alike bear testimony that He has done, is to break down the barrier of sin and re-establish the relations between God and man. That work of reconciliation is as serious as the character of God which underlies it. The profound element to be dealt with is the reaction of God to sin, the condemnation which falls by His nature upon it. And Christ deals with it in a great and serious way.

> He does not treat it as if it were merely subjective—an illusion from which man has to be delivered. He does not put it away by disregarding it, and telling us to disregard it. He puts it away by bearing it. He removes it from us by taking it upon Himself, . . . by submitting to that death in which God's condemnation of sin is expressed . . . To bear sin is not an ambiguous expression. It means to underlie its responsibility and to receive its consequences: to say that Christ *bore* our sins is precisely the same thing as to say that He died for our sins; it needs no other interpretation, and admits of no other.[42]

He took to Himself the final consequences of our sin and did for us what we could never do for ourselves, yet 'what had to be done if sinners were to be saved: for how could men be saved if there were not made in humanity an acknowledgment of all that sin is to God, and of the justice of all that is entailed by sin under God's constitution of the world ?'[43]

Denney spent the greater part of his life seeking to deepen his understanding of the cross and to clarify his expression of it. He found here depths which go greatly beyond the reach of mind and soul, but he found in it a core of truth as simple as its greatness, that it cannot be understood apart from the recognition that in the cross we see the sinless One dying the death of the sinful.

> On the cross the sinless Son of God, in love to man and in obedience to the Father, entered submissively into that tragic experience in which sinful men realize all that sin means. He tasted death for every man. The last and deepest thing we can say about His relation to our sins is that He died for them, that He bore them in His own body on the tree: if we could not say this, we could not say that He knew by experience all that sinful men find to be involved in their sin, nor could we say that He had been made perfect in love.[44]

This is the meaning we saw outlined in the heart of the New Testament. For Denney, it is the heart of the experience of Christian truth and life.

The Symbol of the Experience

How can we describe our experience of what Christ has done for us ? What symbol can we use to express the reality which we know here ? Denney was not insistent upon a particular formula to represent what takes place in the atonement. He did not contend that some particular 'theory of the atonement' be held as the ultimate truth involved. He was much more concerned that the reality be realized than that a particular word concept be formally accepted. He despised labels. Said he, 'No one was ever saved by an abstract noun.'[45]

Needless to say, however, he could not leave the matter at that, without striving to find some form which was the best symbol of communication. As he searched for a word which would give expression to the fact of the atonement, he seemed to settle upon two which came as close to it as any we have in our language.

(1) 'Substitute'. The first of these was the word 'substitute'. Denney has often been counted as a strict proponent of the 'substitutionary theory', but it was a designation which he himself sought to deny or

correct in his own lifetime, feeling that his beliefs—in line with the New Testament—were a great deal more free and vital than the rigid formulas of orthodoxy sometimes associated with that theory. Nevertheless, he felt that there was that within the faith of the New Testament and the truth of Christian experience which makes the word 'substitute' a vital symbol of the reality. 'If Christ died the death in which sin had involved us—if in His death He took the responsibility for our sins upon Himself—no word is equal to this which falls short of what is meant by calling Him our substitute.'[46]

If he could have found a word which suited this meaning better he would have used it. He tried working with the word 'representative', put forward by many and having some basis in the New Testament, but he felt that this carries with it the implication that we are capable of presenting ourselves to God in the person of our representative and thus keeps us from feeling our complete debt to Christ. He insisted that it is only as Christ stands in our place that we are brought into that relation to Him which makes Him our representative. So it was that he held to the word 'substitute', feeling that only in such an expression are we enabled to interpret the death of Christ as the demonstration of love to sinners which it is. This is not a mechanical conception of the transfer of merit in the analogy of an account. It is too personal and spiritual for that. 'He came into our lot as sinners, and was baptized with our baptism; but this truth, essential as it is to the Gospel, is spiritual, and not a truth to be expressed in terms of book-keeping.'[47]

(2) 'Propitiation'. The second word which Denney employed frequently to describe the work of Christ is the word 'propitiation'. He found his own experience and understanding to be in line with Paul's thought and thus came to express himself in like terms. He seems particularly to enjoy using the Greek word, $\iota\lambda\alpha\sigma\tau\eta\rho\iota\sigma\nu$, feeling that in so doing he can fill it with all of the meaning which it had for the apostle. The original word, as we have seen, is sacrificial in its connotation, and it is thus that Denney understood it and interpreted it. This 'substitutionary sacrifice' represents the high mark of Denney's expression of his thought concerning the cross.

He returned to the concept lying within these symbols again and again, seeking to shed new light on its meaning for himself and for others. He used more illustrations to try to make this one point clear than on any other part of his theology. One image he gives is that of a man sitting on the end of a pier enjoying a summer's day when someone comes and jumps into the water drowning himself to prove his love.

The man on the pier might be much in need of love, but this act would be completely unintelligible. But if, on the other hand, the man had fallen over the pier and was drowning and someone dived into the water and, at the cost of making the man's peril his own, saved him from death, then that would be an intelligible act and one would say, 'Greater love hath no man than this'. In that case, said Denney, 'there would be an intelligible relation between the sacrifice which love made and the necessity from which it redeemed'. And then he continued,

> There must be such an intelligible relation between the death of Christ—the great act in which His love to sinners is demonstrated—and the sin of the world for which in His blood He is the propitiation . . . I have not yet seen any intelligible relation established between them except that which is the key to the whole of New Testament teaching, and which bids us to say, as we look at the cross, *He* bore *our* sins, *He* died *our* death. It is *so* His love constrains us.[48]

The Results of the Experience: Revelation

When we ask what Christ's propitiatory death for our sin accomplishes, Denney answers that it holds forth for us the two realities of *revelation* and *reconciliation*. From this point in experience we can see God and ourselves and can know the fellowship for which we were intended.

God is revealed to us in the cross as at no other place. The quality which is most clearly revealed, according to Denney, is *God's righteousness*. He seems to feel that this incorporates the deepest meaning of God's justice and, at the same time, provides the love of God with the moral content which is necessary to keep our thoughts concerning it from devolving into sentiment. At the cross God discloses that sin is not to be dealt with lightly, that He can have no part with it, that it stands under His abiding condemnation and that it costs this much to conquer it. This is the first aspect of God's righteousness, Denney maintained, and it is a revelation with searching spiritual implications for the believer.

> God's righteousness is demonstrated at the cross, because there, in Christ's death, it is made once for all apparent that He does not palter with sin; the doom of sin falls by His appointment on the redeemer. And it is possible, at the same time, to accept as righteous those who by faith unite themselves to Christ upon the cross, and identify themselves with Him in His death: for in doing so they submit to the divine sentence upon sin, and at bottom become right with God.[49]

Some will counter that this hard, awesome side of God's righteousness is incompatible with the conception of the love and the mercy of God, but Denney insists that there is no way to understand the love and mercy of God apart from the justness of His judgment upon sin. They are not separate parts of God's character; they are the single expression of the righteous love of God, and this is what the cross reveals to us.

> The great lesson that the cross teaches is that God's mercy to the sinful comes through His judgment upon sin. The pardon which is preached in Jesus Christ has the awful virtue of God's condemnation in it as well as the tenderness of His love to the sinful; it expresses the self-preserving as well as the self-communicating side of the divine nature; it is wrought, as it were, in one piece out of the judgment and the mercy of God; and in this is the secret of its power.[50]

To stop short of this is to fail to secure in one's understanding the righteousness of God, a righteousness which for Denney is forever made certain in the cross.

Even as we have considered the awful nature of God's righteousness we have found ourselves confronted as well by *His grace*. God has condemned our sin but has provided a redeemer from our sin. In fact, it is only as we see the work of the redeemer that we understand the full weight of the condemnation. God provides the means of atonement in the person of the Son, and the Son has dealt with the guilt and the power of sin in a way which has been true to the righteousness of God. This is the meaning of God's grace, and Denney never interprets that grace without the cross of Christ being at its heart. 'Grace', said Denney in one of his classic definitions, 'is the love of God, spontaneous, beautiful, unearned, at work in Jesus Christ for the salvation of sinful men.'[51] The grace of God contains suffering. Denney used an analogy from human life to make the reality of this clear. He cited the case of a home in which the husband has wounded his wife's love. And what happens? It may be that after a while the offender begins to forgive himself and, on the cheap solution of letting bygones be bygones, tries to go on as though nothing had happened, never allowing himself to recognize that at heart there has been no reconciliation. Too many people, Denney observed, have taken this as analogous to God's forgiveness and have thereby failed to understand the reconciliation which God offers in Christ. He goes on in earnest tones:

> But sometimes what takes place is quite different, far more wonderful, far more divine. There is such an experience as a real reconcilia-

tion, in which the offender does not forgive himself but is forgiven. And what is the peculiarity of this experience, by which it is differentiated from the other? It is this: the centre of moral interest is transferred at once from the offender to the offended . . . I can believe that it is possible for love to forgive anything—for the love of a wife to pardon things in her husband that broke her pride, her hope, and her trust in him; but I can believe also, or rather I cannot but believe, that just in proportion to the purity and divineness of her nature, must that forgiveness come out of an agony in which it would not be amazing if she suddenly fell down dead. There is all this difference between forgiving oneself, which is so easy, so common, and so degrading; and being forgiven by a love which has borne our sins, which is so tragic, so subduing, so regenerating. Real forgiveness, forgiveness by another whom we have wronged, and in whom there is a love, which forgiveness reveals, able at once to bear the wrong and to inspire the penitence through which we can rise above it, is always tragic . . . It is tragic for God—a solemn and awful experience, if we may put it so, for Him to forgive; just as to be forgiven is tragic—a solemn and awful experience for us . . . To evade this . . . is to pluck the heart out of the Christian religion. It is to stifle praise in the birth, and cut devotion at the root.[52]

It is this, Denney asserted, which is the great distinction in terms of forgiveness between the Old Testament and the New. The New Testament sees what was as yet impossible to the Old: the cost at which forgiveness comes to men. 'The Old Testament felt that it was wonderful, but the New Testament can say that it is as wonderful as the Passion of Jesus.'[53]

This, then, is also the point of revelation of *the love of God*. Denney felt, as we have seen, that the source of reconciliation lay in God's love; but he felt as well that we know God's love ultimately only through that reconciliation. We do not guess that God is love and therefore assume His forgiveness; we know His forgiveness in Christ and thereby we know the love of God. It is because God in His righteousness deals with sin—graciously, tragically—so as to make it possible for us to experience forgiveness and reconciliation that we can say in conclusive terms that God is love. This is the final truth, the supreme law of the world, revealed once and for all in the cross of Christ. Said Denney,

What is revealed at the cross is redeeming love, and it is revealed as the last reality in the universe, the eternal truth of what God is. It is before the foundation of the world; nay the very foundations of the world are laid in it . . . You wish to know the final truth about God? Here it is, eternal love, bearing sin.[54]

It is not surprising to find that his view of love revealed in the atonement did not fit easily into the thought frames of the liberal theologians of Denney's day. When they tried to make the cross less than that which he saw it to be, it brought from him the deepest cries of his soul. 'God is love, they say, and therefore He does not require a propitiation. God is love, say the apostles, and therefore He provides a propriation!'[55] It was this which called forth from him one of his most familiar statements. He was speaking of men who minimize the importance of the cross. 'If I had the choice', he said, 'between being such a person or a Roman Catholic priest, I had rather be the priest lifting up the crucifix to a dying man, and saying, "*God loves like that!*" '[56] One who heard him wrote, 'It was said with such a quiet intensity that it burned itself upon the mind ineffaceably.'[57]

The Results of the Experience: Reconciliation

The cross brings as its result in our experience not only revelation, but reconciliation. Or rather, here we know the revelation of God because here we know our reconciliation with Him. Denney felt that we must recognize that there is a sense in which in the cross *God is reconciled to man*. While he does not speak of God as being the object of reconciliation, he would insist that the atonement in Christ clearly made a difference to God and that the simplest way of stating this is to say that God is reconciled to man. This is not a point in theology which can find its affirmation in our vital experience, but it is a necessary inference from all that we do experience in the cross. According to Denney, 'The world with Christ and His Passion in it is a different place from the world without Christ and His Passion in it. It is a different place to God, and God's attitude to it is different.'[58] This is a point on which Denney has been criticized more than once, for some have felt that he was here, in effect, denying the primary place of the love of God. But Denney answers,

> When we say that because God is love, immutably and eternally love, therefore He does not need to be and cannot be reconciled, we are imputing immutability to God in a sense which practically denies that He is the living God . . . If to be forgiven is a real experience, so is to forgive: it makes a difference to God as well as to us.[59]

This is what we mean when we speak of an objective atonement and it is upon this that reconciliation is based. Denney realized that this was a doctrine which could easily be exaggerated, and sought carefully—particularly in his last work—to avoid creating any difficulties in his presentation of it, while he insisted upon its truth. 'Reduced to its simplest expression', he wrote, 'what an objective atonement means is that but for Christ and His Passion God would not *be* to us what He is.'[60] It was in this sense that he quoted the familiar words of Charles Wesley's hymn, viewing them from a rather startling angle: 'Even if no man should ever say, "Thou, O Christ, are all I want; more than all in Thee I find," God says it.'[61]

On the basis of that objective atonement we can speak of the reality of *man's reconciliation to God*. This is the existential response in reconciliation to which Denney holds firmly. 'If a man with the sense of his sin on him sees what Christ on His cross means, there is only one thing for him to do—one thing which is inevitably demanded in that moral situation: to abandon himself to the sin-bearing love which appeals to Him in Christ and to do so unreservedly, unconditionally, and for ever.'[62] This is the meaning of faith, and Denney maintained that it is the whole of Christianity subjectively or experimentally, just as Christ the propitiation is the whole of it objectively or historically, and it is impossible to supplement either the one or the other.

> Redeeming love, displayed in the crucified Christ, is the sum of God's word to the world; and all that that word demands from those who would be right with God is the final and unconditional abandonment of the soul to the redeeming love itself . . . This is faith; it is believing God, and when we so believe Him, He counts it to us for righteousness. He cannot ask from us anything more or less or other than faith. It is the one thing which does justice alike to Him and to us. It is not a part of Christianity, but the whole of it.[63]

He could become aroused when he encountered men who made light of the place of faith and who tried to make good the deficiencies which they found in it by a doctrine of works. He felt that their view of faith was too shallow to be valid, and sought in his own turn to present faith in its most profound terms:

> There is nothing superficial in what the New Testament calls faith, in its relation to the ultimate truth in God; on the contrary, faith exhausts in itself the being of man in this direction; it is his absolute committal of himself for ever to the sin-bearing love of God for salvation. It is not simply the act of an instant, it is the attitude of a life; it is the one right thing at the moment when a man abandons himself to Christ, and it is the one thing which keeps him right with God for ever.[64]

Faith is a free act of response on our part. It involves a free moral choice on the part of the individual, which gives a quality of crisis to the presentation of the cross and to the response which is given. As

Denney once put it, 'God has not come into the world in Christ—Christ has not hung upon the cross bearing the sin of the world—to be talked about, but to become the supreme reality in the life of men, or to be excluded from that place.'[65] Or again, he said, 'There is that in the gospel with which no one is allowed to argue. All we can do is to believe or to disbelieve; to give it in our life the place of the final reality to which everything else must give way, or to refuse it that place.'[66] One of his favorite figures for the significance of the act of faith was that of going into debt to Christ; it is the placing of our lives in obligation to Him, humbling ourselves that we might glory in Him.

It is easily recognizable that repentance and faith are closely related, and it is not surprising to find them practically united in Denney's thought. They are as real as the experience of the cross, and they are dependent upon that experience. This is clear in the matter of repentance.

> Repentance is an adequate sense not of our folly, nor of our misery, but of our sin: as the New Testament puts it, it is repentance toward God. It is the consciousness of what our sin is to Him: of the wrong it does to His holiness, of the wound which it inflicts on His love ... It is the simple truth that that sorrow of heart, that healing and sanctifying pain in which sin is really put away, is not ours in independence of God; it is a saving grace which is begotten in the soul under that impression of sin which it owes to the revelation of God in Christ.[67]

This note of repentance in faith in response to the cross of Christ moves a sinful man into God's attitude toward sin, and in giving himself in faith to God he is free from the bondage of living in sin and dying under its condemnation. 'The blood of Christ', Denney commented, 'does not cloak, it cleanses from all sin.' And then he added, 'The very wonder of it is the evidence of its truth. It is not too good to be true; it is too good and too great not to be true ... The atoning death of Jesus is the supreme miracle of grace, and its effects in human nature are no less wonderful than the power by which they are wrought. It cleanses from all sin.'[68] So, in this trusting commitment of faith a man comes into the living personal fellowship with God for which he was intended. It brings him into the divine-human relationship for which he was created by God and to which God has sought to bring him in the cross of Christ.

> When a man believes in this sense, he does the only thing which it is right to do in the presence of Christ, and it puts him right with God. It really puts him right. There is nothing imaginary or fictitious

F

about it. Sinner as he is, his whole being comes into a new relation to God through his faith, a relation in which there is no more condemnation. God justifies the ungodly man on the basis of his faith in Jesus, and there is nothing unreal about the justification. He proclaims and treats him as one who is right with Himself. And he *is* right with Himself. As long as he maintains the attitude of faith he remains right, nor is there any other attitude in which he can ever be right. Christ makes for ever the same appeal, which demands forever the same response, and in that appeal and response Christianity, including the gospel message and the Christian life, is exhausted.[69]

Denney has not said the last word on the atonement. But he has certainly given us a profound and an inspiring word, one which well-nigh plumbs the depths of New Testament expression and which goes far toward satisfying the most poignant feelings in the experience of believers. He has given us as well a full view of how real and vital was his own devotion and commitment to the cross of Christ. As we turn to consider other areas of his thought, we do not turn from the cross. Rather it is the cross which leads us through his theology. It was the atonement which drew Denney's thinking into other areas and as we consider the variety of his insights we cannot but see that they are all of them sealed with the sign of the cross. Mackintosh once said, 'From start to finish, Calvary was the centre of his world. He drank in life from the thought of Christ crucified, and poured out in burning words the convictions it quickened in his mind.'[70] There are more burning words to come.

V

AT HIS OWN ESTIMATE
The Person of Christ

To be a Christian means, in one aspect of it, to take Christ at His own estimate.[1]

CHRIST stands alone in all the history of the world. He holds a place in the faith of Christians which is totally distinct from the place held by the founders of other religions in the minds of their followers. He is infinitely more to those who believe in Him than Moses is to the Jew, or Sakya Muni is to the Buddhist, or Mohammed is to the Moslem. These men were important, exceedingly so, to the minds of millions, but their importance is primarily historical. They gave the initial impulse to certain movements in history, stamping them somewhat with their own personalities, but they did no more and they were no more than that. But it is not so with Christ; He is unique.

This contrast Denney saw clearly and he was insistent that Christian faith and theology should understand and emphasize the absolute importance of the Christ. 'The Christian religion depends', he said, 'not only upon what He was, but upon what He is. It involves the individual believer in a direct relation to Him, not simply an appropriation of His ideas, but a devotion to His person.'[2] All things in Christian faith and life are referred to Him, and in Him all things are gathered together into one. This absolute and ultimate significance of Christ is the characteristic mark of the Christian religion.

Therefore, theology which would be called by the name Christian must give itself to the task of understanding and interpreting Christ; apart from that it is not worthy of the name. 'In a sense', Denney observed, 'it is Christ who is the great problem of the Christian theologian; our task is to answer His own question, "Whom say ye that I am?"'[3] Denney made no narrow, tradition-bound approach to the solution of that problem, but gave himself with a fearless honesty to the statement of the real meaning of Christ's Person and His work.

His Person and His Work

It was a matter of strong conviction with him that the work of Christ and the Person of Christ must be seen and interpreted together. Nor did he stop at this point. He felt that we fail to arrive at a proper interpretation of the Person of Christ if we approach it apart from His work, and that it is only as we see Him in the light of His work, interpreting Who He is in terms of what He has done, that we can come to an understanding of Christ which is consistent with the truth of Christian experience from New Testament times to our own. It is because we have experience of His power of reconciliation that we seek to understand the source of that power in His Person. Therefore we have first considered Denney's teaching on the atonement, for that is primary for him. 'The doctrine of the atonement is the proper evangelical foundation for a doctrine of the Person of Christ. To put it in the shortest possible form, Christ is the Person Who can do this work for us.'[4]

Starting from this position in answering the questions of Christology we are starting from a basis in experience. As He confronts us as our Reconciler we find in Him the expression of the judgment and the mercy of God with regard to our sins. He is not our gift to God, He is God's gift to us; and this raises for us the question which we must answer as to His relationship to God. However, He is given to us in a life and work which is certainly human and which answers the very problem which confronts all mankind; and this raises for us the similarly crucial question of His relationship to men. It is the doctrine of the atonement which makes certain Christ's place in the gospel, and which makes certain as well that we must have a doctrine of His Person. As Denney put it,

> The doctrine of the atonement signifies that we owe to Christ and to His finished work our whole being as Christians . . . He did something that made an infinite difference, and that puts us under an infinite obligation: He bore our sins. That secures His place in the Gospel and in the adoration of the church. That is the impulse and justification of all Christologies.[5]

It is necessary to underline this point more definitely because it is a conception around which a good bit of theological controversy has gathered. Indeed, there were many in Denney's day who were suggesting just the opposite approach to theology. For them, the important matter was the incarnation, and the task of theology was to concentrate attention there apart from any thought of the atonement. There were many reasons for taking such an approach: some speculative, the desire to relate the incarnation with the cosmic process—some ethical, the desire to broaden the appeal of the life of Christ—some dogmatic, the desire to prove that so great a fact as the incarnation was not simply an afterthought provided for remedial purposes. All of these combined to produce one of the most characteristic aspects of the day of liberalism, the movement 'back to Christ', the concentration upon the incarnation as primary. Denney disparaged this approach, fearing the extremes to which it could lead. We have seen some of these extremes carried out, e.g., in the numerous attempts to portray romantically 'the life of Jesus', and have since come to see the validity of Denney's emphasis.

He held, first of all, that the approach through the incarnation is not in keeping with the message of the New Testament. The New Testament does not speak of an incarnation which can be understood apart from its relation to atonement. In point of fact, the New Testament insists that the incarnation was a means to atonement and to reverse the emphasis, according to Denney, is to leave the field of New Testament thinking.

It shifts the centre of gravity in the New Testament . . . It is not in His being here, but in His being here as a propitiation for the sins of the world, that the love of God is revealed. Not Bethlehem, but Calvary, is the focus of revelation, and any construction of Christianity which ignores or denies this distorts Christianity by putting it out of focus.[6]

In the second place, Denney argued that the approach to faith and theology through the incarnation is concerned with metaphysical rather than with moral problems. If this approach is carried out, then the incarnation is seen in speculative terms and not in terms of human need and Christian experience, and that is to mistake both the problem and the solution which it is the responsibility of Christian theology to consider. If theology is to be approached existentially, then Christology flows out of soteriology. In the third place, this approach leads to sentimentality. Said Denney,

The Christmas celebrations in many churches supply all the proof that is needed: they are an appeal to anything and everything in man except that to which the gospel is designed to appeal. The New Testament is just as little sentimental as it is metaphysical: it is ethical, not metaphysical; passionate, not sentimental.[7]

All of which serves not to depreciate the importance of the incarnation, but rather to show that its importance lies in its relationship to the atonement.

Denney is willing to say further that it is only as we see the cross as a part of the whole life of Christ that we see His life aright: 'He lived in the same spirit in which He died, and in a true sense we are in contact with the Passion and the Atonement whenever we are in contact with the soul of Jesus.'[8] Denney is insistent upon this, feeling that it is true not only to the Scriptural record of Christ but also to the witness of His life in our experience. 'Christ's life attains its true interpretation only as we find in it everywhere the power and purpose of His death.' And then he goes on, 'His life is part of His death: a deliberate and conscious descent, ever deeper and deeper, into the dark valley where at the last hour the last reality of sin was to be met and borne.'[9] The center of Denney's faith and theology, indeed of his life, is not simply the Christ, it is the Christ of the cross. It is in the light of this emphasis that he would direct our attention to the Person of Christ, feeling that from this perspective we are driven all the more forcibly to ask the questions of Christology and that from this basis we are enabled to find the answers which are true to Christian experience.

> The atonement always says to us, 'Consider how great this Man was!' As long as it holds its place in the preaching of the gospel, and asserts itself in the church, as it does in the New Testament, as the supreme inspiration to praise, so long will Christians find in the Person of their Lord a subject of high and reverent thought.[10]

The Christ of New Testament Faith

What then are we to say in answer to the question of Christology, the question which Jesus Himself bids His disciples to answer: 'Who do you say that I am?' What are we as Christians to say concerning this Christ of the cross? Denney feels that our answer must be sought in terms of that which was given by the apostles themselves, not simply on the particular historical occasion at Caesarea Philippi, but as they declared and interpreted their faith in all those ways which have found expression in the writings of the New Testament. The witness of the New Testament to Christ is the primary point of our interest and the normative basis for the construction of Christology.

Denney gave himself to a thorough and detailed study of the place and interpretation of Christ in the minds of the writers of the New Testament. We must begin with what they thought of Him. In following the outline of his approach, there are certain things we should understand about his very careful and specific procedure. In the first place, he limits himself in this aspect of his study to those statements which are clearly expressive of the mind of the writers themselves. For example, in dealing with the Synoptic Gospels he is careful to consider only the observations of the writers and not the statements of Christ or of others. In the second place, he limits himself to their interests as well. He is not concerned to establish metaphysical distinctions about the nature of Christ, but concentrates on that which was of significance to the apostles, the religious conviction which they had concerning Jesus and the religious Christology which comes naturally from that. In the third place, he does not debate at this point the relative value of things which are said about Christ; he simply points out that they are said and that they represent a part of the vital faith of the New Testament.

He directs our attention, in the first instance, to the place of Christ in *the primitive Christian preaching*. The most important point to consider here is that from the very beginning there clearly is a Christology. The disciples could not help putting to themselves, in the light of Jesus' completed ministry, the question which He had put to them earlier. From the first they sought to say Who He is. The tense is important. As Peter proclaimed the primitive *kerygma* he did not think of Christ as a figure of the past; he had seen Him as the risen Christ and had felt His presence in the moving of the Holy Spirit. It was in virtue of this that Jesus commanded Peter's life and faith and filled his religious world and his message to men. The apostle begins his message with the historical person of Jesus. Said Denney, 'The Christ of faith was the Jesus of history.'[11] But, having begun with that historical basis, the apostle moves on to proclaim that this Jesus is the exalted Christ.

> The characteristic of this primitive Christianity is not the belief that Jesus was the Christ, but the belief that He *is* the Christ. He was while on earth what all men had seen and known—a man approved of God by His might in word and deed; He is now what the preaching of the apostles declares Him to be—both Lord and Christ.[12]

The proclamation of Jesus as the Christ embodied the truth that He is King, that He is the Person through Whom God's Kingdom comes. This is the simplest interpretation we can give to the words, but in doing so we are asserting that in the earliest faith Jesus held that solitary place of sovereignty which the Church gives to Him still. This is done in the most intimate awareness of the details of His life and death and exaltation. As Denney summed it up,

He is the Christ, the Prince of Life, Lord of all, Judge of the living and the dead, at God's right hand, the Giver of the Spirit, the ful-filler of all the promises of God. He is not the first of Christians or the best of men, but something absolutely different from this. The apostles and their converts are not persons who share the faith of Jesus; they are persons who have Jesus as the object of their faith, and who believe in God through Him.[13]

Next, Denney turns our attention to the place of Christ in the faith of *Paul*. He begins by showing how Paul's teaching had its roots in the primitive Christian society in which Jesus was intimately remembered, and thus was tied to the historical reality. But Paul's own Christian experience began with the appearance to him of the risen Saviour; the experience on the Damascus road was the starting place in his thinking about Christ. Like Peter, then, it is the risen Jesus who is the object of faith. Denney speaks of 'the absolute religious significance of Christ'[14] for Paul, and proceeds to show how Paul reveals this in various ways. It comes out casually—as he greets his fellows in the name of God the Father and the Lord Jesus Christ; it comes out in a word—as he speaks of Him without qualifying phrases as 'the Son'[15]; it expresses itself in passages where he contrasts Him with men—as he speaks of Paul and Apollos and Christ; it can be seen in the two great religious controversies in which the apostle was engaged—whether faith in Christ should be augmented by the keeping of the Mosaic law and whether Christ should be supplemented by angelic mediators, to both of which Paul's answer in its simplest terms is that Christ is *all*.

Denney carries his investigation a step further and outlines three forms in which Christ is presented by the apostle. This is not to say that Paul's faith in Christ shifted its ground, but rather to say that the basic truth of Christ came to mean more and more to him as he grew in faith and knowledge and he sought to make it grow in meaning for the Church. At the first stage, as seen in the Epistle to the Thessa-lonians, Paul thought of Him as the historical Christ who had lived and died and been exalted, his Saviour and Lord. 'Christianity', wrote Denney, 'may exist without any speculative Christology, but it never existed and never can exist without faith in a living Saviour.'[16] Paul had this personal faith from the very beginning. The second stage in Paul's Christology is marked by the controversial epistles of the third missionary journey—Corinthians, Galatians, Romans—in which Paul speaks not only about the Individual to whom his faith holds firmly but adds the interpretation of Christ as a representative, typical or universal Person, who is to the new Christian humanity what Adam was to the old. In the third stage, seen in the Epistle to the Colossians, Paul carries faith's thought to its conclusion and presents to us not simply an historical individual nor just a representative person for all men, but a person who can only be called eternal and divine. Here we are presented with the Christ who is nothing less than the eternal truth and being of God; no one knows what anything is—God, the universe, redemption, the Church—apart from Him. Even here Paul was not a speculative philosopher.

> Paul does not . . . invest Christ in a character and greatness which have no relation to His true nature, merely to stop a hole in his philosophy. On the contrary, the presence of God in Christ—His presence in the eternal truth of His being and character—is for Paul the primary certainty; and that certainty carries with it for him the requirement of a specifically Christian view of the universe. He would not be true to Christ, as Christ had revealed Himself to him in experience unless he had the courage to *Christianize* all his thoughts of God and the world.[17]

This is a startling conception on the part of the apostle, as profound as it is daring. While it stands in line with what we have considered as the faith of the primitive Church, it has taken that faith and exhausted its implications, 'Christianizing' the universe, reconstituting it with Him as its center, as the principle of its unity, and as its goal.

Denney next leads us to the study of *the Epistle to the Hebrews*. Here we find what Denney calls 'the most humanitarian of apostolic writings',[18] in which the man Jesus is recalled in 'the days of His flesh'. At the same time, the author has deep theological interests, and we discover in him the insistence that everything in the relationship between God and men is determined by Christ. Denney points out that this paradox provides for Jesus in the mind of the author a place in the true religion which belongs to Him alone.

Moving on to consider *the First Epistle of Peter*, Denney indicates that the same emphases seen in the early chapters of Acts are clearly noticeable here. Though Christ's historical life is intimately remembered, He stands in this letter as seen in His risen power and in His unique role between God and men.

> Jesus is not to the writer one of us, who shares a faith in God which is independently accessible to all men; He is the Person to Whom alone the Christian religion owes its character and its being; God would be a word of another meaning to us but for Him. With the

fullest recognition of what Jesus was and suffered as a man upon earth, the risen Lord, in Whom the writer believes, stands on the divine side of reality, and is the channel through which all God's power flows to men for their salvation.[19]

The Epistle of James is taken up next and it is noted that the writer says comparatively little about Christ and a great deal more about the life of the Christian. Denney's comment is that 'he may or may not have had theologizing interests, though he found no call to exhibit them in this letter; but it is clear that in his religion Christ occupied the central and controlling place'.[20]

The remaining *Catholic Epistles*—Jude and II Peter—are recognized by Denney to be late in their date of origin, but they nevertheless bear similar witness to the place of Jesus in the mind and life of the early Church, and by their date serve to prove that the later witness of the Church was one with that of the earliest believers, not an evolution beyond their primitive position.

As Denney turns to *the Synoptic Gospels*, he seeks to confine himself to 'that minimum of matter in which the mind of the evangelist can be clearly distinguished from that of his subject'.[21] In *the Gospel according to Mark*, we find the same lofty conception of the person and place of Jesus which we have seen since the early *kerygma*. From the very first, it seems that 'for Mark, Jesus is not so much a preacher of the Gospel, though he says that He came proclaiming the Gospel of God; He is the subject of the Gospel and its contents . . . The message itself which is called Gospel is embodied in Him, and the only way to deliver it is to make Him visible.'[22] Denney emphasizes particularly the place of the baptism of Jesus in the Christology of Mark, as the beginning of His ministry and as the key to its meaning:

> From that hour He was all that in the faith and experience of Christians He ever came to be. But He could not tell what He was as one can impart a piece of indifferent information to another. He had to reveal Himself as what He was, in life and word and works; He had to be discovered as what He was by men who associated with Him in obedience, trust, and love.[23]

The Gospel according to Matthew gives much the same Christological impression, although we find here the characteristic interest of the author in showing Jesus to be the fulfillment of the Old Testament prophecy. Said Denney,

> What Matthew is assured of is that the whole divine intention which pervades the ancient revelation has been consummated at last, and

that the consummation is Jesus. The argument from prophecy that Jesus is the Christ is not for us an argument that this or that detail in the life of Jesus answers to this or that phrase in the Hebrew scriptures; it is the argument that the Old Testament and the New are one and continuous, and that what God is preparing in the one He has achieved in the other . . . The unity of the Old Testament and the New, which makes Jesus the centre and the key to God's purposes, was the core of the evangelist's religious convictions, and it is in harmony with the place assigned to Jesus in the common faith.[24]

The use which the evangelist makes of titles to refer to Jesus and his treatment of the post-resurrection accounts further substantiate the loftiness of his view of Christ.

The Gospel according to Luke brings us to the same conclusion as to the Person of Christ, which is apparent in the author's citing of prophecies fulfilled and the use of titles for Jesus, such as 'the Son of Man' and 'the Holy One of God'. At the same time, Luke combines an intense interest in His resurrection and in His humanity, and goes on to indicate the universal scope of the gospel and therefore the universal place of absolute importance which is assigned to Christ.

Under the discussion of *the Johannine writings*, Denney first considers the Apocalypse, showing that a great deal of the work is in the language of worship giving Christ, with complete abandonment, all that the soul can ever give to God.

The writer's Christology may mingle naively archaic elements like the lion of the tribe of Judah, or the iron sceptre which dashes nations in pieces, with speculative ideas like the first principle of creation or the eternal divine word—it matters not. What his work reveals is that Jesus is practically greater than any or all these ways of representing Him; neither the imagination of the Jew nor the philosophical faculty of the Greek can embody Him; in the faith and life of the Seer He has an importance to which neither is adequate; the only true name for Him is one which is above every name.[25]

In the Epistles of John we find a determined effort to justify historically the place of Christ in faith. There is increased use of the conception of 'the Son', and it is a term as absolute in its significance as 'the Father'. It is to the Father in and through the Son that the author looks for all truth and eternal life. For its life the world is dependent upon the saving work of the Son. Denney asserts that 'it is only excessive familiarity which can deaden our minds to assertions so stupendous'.[26] There is a persistent emphasis as well upon the reality of the human life of Jesus, and so strong a term as 'antichrist' is identified with the denial of Jesus Christ as having come in the flesh. 'It is this unity of the historical and the eternal,' wrote Denney, 'this eternal and divine significance of the historical, which is the very stamp and seal of the Christian religion.'[27]

Passing on to the Fourth Gospel, Denney is willing to treat the way in which Jesus presents Himself in the pages of this gospel as embodying the evangelist's own sense of His place and significance for faith. Denney points to the prologue as introducing the theme of Christology and notes that here the author is dealing with the same universal significance of Christ which we saw particularly in the later writing of Paul. The interest is not speculative here in the prologue, Denney maintained. 'There is not a single technical term. The writer has no philosophical problems or conundrums for the solving of which he makes use of the category of the Logos. The one immeasurable reality which fills and holds his mind is Jesus.'[28] That the term Logos is taken over from Greek thought he readily admits; but in the light of the evangelist's use of it he adds, 'Though he borrows the conception, he does not borrow from it.'[29] In the body of the gospel we find the writer fulfilling his declared purpose of presenting Jesus as the Christ, the Son of God, and doing it by depicting His relation of God, to the men about Him and to the task of regeneration and atonement.

> The Lamb of God that taketh away the sin of the world—the Son of Man uplifted on the Cross as Moses lifted up the Serpent in the Wilderness—the Only-begotten sent of God as a propitiation for our sins: these are one figure, dominating thought and inspiring faith . . . In this character, as in every other, Jesus stands alone. It is in Him and in His death, in no other person and no other act, that for the New Testament Christian sin is annulled. Here above all, we may say, for New Testament faith, there is none other name.[30]

The Answer of the Apostles

On the basis of this ground which Denney's study has covered it is possible to come to some fundamental conclusions concerning the answer which the apostles themselves found to Jesus' searching question: 'Who do you say that I am?'

To begin with, we find that all of the New Testament writers were *deeply concerned with the question of Christology*. They made it a matter of primary importance to bear witness to the answer which they had found. This impressed Denney as he thought of its significance, and it was one of the basic reasons why he approached theology in terms of the work and the Person of Christ.

In the apostolic writings we find a theology, so to speak, involved; but a Christology fully and explicitly developed. It did not content the New Testament writers to recognize that Christ had for their hearts the religious value of God; they were impelled, or rather, let us say, were constrained, under the teaching and guidance of the Spirit, to set Christ in such a relation, objective and real, to God and the world, as justified that judgment of the heart.[31]

In the second place, we find that there is *a genuine unity of thought in their statements about Jesus.* That there are differences there is no question, but neither is there any question as to their common faith in Him and their common religious convictions about Him. Denney's study has served to prove that there is such a thing as a self-consistent New Testament, and a self-consistent Christian faith, and that that one-ness is based upon Christ. We shall return to this important considera-tion in our study of the Scripture.

Thirdly, the common convictions of the New Testament writers about Christ were *held in the context of the Old Testament prophecies concerning the Messiah.* Denney's cryptic word for this was, 'Jewish disciples had a Christology before they became believers in Jesus as the Christ'.[32] This is not to say that their impressions of Christ were limited to the forms of the Old Testament, for that is clearly not the case; but it is to say that they found in Him the fulfillment of God's deepest scriptural promises, and without fail they spoke of Him as 'the Messiah', 'the Christ'.

In addition, we find that *their point of origin is the resurrection and exaltation of Jesus.* This is the beginning of the content which they put into the title 'the Christ', and it is the place where our understanding of their Christology must start. It was in the light of this grand reality that they spoke of Him as their Lord. Said Denney,

Not a single New Testament writer, unless he is engaged in simply recording Christ's early life, thinks of Him as He lived on earth. They all think of Him as He lives now, on the throne of the universe, with angels and principalities and powers put under Him. His sovereignty in glory is not a thing which may or may not, as one please, be added to the religious appreciation of His life on earth as having the value of a revelation of God; it is the first and last and dominating element in the Christian consciousness of the New Testament.[33]

In the fifth place, we have found that *their Christology is bound to-gether by their common experience of forgiveness of sins in His name.* This is the motive behind their lives and their message and in this they are united. Denney speaks of that unity in terms of 'a common religious relation to Christ, a common debt to Him, a common sense that everything in the relations of God and man must be and is determined by Him'.[34] The Christ they proclaim is their Saviour.

As a sixth conclusion, it is quite evident that for the writers of the New Testament *Jesus is uniquely related to God*. He stands in a place which is entirely His own, a place of absolute significance, as Denney's study has shown.

> The apostolic writers are agreed in the idea that there is a transcendent element in what is now called the Godhead of Christ . . . They are agreed that His appearance on earth is of the nature of an Incarnation. He is not a saint offered by humanity to God; He is the Son Who has come from the Father into the world.[35]

This is in the thought of every one of the New Testament writers, and they sought to express this in ideas such as that of Christ's pre-existence and that of the Logos. What these ultimately mean is that the work of redemption which Christ has accomplished cannot be understood unless all that is involved in His eternal existence lies behind it. Such a work requires that He should be eternally and essentially related to God. It is the extension of His work to that necessary conclusion wherein He not only mediates in redemption but actually mediates in the creation of the world which is to be the stage of that redemption. If it were not so, no one with his roots in nature could understand and accept Christ when He appeared. 'Creation', wrote Denney, 'must in the last resort be in alliance with the God and Father of our Lord Jesus Christ, and in league with His purposes . . . It must be built on redemption lines . . . It must be built on Christian lines; the world in which Christians live must be essentially a Christian world.'[36] Denney put this as strongly as he possibly could, straining words to the limits of their meaning.

> If there is any region of reality which does not depend for its meaning and value on its relation to Him—if the truth with which we come in contact in Him is not the ultimate truth of God, the master light of all our seeing—then His importance is only relative, and He has not the abiding place in religion which requires that He should be preached at all. But in reality He is a Person so great that all nature and history and religion have to be interpreted through Him. All we call being, and all we call redemption, need Him to explain them. The love revealed in Him is the key to all mysteries. The categories we use to make His redemption intelligible are the only categories by which we can completely understand anything. Once Christ's

absolute significance has become clear to us, . . . we discover that our task, if we would understand the system of things in which we live, is not to find natural law in the spiritual world, but rather to find spiritual law—indeed, specifically Christian law—in the natural world.[37]

Finally, the New Testament writers present *a common belief in a real incarnation*. This has been assumed throughout, but it is possible now to see how much it meant. All of this which we have recognized to be a part of their understanding of the Christ was embodied in the historical Jesus whom they knew intimately as a man. There was a constant balancing in their minds of these two elements of His single nature; He was absolutely human, and He was absolutely divine.

The Two Natures and the Virgin Birth

There are, in addition, two points of Christological interest which Denney touched upon at one time or another, and which logically follow from this discussion. The first of these is the matter of the two natures in Christ. This is the type of speculative question with which he could never have become absorbed, but he did seek to think through its implications and he does have a contribution to make to our understanding at this point as well. This matter of the two natures—the divine and the human—in Christ is a technical approach to thought which is not familiar to the New Testament itself, but which comes naturally from the New Testament writers' doctrine of Christ. Its prominence in the later history of the Church and its consequent place in the creeds have led many to cling to certain formulas about the two natures. Denney feels that this is not very helpful and maintains that the proper procedure is to go to the New Testament and look at Christ Himself.

The formula of two natures in one person does not adequately reproduce the impression which He makes. He is all one—that is the very strongest conviction we have: the simplicity, the unity, the consistency of His law, is the final impression it leaves. The divine and the human are not distinct, and the incomprehensible artificialities of the *communicatio idiomatum* cannot avail at once to maintain their distinctness and deny it. All that is divine in Him is human, all that is human is divine. He is not separately, or even distinctly, Son of God and Son of Man; it is the Son of God Who is Son of Man; the Son of Man Who is Son of God. Great is the mystery of godliness: great, that is, is the open secret of the true religion—*God* was manifested *in the flesh*.[38]

One of the liberating truths which his students recall having presented to them was that of the wholeness of personal life and the falseness which lay alongside the truth in the distinction between divinity and humanity. He used to say to his classes, 'Christ's divinity was *because of*, not in spite of, His humanity'.[39] He drew an effective comparison between Peter and Paul in this matter, showing that while Peter began with the knowledge of the historical Jesus, Paul's Christian knowledge opened with the appearance of the risen Christ, yet, in spite of their different points of origin, both of them came to the same conclusion as to the divinity and the humanity of Jesus.

The other matter of additional interest is that of the manner of the incarnation, which has come to be known as the question of the supernatural birth, or the virgin birth. Denney feels that this should be regarded as an appended issue, not as a basic point of Christology. The basic matter is the conception of the Person and power and claims of Christ, and the supernatural birth will only have meaning as it is accepted in the light of that prior concept. He does not think that the virgin birth makes the incarnation any more intelligible, nor that it enables us to define relations any more clearly. 'This only it compels us to say', he wrote, 'that in whatever sense personality is to be ascribed to the Word, that same personality is the centre of the life which began at Bethlehem.'[40] Elsewhere he commented, 'It is in harmony with that unique relation to God and man which is of the essence of His consciousness, that there should be something unique in the mode of His entrance into the world as well as in that of His leaving it.'[41] On this basis of understanding he accepted the supernatural birth.

Christ's Testimony to Himself

Denney pushes on further in his Christological studies and enters an area which he regarded as being of the utmost importance. Granting the religious attitude to Christ which we have seen throughout the New Testament, the more basic question is: Can the Christian religion, as the New Testament exhibits it, justify itself by appeal to Jesus? Granting that the spiritual phenomenon is a common conviction concerning Christ, is Christ's own self-revelation sufficient to sustain it? Or, to put it differently: is the mind of Christians about Christ supported by the mind of Christ about Himself? This was important for Denney because he realized its importance for the Church. It is to this that the Church must look for historical assurance of its faith.

There are three assumptions which one must make at the beginning of a study of Jesus' consciousness of Himself. The first is that it is possible and necessary to seek the mind of Christ here. Some philosophical theologians and historical critics would deny this, on widely differing grounds. We need only remind ourselves that Denney does not accept either the one or the other, but holds in the light of the New Testament that Christianity is an historical religion.[42] Said he, 'The philosophical appeal would give us a Christianity without Jesus, and the historical one would give us a Jesus Who could take no responsibility for anything that has ever been called Christian.'[43] The second assumption is that we can move back to the self-consciousness of Jesus in a way which is historically unimpeachable. In Denney's study, he builds upon sound historical criticism and is unwilling to consider any material which is questionable on scientifically critical grounds. He limits his study to only the primitive material found in the two earliest gospel sources, Mark and 'Q'—which latter refers to the source of the material common to Matthew and Luke. In the third place, it is assumed that the resurrection is accepted as an historical reality and that what the apostles knew of the self-revelation of Jesus was made of eternal significance because of His exaltation. This will be considered in detail in the following chapter.

Denney's treatment of this subject absorbed a great deal of his interest and we see it breaking forth in several places in his work.[44] One by one he takes up the relevant items in the account of the life of Jesus from the baptism to the passion. His argument is clear and convincing and builds up by cumulative effect to the answer to which it leads. It is unfortunate that we shall not be able to touch on each step in his path, but a few examples of his approach will help us to understand his conclusion.

In both Mark and 'Q', Jesus is introduced in connection with *His baptism*. This was certainly the occasion of an extraordinary spiritual experience for Jesus and we have in the oldest records something of the impression of it which He was able to share with His disciples. The fusion of the two prophetic strains in the voice from heaven has already been mentioned, and what the whole experience declares is that 'Jesus stands before us from the very beginning of our knowledge of Him as a Person uniquely endowed, with a consciousness of Himself and of His vocation as unique as His spiritual power.'[45] His ministry is from its point of origin the ministry of 'the Son', and Jesus accepts not only the task but the title from the Father. Said Denney,

On the banks of the Jordan as in the courts of the Temple Jesus was

G

about His Father's business. His consciousness of Himself, as determined by the heavenly voice, was solitary, incomparable, incommunicable; but it was the consciousness of one who before it and in it and through it called God Father; it was not official, but personal and ethical, filial and spiritual throughout.[46]

Jesus was greater than any name which was applied to Him, and He gives to the Messianic appellations more content by His Person than they can ever give to Him. Yet it is by His awareness of the appropriateness of such names as 'Son' that we can appreciate that from the beginning He was conscious of His unusual and absolute significance.

Closely associated with the baptism is the narrative of *the temptations of Jesus*. Though given differently in the two basic sources, they are one in their major intent. The temptations are relative to the character in which He is introduced at the baptism; it is only as the Son that He undergoes temptation at all. His Kingship is accepted, and the questions raised before Him in the wilderness are as to how His sovereignty is to be realized. His victory over them is the vindication of His right as Son and King. As Denney put it,

> The temptations . . . show how the Kingdom of God is in the mind of Jesus essentially bound up with Himself . . . To His own mind the coming of the Kingdom is involved in His victory over these temptations. His initial triumph, in principle, over all the assaults of Satan—His resolute turning away, from the very beginning, from every false path—the entrance into the world and into the life of man of a Person thus victorious—are a revelation of what the Kingdom is and a guarantee that at whatever cost it will prevail.[47]

That this is how the New Testament writers conceived of Jesus there will be no question; what is of unusual importance is that from the beginning this was His conception of Himself.

The revelation of His self-consciousness comes to us in another way, as *He calls men to follow Him* and places upon them the task of discipleship. That He called the twelve seems indisputably historical, and it can be appreciated as an act of symbolic meaning. In choosing the twelve, it seems clear that the new Israel of God was before His mind —with its twelve tribes—and thus it becomes evident what He must have thought of Himself. He uses no lofty name for Himself, but, adds Denney, 'He acts, unassumingly so far as the outward form goes, yet in a way which indicates His conviction that the fulfillment of all God's purposes—for nothing less is involved in the re-constitution of God's people—is to come through Him.'[48] When He sends the twelve on the preliminary or experimental mission,[49] He gives them a commission

then decided for ever by their relation to Himself, He only concentrates into one tremendous expression what is the burden of His self-revelation from beginning to end.'[59] All of this is contained in the title which He Himself used, the Son of Man.

It would be helpful for us to consider one example of *the miracles* which Jesus performed and in which He revealed His consciousness of Himself. A typical 'mighty work' is found in the healing of the paralytic in Mark 2.1-12. On this man He works the comprehensive miracle of redemption, forgiving all his iniquities, healing all his diseases. In this connection, Denney comments,

> It is not declarations we have to do with, here or anywhere in the Gospels, but achievements. Jesus no more told the man his sins were forgiven than He told him he was not lame. With the same word of redemptive power He lifted the disabling touch of sin from his soul and of paralysis from his limbs, and in doing so revealed what He was.[60]

Jesus was declaring Himself to be the bearer of God's salvation and it was evident that He was conscious of the power of God in Him for the deliverance of man from all his sorest needs. On the matter of miracles, Denney feels that it is important to see them as a part of the total picture of Christ's ministry and of His self-consciousness. He points out that the accounts of miracles are in the oldest stratum of apostolic tradition, and that they must be considered in the light of one's acceptance of the supreme miracle of the resurrection. In connection with such miracles as the one considered, he made the observation, 'The healings worked by Jesus were personal, not scientific achievements . . . Jesus did not come to teach medicine or psychology, but to reveal the Father in delivering men from all that disabled and ruined life.'[61]

These passages, and a great many more, reveal the consciousness of Jesus as to His place in the world. What He is, of course, cannot be fully told, unless it has been in a sense discovered. These factors we have considered were seen and heard by the twelve, and *at Caesarea Philippi* Jesus turns from the crowd and concentrates upon these few, seeking to find if they have penetrated His secret, if He has shown them Who He knows Himself to be (cf. Mark 8.27 f., and its parallels). Denney comments that 'the question, it might almost be said, is more significant than the answers. Jesus is not only conscious that He is a problem to men, He assumes that He ought to be.'[62] When the disciples answered that the people recognized that He was someone extraordinary, perhaps one of the prophets come to life again, Denney observes that these must have been people who scarcely knew Jesus: 'No one who had been in His company could imagine that He was any one *redivivus*, any one but Himself. He was not the reanimation of any dead past, but an absolutely living Person, with His hand on the present and the future.'[63] It was this experiential knowledge of Him which prompted Peter to answer for the group, 'Thou art the Christ.' We have already had cause to consider what that term meant, and we know that, at the very least, they were calling Him their King. Jesus accepted their confession at their level and then proceeded to fill their concept of the Christ with the content of His own life and work. What He disclosed to them was the path of the cross which the Christ was to take. Denney's summary paraphrase of this whole section gives us the core of the point which he is seeking to make here, and at the same time gives us an example of his effective use of paraphrasing:

> It is as though Jesus were saying to His disciples all through this period, I am indeed the Messiah, the Person through Whom God's Kingdom with all its hopes and blessings is to be realized, and you are right to recognize Me as such. But the Kingdom is not what you think, and as little is the vocation of the King. The Son of Man must suffer many things, and be rejected, and be killed. His death is divinely necessary; it has to be faced in the path along which the Father calls Him. The loyalty which you rightly exhibit when you call Me 'the Christ' must be loyalty to One Who dies in the Christ's vocation.[64]

In presenting Jesus as the Saviour of the world because of His offering up of His life for the lives of all, the New Testament Christians were being true to the revelation which Jesus Himself had given them of Who He was and what He was to do. 'If the Church was conscious of being redeemed through His passion, He was conscious that through His passion He became its Redeemer.'[65]

We shall conclude this survey with the narrative of *the Last Supper* (cf. Mark 14.22 f., and its parallels). The historicity of this important occasion seems certain, and on both critical and logical grounds the central statements of Jesus at the table are trustworthy. The words, 'This is my body . . .', have from the beginning spoken unambiguously to the Christian mind of His passion, of the covenant in His blood, of His place in the transcendent Kingdom. It is impossible to put Him in a more central and commanding place, and it is the place which He has in that very night claimed as His own. It is assumed in the words which He speaks and in the symbols which He uses, before anyone has seen what they actually involve. Thus, Denney concludes,

The same wonderful Person whose incommensurable greatness had already flashed upon us in this scene or that of the Gospel history here rises as it were to His full stature before our eye, and shows us the ultimate meaning of His Presence and His work in the world. The revelation is one that justifies all that Christians have ever felt or said of their debt to Jesus, and it is one of the services the Supper does to the Church, that it recalls Christians periodically to the things which are fundamental in their faith—the atoning death of Jesus, fellowship with God through Him, the assurance of immortality. We do not feel it presumptuous to conceive such thoughts or to accept them as true; they are in the mind of Christ before they are in our minds, and we rest on them as realities in Him.[66]

The Freedom of Faith in Christ

It seems clear, on the basis of this review, that Christianity as it is revealed in its normative form in the New Testament can be justified in the mind of Christ. As we look at Him we see One who is not only equal to the place which Christian faith gives to Him, but who accepts and assumes that place naturally and spontaneously as His own. To put it in Denney's pungent phrase, 'To be a Christian means, in one aspect of it, to take Christ at His own estimate.'[67] This is the justification and the assurance of the historical Christian faith, and in this fact the right of evangelical Christianity is secured. Historical Christianity has sought to make Christ all in all, determining every relation both to God and man. This is exactly what we have seen to be the conception of Christ in the New Testament, and it is a conception which He not only vindicates, but to which He call us. Said Denney,

> There can be no Christianity at all, in the only sense in which Christianity can be seen in the New Testament, in the only sense in which it is a religion answering to the mind of Christ about His own place and calling, unless Christ is established in the place which the faith of the Church has always given Him. He must have His place because He claims it and because it is His due.[68]

This approach to Christianity through the mind of Christ, Denney maintains, secures the right of complete intellectual freedom. 'To be true Christians we are thus bound to Him; but we are not bound to anything else.'[69] We are not bound to any man's statement of what He is or has done; we are not bound to any church's rendering of His person or His vocation; we are not bound to any particular form of Christology; we are not bound to any formal doctrine of the work of Christ. When we insist on placing laws upon our faith in Christ we are striking at the very root of that faith and are endangering our intellectual integrity and that of the Church. As Denney put it, 'We are bound to Christ, and would see all men so bound; but we must leave it to Christ to establish His ascendancy over men in His own way—by the power of what He is and of what He has done—and not seek to secure it before hand by the imposition of chains of our forging.'[70] It was in line with this conclusion that Denney offered the creed which seemed to him to express the essence of the Christian faith and around which he sought to unite the Church. We shall consider that creed in connection with his discussion of the Church, but we should not forget that his suggestion came out of this background of study and commitment to the deepest reality in the field of Christology.

Denney was seeking to draw the mind of the Church and the focus of individual commitment back to the Christ of the cross. There were many in his day who were seeking to emphasize the historical Jesus and who were making the cry, 'Back to Christ', a slogan for their procedure of separating the historical figure from what they conceived to the entangling theology of Paul and the other New Testament writers. What they came forward with was the Galilean teacher whose doctrine of the Fatherhood of God and the brotherhood of men fell comfortably upon twentieth century ears. To them, Denney was saying, 'Back to Christ' indeed! But when we come to Him we must take Him at His own word. Denney's treatment of the subject, even in the brief review which we have of it here, shows that in the very earliest documentary sources we hear—and overhear—His indisputable claim to be all that the New Testament writers were ever to call Him. 'Never man spake as this man—about Himself. He stands alone, not only in the faith of His followers, but in His own apprehension of what He is to God and man.'[71]

On the other hand, there were those who were seeking to present the truths of Christ in the form of an absolute idealism which stands independent of historical material. Denney's reply to them, also, is to look carefully at the data. To touch Christ at all is to touch historical realities, yet it is to touch One who was fully aware that in the midst of history He was of transcendent and eternal significance.

> The certainty of faith that in Jesus Christ the historical and the eternal are united, and the very truth of God put within the reach of men dwelling on the earth, is the fundamental and specifically Christian experience, without which neither Christian religion nor Christian theology can exist. But the fulness of eternal truth is only given to faith historically, and we must always revert to what we have in Christ as the measure for rationalized religion.[72]

It was this place of Christ as the ultimate authority for faith and theology which Denney was seeking to secure. From the New Testament itself he had learned that as men come into intimate contact with Christ as He actually lived in history they come to know who He is and become His own. He was conscious that throughout the life of Christ there was the presence of the intended Messianic secret, 'the riddle of the New Testament'; that Christ was fully aware that the truth of Himself could not simply be told, that it must be revealed on the one side and perceived at first-hand on the other. Our joy as Christians is thus to know Him, and thus to make Him known. Our faith is founded upon Christ and upon Christ alone, and our theology must be built upon the sure, personal knowledge of Him whom to know aright is life. He is our gospel and He is our authority.

All that is creative and normative in the Christian consciousness depends upon Him . . . Mere conceptions soon become barren; definitions the most curious and precise become curiously unreal; nothing but personality and life is infinitely inspiring . . . The Bible is our text-book because it puts us in communication with Him; but He is our authority. We must always fail more or less decidedly unless our whole thoughts are inspired and controlled by Him who says, *I* am the Truth.[73]

VI

IN THE PRESENT TENSE
The Resurrection

No apostle, no New Testament writer, ever remembered Christ.[1]

'THE Christian religion', said Denney, 'depends not on what Christ was, merely, but on what He is; not simply on what He did, but on what He does.'[2] The Church throughout history has proclaimed that Christ did not cease to be when He died and was buried, but that He rose from the dead, ascended into heaven and sits at the right hand of God the Father. The testimony to this truth is one of the strongest elements in Denney's theology, and we have not read him aright until we have read him in the light of the resurrection.

The Christ of the cross is the living Christ, and the Christian faith —in touch with the New Testament—is the faith of men who believe that Christ is risen and that He reigns and that they themselves are in fellowship with a living Lord. Who He was and what He did are indispensable to faith and theology, but if we are to have any reality in either, then we must understand that the historical has become present and eternal. We must know that He lives and that He fulfills His vocation as the Son in the present hour. This truth we know through the fact of the resurrection as it is apprehended by faith. This is clearly the witness of the New Testament. Denney's cryptic word was: 'No apostle, no New Testament writer, ever *remembered* Christ.' And then he proceeded to expand and explain that paradox:

> They never thought of Him as belonging to the past. The exalted Lord was lifted above the conditions of time and space; when they thought of Him memory was transmuted into faith; in all the virtue of the life they had known on earth He was Almighty, ever present, the Living King of Grace.[3]

The Importance of the Resurrection

Apart from the reality of the resurrection and the faith in that fact which is exhibited in the New Testament, there could be no such thing as the Christian religion in any sense which history would justify. But for the resurrection Christianity could never have been born; without the proclamation of it, assent would have died within a generation. Denney leaves no doubt in the mind of anyone who reads his works that the exaltation of Christ is of this absolute importance. The life and death of Christ are not moved by this from their central place; rather, it is only as we see His life and death in this eternal perspective that they hold their place as the core of Christian experience and thought. Denney insisted that this was the meaning of the apostles' emphasis upon the resurrection. 'Except as Risen and Exalted they never preached Jesus at all. It was his Resurrection and Exaltation which made Him Lord and Christ, and gave Him His place in their faith and life.'[4] They would never have recognized His eternal significance apart from this fact, and neither would we. Thus it was that, as Denney counselled men about preaching, he urged them to lift before people the Person and work of Jesus as they are presented in the gospels. But then he added,

> When we preach from the Gospels, and see what Jesus was, and said, and did, and suffered, let us remember to make the application in the present tense. Never preach about the historical Christ; preach about the living, sovereign Christ—nay, rather preach *Him*, present in the grace of His earthly life and death, and in the omnipotence of His power to save.[5]

Denney's contention was that to fail to see the significance of the present, living Christ was to fail to understand the meaning of faith and religion. Faith must have its object in the present, and the Person who so inspires belief in the pages of the New Testament is a living Person whose presence with us here and now is the object and the inspiration of our Christian faith.

There are those who feel that this is impossible, and others who feel that this is unnecessary. Many were engaged in the 'Back to Christ' movement precisely because they did not believe any longer in His present existence or His heavenly reign and felt that all that was necessary was an appreciation of His earthly life and an allegiance to His principles. Denney's patience ran short with such an approach:

> They go back to gaze upon the great Teacher of Nazareth, as they call Him, not in the spirit of religious faith, but simply in that of aesthetic appreciation. They introduce into the Gospels the realism of the modern novelist, and try to reproduce Christ as He lived, moved, taught and suffered nineteen hundred years ago; they

dwell tenderly—not to say sentimentally—on the figure they evoke; and there is a kind of emotion accompanying this contemplation, which is supposed to be religious, and to have some kind of healing or saving efficacy in the soul ... Surely it is obvious that the historical imagination, carried even to its highest power, and suffused with the tenderest feelings, is not the same as religious faith, and cannot do its work.[6]

Elsewhere he wrote, 'They may reverence the figure preserved for us by the evangelists as the ideal of humanity, the supreme attainment of the race in the field of character; but they can have no relation to Jesus resembling that in which New Testament Christians lived and moved and had their being.'[7] On the other hand, there are those who are so preoccupied with the spiritual significance of the resurrection that they are willing to give up the historicity of the fact of it. This is the more subtle of the two; it was the popular distinction of Harnack between 'the Easter Faith' and 'the Easter Message'.[8]

Denney maintains that the answer to both positions is a thorough study of the facts and the meaning of the facts as they are presented to us. Both of the unsatisfactory approaches to the resurrection are founded upon dogmatic assertion and it does little good to meet dogma with dogma. What is needed is an analysis of the New Testament evidence, its worth and its meaning.

The Historical Evidence for the Resurrection

It seemed to Denney that a great deal of the difficulty in this area is due to the fact that the survey of the evidence for the resurrection has so frequently begun at the wrong end. Men starting their study with the gospel narratives inevitably become involved in literary and historical questions which seem almost insoluble, and these difficulties become attached to the ressurrection itself and to the whole New Testament faith. Denney holds that this is the wrong direction in which to move, that the important fact to begin with is the presence of an intensely powerful faith in the resurrection before any of the New Testament books came to be. If it had not been for that faith not one of them would have been written.

It is not this or that in the New Testament—it is not the story of the empty tomb, or of the appearing of Jesus in Jerusalem or in Galilee —which is the primary evidence for the Resurrection; it is the New Testament itself. The life that throbs in it from beginning to end, the life that always fills us again with wonder as it beats upon us from its pages, is the life which the Risen Saviour has quickened in

Christian souls. The evidence for the Resurrection of Jesus is the existence of the Church in that extraordinary spiritual vitality which confronts us in the New Testament. This is its own explanation of its being.[9]

The oldest historical evidence which we have is to be found in I Cor. 15. There Paul testifies that the gospel which he had preached to the Corinthians was the common Christian tradition which he himself had been taught just a few years after the events of Christ's life. Thus, says Denney, it is possible to isolate a primitive *kerygma* and to recognize that at a date quite close to the alleged events themselves we find that fundamental facts of Christianity are being taught in the early Church. These include the facts that Christ died for our sins, that He was buried, that He rose on the third day and remains in a state of exaltation, and that He appeared to certain persons.

Denney comments that the mention of the burial is important for it helps us to understand what is meant by the rising. The primitive Church would never have understood the meaning of a spiritual resurrection or a rising again simply in the faith of the followers. 'The rising is relative to the grave and the burial, and if we cannot speak of a bodily resurrection we should not speak of resurrection at all.'[10] At the same time, he feels that the mention of the third day is significant, for it explains the change from the Sabbath and is a further proof of the magnitude of the event which took place on that day. Denney commented succinctly, 'Every Sunday as it comes round is a new argument for the Resurrection.'[11] There is another detail of importance, the use of the perfect tense in $\dot{\epsilon}\gamma\dot{\eta}\gamma\epsilon\rho\tau\alpha\iota$, 'He has been raised'. Denney argues that this signifies that Christ rose and remains in the risen state. He does not come back to this former life at all but gives us the revelation of life in the new order, a life which has conquered sin and death. The early Christians understood this and proclaimed it. The list of witnesses is not exhaustive but it is sufficient to make the case perfectly clear and to answer the specific problems of the church in Corinth. Last of all, Paul lists himself as a witness. Denney insists that what Paul had seen was not simply an illusion, and, although we cannot penetrate into his experience, we know that it left no doubt at all that Jesus of Nazareth, who had been crucified, was exalted to the right hand of the Father in power and glory. 'The same Jesus whose body had been broken on the Cross had manifested Himself to Paul in divine splendour and power; ... the exaltation of Jesus was as real as His crucifixion.'[12]

This is strong evidence, if we may take it as historically valid. However, there are some who would say that it is not possible so to take it, that these 'appearances' were subjective, and represented the moods of those to whom they occurred. Denney counters that this estimate of the early testimony means that 'it is to be treated as a pathological phenomenon; it belongs to the disease and disorder, not to the health and sanity of the human spirit. Paul and the other apostles no doubt had visions of Jesus in power and glory, but they ought not to have had them. Unless their brains had been overheated they would not have had them. It can never be anything but a pity that they did have them.'[13] It was difficult for Denney to take this sort of dogmatic criticism seriously, and he feels that the whole area of historical testimony is put in doubt if such an abstract denial of an historical event is allowed. The historical witnesses stand true to experience and it is in the area of experience that their testimony has meaning.

> The Resurrection is not attested to metaphysicians or psychologists as a thing in itself; it is preached to sinful men, in its divine significance for their salvation, and it is in this concrete reality alone that it exists or has interest for the primitive witnesses.[14]

The Moral Evidence

On the basis of the historical evidence, Denney directs our attention to three ways in which the testimony to the resurrection is morally related to experience, and therefore needs to be appreciated as moral evidence.

The first consideration here is that of *the Person*. It is the resurrection of Jesus to which they testify and if there had been the assertion of the resurrection of anyone else the presumption would have been against the witnesses. 'The Resurrection', said Denney, 'was that of one in whom His friends had recognized, while He lived, a power and goodness beyond the measure of humanity, and they were sensible when it took place that it was in keeping with all they had known, hoped, and believed in Him.'[15] The apostles were not simply proclaiming resurrection in general, they were proclaiming the resurrection of Jesus. This is not to say that their memory of Him was such as would demand a vindication of His principles and therefore produced the Easter message. It is in precisely the opposite direction that Denney is moving. The disciples did not simply brood over the loss of Jesus and from that mood produce a resurrection story. If they had done so they would have been limited to the memories which made them brood. But they were not so limited. Jesus did not appear to them as they had known

Him, in the simplicity and the familiarity of the life they had known; He appeared as One who was exalted in glory and power. 'It was no coming to life again in the memory of the dear familiar friend whom even death could not dislodge from the heart; it was something transcendently and unimaginably new, and it needs a cause proportioned to it to explain its presence.'[16]

The second moral consideration concerns *the preaching* of the resurrection. Denney sought to make this point clear in the light of the New Testament preaching of the risen Lord.

> The apostles did not preach the resurrection of Jesus itself as a mere fact; what they preached was the Gospel of the Resurrection. It was the fact read out to the mind, heart, and conscience of men in its divine significance—the fact and its interpretation as indissolubly one, and constituting a supreme appeal on the part of God to man.[17]

Their proclamation was the historical testimony of men who can say, 'We have seen the Lord'—that is the point of attachment within history. But the fact was never proclaimed apart from its meaning and purpose in the relations of God and man. Its moral significance cannot be separated from it, and as we consider it as it was preached we find in it an appeal not simply to the scientific and historical interests of men's minds but an appeal to the whole man. This does not provide us with the right to judge others, but it does certify to us the truth that the acceptance and understanding of the resurrection is dependent to some extent on the moral quality of the individual.

The third consideration is the fact of *the power* of the resurrection. This is the most important moral factor and the most certain. We have already touched on this in the recognition that the spiritual vitality and strength of the Church whose life is reflected in the New Testament is the primary evidence for the resurrection. The point here is simply that the Church itself was conscious of that fact from the beginning and that as that power is felt the historical reality of the resurrection finds its strongest moral proof.

It is significant that in the earliest great treatment of this subject— I Cor. 15—Paul takes into account and unites both the historical and the moral evidence for the resurrection. The historical evidence comes first: that part of the chapter which we have already considered. Denney observed, 'It cannot be repeated too often that this is fundamental. If there had not been men who could say this, there would never have been such a thing in the world as Christian life, with the

evidence for the Resurrection which it brings.'[18] Upon this foundation
in fact Paul builds with evidence which is moral or spiritual in nature
and which in its proper place is of the highest value. Denney sums up
Paul's argument when he says,

> To put it broadly, Christian experience in all its forms implies the
> Resurrection. State the content of this experience as you will, take
> any aspect or illustration of it you please, and if you deny the Resur-
> rection, instead of being the highest and truest form of human life,
> such experience must be considered a thing illegitimate, abnormal,
> delusive.[19]

Paul wrote, 'If Christ has not been raised, then our preaching is in
vain.'[20] But Paul knew that his preaching was not in vain, and that it
must have a power behind it which corresponded to the effects which
it produced, and he saw that to be the power of the risen Christ. 'And
your faith is in vain,' he added. But the experience of reconciliation
was more real to Paul and his fellow-Christians than anything else in
life and he asserts that its reality is one with that of the resurrection.
He went on, 'Then those also who have fallen asleep in Christ have
perished.'[21] He is convinced that the resurrection is as certain as the
fidelity of God to those who trust Him even to death. And the apostle
adds, 'If in this life only we have hope in Christ, we are of all men
most to be pitied.'[22] This last word has been criticized on the ground
that a man should live the best life irrespective of a life beyond. Denney's retort is typical:

> It is hardly profitable to discuss the kind of life a man will live quite
> irrespective of conditions. Life is determined by the kind of motives
> which enter into it. If a man believes as Paul did in the Risen Christ
> and in the immortal life beyond death, motives from that sphere of
> reality will enter into his life here, and give it a new character; and it
> will be time enough to disparage the morality of this verse when we
> find the people who dispense with the apostolic motive leading the
> apostolic life.[23]

Such moral qualifications can easily be over-emphasized or overstated so that they become a caricature of the truth and distort the
understanding of the resurrection. What Paul is saying is that the
resurrection and faith in it are not isolated phenomena. When we
consider the validity of the resurrection, we must consider it in the
context of the Christian consciousness of reconciliation, the Christian
hope of immortality, the Christian witness in life; these things are
inseparably tied up with the resurrection and are dependent upon it.

These moral considerations, however, are not the deciding factor. The basic matter is the historical evidence which is clearly before us. As Denney summed it up,

> With some sense of the character of Jesus, with some perception of the *Gospel* of the Resurrection, the appeal which God makes through it to sinful man, with some knowledge of what it has produced in human life—one is invited to accept the testimony of witnesses who say, 'We have seen the Lord'.[24]

It is this total complex of evidence which stands as the testimony to the resurrection. It does not speak to men's scientific interests apart from their spiritual needs, nor to their hearts apart from their minds. It speaks as a whole to the whole of man.

The Narratives of the Resurrection

It is possible to approach the narrative accounts of the resurrection and of Jesus' post-resurrection appearances from the ground of evidence already made firm, and to do so with a better understanding of what they are seeking to do. The stories in the gospels and in the Book of Acts are not seeking to submit evidence so much as to give meaning to the evidence already in hand. These stories are not essential to faith in the resurrection, according to Denney, but they are helpful in our interpretation of it. They carry with them questions which should be answered in order that their interpretation might be made more clear. Denney deals primarily with three features in the narratives which have been the subjects of a good bit of discussion.

The first of these is the sequence of the appearances of Jesus. Denney readily admits that there is inconsistency if not contradiction in the narratives at this point, but he indicates that this shows clearly the uniform testimony to the excitement of those days and assumes that there would have been discrepancies in detail even if records had been made immediately. The fact that the gospels as we have them were not written down till after the time of Paul's death would indicate that the accounts, while true to the general import of what the Church had known from the beginning, were not able to make and were not seeking to make every detail certain.

A second point of difficulty is in the seeming progressive materialization of the appearances of Jesus. Denney insists on the matter of the empty grave, for reasons which we have considered, but on such details as Jesus' eating and drinking he is willing to attribute to Luke a tendency to materialize the supernatural. He wrote, 'To reject the

H

eating is not to reject the Resurrection Life of Jesus, it is to pre-
serve it in its truth as a revelation of life at a new level—life in which
eating and drinking are as inappropriate as marrying or giving in
marriage.'[25]

The third point of discussion is the matter of the place of Jesus'
appearing. Carrying out a detailed analysis of the sources in the construction of the narrative, Denney argues that the solution to the
problem of the contradictory accounts found in Matthew and Luke lies
in an understanding of the evangelists' points of view. 'The aim of the
various writers', he commented, '—their conception of an evangelist's
function—seems to have been this: believing in the Resurrection
themselves, and writing for those who believed in it, they aimed at
giving such an account of it as should bring out its permanent significance for the Church.'[26] They were not concerned to give a systematic
or exhaustive account of the evidence for the resurrection, and it seems
likely that they condensed their accounts in order to fulfill their purpose
and the interest of the Church in concentrating on the meaning of the
event. Their differing perspectives go a great deal of the way in explaining their differences: Matthew, resting on the authority of an original
disciple, placing his representative or typical scene in the familiar
region of Galilee; Luke, knowing Christianity only as a faith with 'its
cradle and capital at Jerusalem',[27] placing his single scene there.

It is not necessary to dwell on these details further, for it is clear by
this what Denney was seeking to do. He was perfectly willing to face
any representations of doubt, feeling that the truth is sufficient to
answer them all and that the most forceful weapon in the believer's
hand is his awareness and perception of the facts.

The Meaning of the Resurrection

The meaning of the resurrection is best seen in terms of the realities
to which it is related. Denney never thought of the resurrection as an
individual or isolated fact. It was intimately connected with Jesus' life
and death on the one hand, and with the ascension into glory and the
continuing ministry of Christ on the other. All of this is apprehended
by the believer in terms of the relationship between the event and
himself, which is made real to him through his faith.

(1) *Christ's Life.* Denney was careful to point out the relationship
between the life of Christ which the disciples knew before the resurrection and that which they knew after it. 'The Resurrection is the
Resurrection of Jesus, and though it lifts Jesus, as it were, into His

place of incommunicable greatness, it is this Person and no other Who is thus transcendently exalted, and there must be some inner relation between what He is and what He was.'[28] This is a part of the moral qualification and support of the resurrection which we have already considered, but it is one which should be emphasized because of its place in Denney's total theology. The meaning of this is that all that we have seen in the preceding chapter as to the significance of the Christ of the cross is made intelligible in terms of eternity and is filled with surpassing meaning and power. Thus the apostles' testimony as to who He *was* is lifted to a new level and conceived of in terms of who He *is*. Denney had a phrase which many remember in which he incorporated the implications of this: 'There is no such thing in the New Testament as an appearance of the Risen Saviour in which He merely appears.'[29] He goes on to explain that Christ always appears to His own, and appears to them in such a way as to enter into personal and intimate communication with them. It was on the basis of such a personal relationship that the apostles came to their firm conviction as to His Person, and in the intimacy of these communications that they united His life into one divine, consistent whole. The testimony which the New Testament bears to Christ is based on the total experience of the disciples from the moment of first contact, through the process of Christ's revelation of Himself, into the living fellowship with the Risen Lord which knows no end.

(2) *Christ's Death*. The resurrection is inseparably related to the work of Christ, as well. It is not surprising to find this one of Denney's most important emphases in the presentation of the resurrection. He did not think of the resurrection apart from the cross, nor the cross apart from the resurrection. They were two aspects of the same reality and when he spoke of one he always included the other in his thought. This, he felt, was true to the mind of the New Testament. At times he would start with the cross and come out at the resurrection:

> The New Testament preaches a Christ Who was dead and is alive, not a Christ Who was alive and is dead ... To preach the Atonement means not only to preach One Who bore our sins in death, but One Who by rising again from the dead demonstrated the final defeat of sin, and One Who comes in the power of His risen life—which means, in the power of the Atonement accepted by God—to make all who commit themselves to Him in faith partakers in His victory.[30]

Or, contrariwise, he would begin at times with the resurrection and come out at the cross:

The New Testament knows only of a living Christ, and all apostolic preaching of the Gospel holds up the living Christ to men. But the living Christ is Christ Who died, and He is never preached apart from His death and from its reconciling power. It is the living Christ, with the virtue of His reconciling death in Him, Who is the burden of the apostolic message.[31]

What makes His atoning death the significant fact that it is is the seal of God's acceptance of it which is revealed in the resurrection. What makes His risen life all meaningful and all powerful to sinful men is the fact that His death is in it. This union of the two is the key to the understanding of them both. As Denney put it pointedly, 'The New Testament writers, though they speak often of Christ's death, never think of a dead Christ: their Christ is One Who became dead and is alive forevermore, and in His immortal life the virtue of His death is present.'[32]

(3) *Christ's Exaltation.* This relationship with His earthly life and death does not exhaust the meaning of the resurrection. It is bound up with the testimony of that which comes after it; it is a part of the exaltation of Christ and marks His entrance into His sovereign glory. Denney draws all of this together:

> The Christ in Whom the apostles believed, the Christ who created Christianity and sustained it, the Christ who was the object of that faith which makes the New Testament to this day the most living book in the world, was the Risen Christ, the Lord of Glory. It was not Jesus the carpenter of Nazareth, it was not even Jesus the prophet of Galilee; nay, it was not even Christ crucified, as a person belonging to history and to the past; it was the crucified Christ *in the heavenly places*, the Lamb as it had been slain *standing in the midst of the throne*, the Universal Redeemer as Universal Lord.[33]

When faith in the resurrection was made certain in the disciples' hearts, when they understood the height of the gospel and the breadth of their task, when He had promised them the gift of spiritual power, then 'He parted from them for the last time in such a way that they knew it was the last; He passed with something like kingly state to the right hand of the Father.'[34] That which took place at what we call the ascension was a point of transition which cannot be ignored. Whatever happened, and Denney sees little reason to question the account given in Acts, it clearly marked for the apostles a solemn close to the period of His resurrection appearances and the exaltation of Christ into a life where contact with Him may be more intimate, but must be purely spiritual. This is important for our Christian theology and for our Christian life.

It is this exalted glory of Christ which prompts Denney to say, 'The crucifix is no adequate symbol of the Christian faith.'[35] This is a statement which should be kept in mind by those who only remember Denney's more familiar saying about the crucifix and who tend to limit his field of interest to the cross. He saw the cross and the glory of Christ in intimate association, and once commented on those who think of the death of Christ as containing the whole truth of the gospel: 'They forget that He is not on the Cross, but on the throne.'[36] He goes on to say that this is a point with regard to the Christian life which is often neglected, but that the true *imitatio Christi* must go even this far and must have the ascension's note of victory and joy or it is incomplete. The type of Christian life which strikes at its height the note of resignation is not adequate to the life in Christ. And to those who would speak of Christianity as 'the religion of sorrow', he retorts,

> There never was a more complete misnomer. It is not the religion of sorrow, but the religion which, because it is inspired by One who lives and was dead, gives the victory over every sorrow, even the crowning sorrows of death and sin. There is not in the New Testament from beginning to end, in the record of the original and genuine Christian life, a single word of despondency or gloom. It is the most buoyant, exhilarating, and joyful book in the world.[37]

The Christian life can have, and should have, this note of triumphant joy because Christ is exalted and we live in His constant presence, 'in the omnipotence of His grace'.[38]

The picture of the exalted Christ is not complete until we perceive the fact of His vocation in the state of exaltation and the meaning of it for our faith and for our lives. The New Testament represents the exalted Lord as carrying on His work above, culminating in His ministry of intercession. Denney pointed out that the apostles seemed to speak of this in a tone of adoration and awe. 'It seems to have impressed them as one of the unimaginable wonders of redemption— something which in love went far beyond all that we could ask or think. When inspired thought touches it, it rests on it as on an unsurpassable height.'[39] This is a part of Christ's priestly function, that continuing part which carries its meaning to the ultimate and presents us with the great high priestly act of Christ, His appearance in the presence of God for us. The Jewish symbolism here is apparent, and its meaning for us is that there is One who through sympathy and sacrifice is able to represent us before God in His continuing vocation as Mediator; so that, as Denney put it, 'when we present our prayers in His name, He presents them again in our name'.[40] As intercessor, we see our redeemer actually carrying out in glory that work of love the foundations of which have been laid in His reconciling cross here in the midst of history. And by that love we are bound irrevocably to Him.

VII

THE TOUCH OF GOD
The Holy Spirit

*Faith itself is not born till the touch of God completes
the spiritual circuit . . . What was remote, inert and unintelligible flames up under the witness of the Spirit into
the present, living, all-powerful love of the Redeemer.*[1]

'It is by the gift of the Holy Spirit that the exalted Lord carries on
His work on earth; He is with us through the Spirit, and in the work
of the Spirit the ends are being secured for which Jesus lived and died.'[2]
So Denney indicates the relationship which exists between the risen
Christ of the cross and the experience of believers. At the same time,
he discloses how important to him in this relationship is the reality of
the Holy Spirit.

The absence of extended reference to the Spirit in the discussion of
the work and the person of Christ might easily confuse us into thinking
that Denney laid little emphasis upon the subject. The exact opposite,
however, is the case. The Spirit has such over-all significance in
Denney's thought that the theme of the Spirit extends to theological
dimensions co-ordinate with those of Christian faith and experience.
Because the Spirit is everywhere through his theology, he seldom
pauses to isolate the term anywhere. To speak of the Spirit is another
way to speak of the experience of God in Christ. Denney's comprehensive view of the nature and work of the Spirit is a key to his unity
of thought, and supplies the underlying note of vitality which we find
in every area of his theology. He sees the Spirit extending to the limits
of the New Testament's expression of the Church's experience. He
once said, 'To understand what is meant by the Spirit is to understand
these two things—the New Testament and the Christian Church . . .
In them and in their mutual relations we have the only adequate
witness to what the Spirit means for Christians.'[3]

In the light of this acknowledgment of the importance of the Spirit,
he sought to clarify the Church's understanding and experience,
recognizing that when we touch doctrine at this point the whole field of

theology is involved. Consequently, he felt that one of the genuine needs of the Church was to study the facts with regard to the place and the work of the Spirit as they are presented to us in the New Testament. 'The Holy Spirit', he commented, 'occupies a place in the New Testament strikingly out of proportion to that which is assigned to Him in most books of theology . . . There seems to be an incapacity, or an unwillingness, to do justice to the Biblical data.'[4] On the one hand, there are those who, in seeking to establish the Christian religion on a scientific and historical basis, devote themselves to evading or explaining away the New Testament references. On the other hand, there are those who seek to secure a pietistic type of Christianity by preoccupying themselves with the doctrine of the Holy Spirit in a way which warps the meaning which it had in the experience of the primitive Church. Denney seeks to lay hold of the New Testament teaching and avoid both these extremes.

The Holy Spirit in the Life of Jesus

Denney pushes back through the New Testament to the life of Jesus as it is presented in the synoptic gospels, and there points out the place of the Spirit in the evangelists' narratives. He recognizes the difficulty of distinguishing between those references which are genuine and those which indicate the reflection into the gospel accounts of experiences which the Church had come to know later. He deals carefully with the critical details, building primarily upon the Gospel according to Mark, and he points out that even restricting ourselves to the best attested passages alone we cannot escape the distinct impression that the whole life of Jesus is depicted as a demonstration of the Spirit.

The earliest gospel reference to the Spirit is in the preaching of John the Baptist, who uses the Spirit to indicate his own impotence as contrasted with the One mightier than himself who would be recognizable by the fact that He would baptize with 'Holy Spirit' because He would be filled with the Spirit Himself. Thus, in His baptism experience Jesus is ushered onto the scene of His ministry in the context of the Spirit. The one idea which would have been dominant in men's minds as they heard that reference to the Spirit would be the teaching of the Old Testament, which seemed to place its emphasis upon the Spirit as the symbol of power, and specifically divine power. Denney observed that, 'The Spirit in the Old Testament means God in act, God putting forth His power.'[5] This note of divine power sets the stage for the ordination of Jesus to His ministry. This took place at His baptism, where, 'Jesus received the Holy Spirit, and in it the attestation of His Sonship, the call to His unique task, and the endowments needed to discharge it.'[6] There is no description of the nature of the Spirit, though the implication is that we may judge from the life of Jesus which follows what the Spirit is. Some further light is thrown on the subject in the narrative of the temptations, in which the first idea of the Spirit —that of divine power—is united with another essential aspect—that of holiness.

> It is at war, in principle, with everything which is unworthy of God; the kingdom which the Son of God is to found in the power of the Spirit is one which can make no kind of compromise with evil. It must be spiritual in its nature—not based on bread; spiritual in its methods—not appealing to miracles which only dazzle the senses or confound the mind; and spiritual in its resources—not deriving any of its strength from alliance with Satan.[7]

From this point of origin we can understand the evangelists' presentation of the whole ministry of Jesus in the light of the Spirit within Him. 'If they do not mention the Spirit at every step', wrote Denney, 'it is because they think of Him as in full possession of it continually.'[8] His ministry was carried out with a quality of vitality and vehemence, and both in His dealing and in His teaching we feel the force of strong emotions. There was such an earnestness about the conduct of His life and work that some could even come to feel that He was beside Himself. Denney pointed out that 'the more we look into the Gospels, the less does the emotionally colourless Saviour of popular art seem to correspond to the historical reality'.[9] There is no trace of any want of self-control, but there is ample testimony to the superhuman intensity with which He carried out his vocation. Through the whole of His life, and particularly in the healing miracles which Mark emphasizes, we get a vivid picture of the work of the Spirit in the work of the Christ.

When Jesus speaks of the Spirit He gives us a further idea of the quality and the holiness which are a part of the Spirit's nature. In such statements as those concerning blaspheming the Spirit,[10] we get the clear indication that 'the Holy Spirit is specifically God's; it brings Him in His power to men, it is the very token and reality of His presence with them'.[11] On the basis of the life of Jesus described in Mark—with support from the material in Matthew and Luke—Denney concludes that we can begin to get an idea of what the Holy Spirit is like.

The Holy Spirit is the Divine power which from His baptism onward wrought in Jesus, making Him mighty in word and deed . . . It takes nothing less than His life itself, from beginning to end to show us what the Spirit means. If the last Evangelist tells us that the Spirit interprets Jesus, the inference from the first is that Jesus also interprets the Spirit, and that only through Him can we know what it means.[12]

The most interesting additional materials which Matthew and Luke add to the basic story are the accounts of Jesus' birth, and the place of the Spirit within them. Denney thinks that the explanation of the Spirit's role in the nativity stories lies in the desire on the part of Matthew and Luke to show that the origin of Jesus' personality lay behind the baptism and that at His introduction to earthly life there was a definite demonstration of God's power.

The Spirit is the power of the Highest, to which the presence of the Son of God in the world is due. In other words, the Divine Sonship of Jesus does not date from His baptism, as that of Christians; it is not with Him as with us an affair of re-birth, but of birth simply; it is native and original, with roots as deep as His being; He is not only υἱὸς θεοῦ ('Son of God'), but μονογενής ('only Son')'[13]

The Holy Spirit in the Book of Acts

Coming to the Book of Acts, we find a strong emphasis upon the Spirit throughout the historical account of the early Church, and numerous passages in which Luke deals directly and formally with the subject. In the opening chapter there is reference to the disciples' contact with the Spirit in an intimate way in the Person of the Risen Lord and the promise of the Spirit's coming upon them in power. This promise was fulfilled at Pentecost, and it is important to understand the implications of that momentous experience. In the first place, the Spirit at Pentecost is inseparably connected with Christ. Denney said,

The Spirit which Christians have and of which they speak is never anything else than the Spirit of Jesus. It is never an undefined impulse or stimulus—a vague excitement originating anyhow and tending anywhither; it is always referred specifically to Jesus, and it is fundamentally a token that He is there in power.[14]

Secondly, there is the representation of the disciples speaking in tongues which Denney treats as imagery in which we need put little emphasis upon the foreign tongues used. 'The miracle of Pentecost is not that the disciples spoke in foreign languages, . . . but that they spoke at all, that they spoke with tongues of fire, and that their speech was a testimony to Jesus, delivered with overwhelming Divine power.'[15] In the third place, there is the connection between the gift of the Spirit and the ability to prophesy. The power of insight which the Spirit gives is recognized all through the Book of Acts and it is the Spirit which is seen as guiding the Church in its thought and activity. Denney adds the note that in this aspect of the Spirit 'there is nothing of the pagan oracle which deals with any question proposed to it: the Spirit gives direction only in the concerns of the Kingdom of the Messiah'.[16] As a fourth point, we should note that there is the important connection in Acts between the Spirit and baptism. After Pentecost, we might have assumed that water-baptism would have been annulled, but what we find is that baptism with the Spirit is regarded as being normally coincident with the baptism with water. It is this receiving of the Spirit which is regarded as the mark of the Christian.

These implications of the Pentecost experience are carried on through the Book of Acts, and are the distinctive signs of the experience of faith within the primitive Church. Wrote Denney, 'In Acts, as elsewhere in the New Testament, the reception of the Spirit is the whole of Christianity.'[17]

The Holy Spirit in the Epistles

The next block of New Testament material which we may consider as a unit is the group of letters written within the wide fellowship of the Church. The dominant personality here is Paul, and in his writings we find the Holy Spirit given a prominence above that which He has anywhere else in the New Testament. There are similarities between his presentation and the account given in Acts. One point of interest in this connection is that, while Paul recognizes the same gifts of the Spirit seen earlier—particularly tongues and prophecy—he is not insensible to their dangers and feels that the Church must be aware of the dangers as well. Denney comments that for Paul, 'The Christian common sense of the community, so to speak, is felt to be more inspired than the most ardent utterance of any individual.'[18] At the same time, there is in Pauline thought a conception of the Spirit which, while implied throughout the New Testament, is made specific and prominent by the apostle to the Gentiles. It is the recognition of a possession of the Spirit which is beyond all particular 'gifts' of a spiritual sort, so that the possession of the Spirit is identified with Christian experience and with Christian life itself. Denney sees this Pauline conception of the Spirit in connection with the apostle's presentation of the truth of the atonement:

In experience, the Spirit is indistinguishable from the assurance that God is sin-bearing love; and to have that assurance in overpowering strength—as the apostle had it through faith in Christ—is to be full of the Holy Spirit . . . Faith and the Spirit are correlative terms. The Spirit describes the Christian life as divinely determined, or as the gift of God; faith describes the very same life as humanly conditioned, a life which from first to last is one of trust in Christ.[19]

This is a point of primary importance to Denney and it is well to note that he draws his thought in the first instance from his study of Paul's conception of the Spirit.

Upon this broad basis of interpretation, it is valuable to look at a few of the particular points which come out of a survey of the Epistles. To begin with, the Spirit is specifically Christian in Paul's thinking. 'It is not the power or the life of God *simpliciter*, but the power or the life of God as God has been manifested in Christ, and especially in His Resurrection and exaltation.'[20] The Spirit glorifies Christ. The apostle's method of making the meaning of the Spirit definite was to depict it constantly in contact with the known facts of the historical Christ. Secondly, the Spirit, for Paul, is one of adoption or sonship. In this close connection with Christ, Paul sees the experiences of the Spirit involving joy and trust, in place of fear and doubt. Thirdly, the Spirit is an emancipator, and in Him there is the complete freedom of the Christian life. The Christian is not under law, but under grace. As he gives himself to the love of God revealed in Christ the Spirit enters his heart and breaks all bondage, becoming everything to him from that point forward. As a fourth point, we should note the Pauline idea that the Spirit is 'an earnest' or a guarantee of eternal life. This is consistent with New Testament thought elsewhere, and is of vital significance for the believer. As Denney commented,

When God has pledged His friendship to men as He did to the patriarchs in ancient days, or as He does to Christians now in making them, through the Spirit, partakers of His own life, He has entered into a relation to them to which death can make no difference. His love outwardly, His Spirit inwardly, both mean immortality.[21]

In the fifth place, there is in Paul's thought the contrast between the Spirit and the flesh. The Spirit represents for him the divine power in the believer which enables him to put to death the nature of sin identified with the flesh. This is the description of our dependence upon the Spirit for all goodness. Finally, there is the Pauline note concerning the Spirit as a source of wisdom and knowledge and revelation. This has no direct parallel in the Synoptics or in Acts, but is based upon the recognition that the Spirit searches all things, even the depths of God. In summing up the Spirit's relationship to us in the apostle's thought, Denney said,

> When God comes to us through the Spirit, all that we were without God comes to an end; all that we were striving in vain to become for God is assured of consummation. As against the sinfulness of the flesh, the Spirit is a Divine power which ensures righteousness; as against the death which is all that sinful flesh has to look forward to, the Spirit is the Divine power which brings the earnest of immortality.[22]

The Holy Spirit in the Johannine Writings

Moving on to the Johannine literature we see that here too the Spirit is given a place of paramount importance. It is necessary to remember that the experience of the Pauline Churches lies behind these books and that this experience has exercised a decided influence upon the presentation of the material. In the Apocalypse, we are told four times that what the author is presenting he himself received when he was 'in the Spirit'. This suggests the carrying further of the Pauline idea of wisdom and revelation being found in the Spirit. It does not mean that he was unbalanced, for in the Epistles to the Seven Churches—'terrible in their calm as in their passion'[23]—he writes with the same confidence that the Spirit is expressing Himself in his words.

It is in the Fourth Gospel that the Spirit takes a natural place at the center of the stage of the life in Christ. What strikes one is the assumption which the writer has that the reader will know what is meant by 'the Spirit'. Said Denney, 'The Gospel is meant for Christians to whom the Spirit is an experience.'[24] Baptism has an important place in the mind of the writer of the Fourth Gospel, and he sees the baptism of Jesus as the symbol or the type for all Christian baptism, for with the baptism of Jesus the symbol and the reality symbolized coincided. From this point onward it is baptism with water and with Spirit. Denney feels also that the sixth chapter is a clear reference to the Lord's Supper, in which the place of the Spirit is the same as that in the other sacrament, assuring the spiritual interpretation of the symbol. In both these cases, it is probable that the evangelist was countering materialistic and superstitious interpretations of the sacraments, and in doing so was emphasizing the proper place of the Spirit in the life of the Church.

Passing on to chapters 14-16, we come to the treatment of the Spirit which gives the best insight into the Johannine concept. Denney observes that 'the Spirit may be said to be the main subject in the discourse in which Jesus prepares the disciples for His departure'.[25] It is at John 14.16 that a new name is given to the Spirit, that of $\Pi\alpha\rho\acute{\alpha}\kappa\lambda\eta\tau\sigma\varsigma$ —'Counselor', 'Comforter'—though it is the name only which is new and not the idea. The strength of the apostles was reinforced by Him as long as He was with them, and when He goes they will find His place taken by the Spirit. Said Denney, 'The presence of the Spirit is Jesus' own presence in spirit.'[26] A Trinitarian conception is implied throughout this whole passage. Further along in the same chapter, we are given more insight into the meaning of the Spirit. He is represented as being personal, with the masculine pronoun used to refer to the Spirit. In addition, He is seen in the function of teaching or revealing, and His teaching is not independent of Jesus but involves bringing to remembrance the words and the works of the Lord. Denney felt it was most important for men to understand what it meant for the Spirit to remind the disciples of the things of Jesus.

> Something is recalled, but it is not only recalled, it is for the first time understood; it is remembered because a key to it has been found; it is not only the dream, so to speak, which is recalled, but the dream and its interpretation together . . . They are remembered in the heart as well as in the brain; they are remembered with an ardour which contemplates, explores, makes discoveries, worships; and when they are reproduced in the Spirit, it is not the unintelligent and misleading truth of an amateur photograph with which we are confronted, but something like the work of a great painter, something which is truer in a manner than the most literal recollection would be.[27]

The climax of the Fourth Gospel's teaching on the Spirit is reached in the passage in 16.7 ff. Here Jesus indicates that His departure is actually for the disciples' benefit, for the Spirit's coming is dependent upon His leaving. It is Jesus Himself Who sends the Spirit and this He does on the ground of His own departure through His death and exaltation. Thus it is that the Spirit comes in all of the power in which Christ Himself lives and reigns, and comes with a two-fold function to perform. The first function of the Spirit is to convict the world (16.8-11) of sin, of righteousness and of judgment. Wrote Denney, 'Sin, righteousness, and judgment are abstract ideas, and come home to men in their reality only when in the power of the Spirit they are interpreted in their connection with Christ.'[28] It is Christ's finished work of redemption and reconciliation which the Spirit takes and applies to the mind and conscience of the world, thereby convicting it. The underlying quality of the Spirit in this convicting of the world is the aspect of power. When we turn to the second function of the Spirit, we find that the underlying quality of the Spirit is that of illumination (16.12-15). The Spirit is conceived of as giving the disciples the necessary comprehension of the full work of Christ. The basic concept of this function is given in verse 12—'I have yet many things to tell you, but you cannot bear them now.' Denney gives the meaning of this as simply as possible: 'Jesus is greater than His words.'[29] Many things have been left unsaid, but the Spirit will open up the full meaning of these things and lead into all the truth.

> The Spirit which He promises as the Spirit of truth will have this as His very task, to initiate them into the whole meaning of Jesus. He will lead them, not into all truth, but into all the truth—that is, the truth which is embodied in Him in all its dimensions.[30]

The Spirit receives from Christ and then reveals to men. Denney insists that we must consider both aspects of the Spirit's function together, that both are important to the work of the Church, and reveal our complete dependence upon the Spirit. The spiritual quality of power to convict gives us the dependence of the preacher upon the Spirit; the spiritual quality of illumination gives us the dependence of the theologian upon the Spirit. Both are drawn together because of the complete and united work which the Spirit performs.

With Denney as our guide it is possible for us to come to some penetrating and far-reaching conclusions with regard to the Holy Spirit and to see the significance of the Spirit for our faith and theology.

The first, and most important, fact concerning the Spirit is that He is the Spirit of Christ. We have seen with each succeeding block of material in the New Testament that this is the basis of their interest and their understanding of the subject. The apostles never thought of the Spirit apart from the Christ. In the Person of Christ they found the Spirit's nature and the meaning of the Spirit's vocation and message. The Spirit is the gift of the exalted Christ, Who—having been anointed with the Spirit Himself—finished His work on earth, entered into His glory and by the promise of the Father was able to bestow this gift upon men. The giving of the Spirit may be understood therefore as the clear sign in our experience of God's acceptance of the work of Christ. This was vital for Denney.

Pentecost was won for us at Calvary; it needed the atonement to make regeneration possible . . . Pentecost is a historical proof—a proof in the domain of fact and experience—that sin has been overcome by Christ's death, and that a divine life is again within the reach of men. It is a seal of the great reconciliation; in the possession of the Holy Spirit men are actually united to God in Christ.[31]

It is therefore possible for us to speak of the Spirit as being Christ's *alter ego*, Whom we meet in experience and Who enables us to accept Christ's reconciling work. He is Christ's Spirit, with Christ's nature in Him. Because of Christ the Spirit is conceived of as a Person. As Denney puts it, 'When we talk of the Spirit as an abstractly supernatural power . . . we are not on Christian ground.'[32] And because of this intimate personal identity the Spirit's work within us draws us not away from Christ, but to Him.

In every sense of the terms the Spirit's work is to testify to Christ—to what He is, to His words, to what He has done and suffered, to what He is to achieve. In this His function, if not His being, as the Spirit of truth is exhausted. And to say that He uses only what is Christ's is not to narrow the range or the means of His action . . . All that belongs to the truth of God's Fatherhood is revealed in the Son, and all that is revealed in the Son is interpreted and vivified by the Spirit.[33]

The Experience of the Spirit

The second fact which we should emphasize is that the New Testament presents the Holy Spirit in terms of experience, not of doctrine. This is one of the most interesting and important contributions which Denney makes to this area of theology.

Familiar as it is to us through the accepted creeds of the Church, such an expression as 'I believe in the Holy Ghost' is entirely foreign to the New Testament. What the apostles asked was not, *Do you believe* in the Holy Spirit? but, *Did you receive* the Holy Spirit when you believed![34]

In line with this, Denney was not disposed to speak of the doctrine of the Holy Spirit, feeling that to introduce a formal statement where in reality we are referring to a vital experience is to leave the world of faith and thought of the New Testament and commit ourselves to a barren intellectual construction of the divine nature which has little to do with Christian faith and little or no Christian value. For this reason, he was looked upon with some misgivings by the staunchly orthodox of his time. No one, however, who has thought through his treatment of the New Testament conception of the Holy Spirit will think that he is not interested in the reality of the Spirit. The point for him was that he was so interested that he could not be satisfied with a formal doctrine. For him, the Holy Spirit is correlative and coextensive with the whole of Christian faith and experience. When some argued that the creed which he suggested for the use of the Church did not mention the Holy Spirit, he replied that one has said what is necessary about the Spirit when he has said, 'I believe' in the Christian sense of commitment.[35]

> The Spirit and faith are correlative terms, and each of them covers, from a different point of view, all that is meant by Christianity. Regarded from the side of God and His grace and power in initiating and maintaining it, Christianity is the Spirit; regarded from the side of man and his action and responsibility in relation to God, it is faith. The two are coextensive, and all Christianity is in each.[36]

This was to his mind clearly the New Testament teaching on the subject and he was strong in his assertion of it. 'Every Christian experience is at one and the same time an experience of faith and an experience in the Spirit.'[37]

But even this is not all, for Denney insists that the whole of Christian experience is in the Holy Spirit. We do not have Christian experiences, but Christian experience, which as a whole can be identified with the Holy Spirit.

> To have an overpowering assurance of the love of God as it is revealed in Christ the propitiation and to be filled with the Holy Spirit are the same thing; and in that one thing lie the promise and the potency of all forms of Christian goodness. Such goodness is never imposed; it is always inspired.[38]

There was a form of positive existentialism in Denney's thought, which insists on grounding all theology in vital experience and which thereby adds dynamic quality to all that he said. And all of this draws ultimate meaning from his interpretation of the Spirit, Who brings all Christian experience into unity. Denney maintained that as long as men believe, as long as they have faith in God through Christ, they will know the meaning of Christian experience in their lives; the Spirit in His role on the divine side of that experience will have His place which no other could possibly take, as ultimate as the reality of Christian faith itself. Christian experience in the New Testament is something totally distinctive and creative, it is the gift and the work of the Spirit. If we

I

would understand the New Testament conception of the Spirit, we must come to know in our own lives the New Testament experience which recognized this reality and spoke of it in personal terms.

The Nature of the Spirit

Of the ways in which the nature of the Spirit is characterized in the New Testament, Denney feels that there are three which are of particular importance. In the first place, the Spirit is represented as being *the Spirit of truth*. This is the function of illumination which is presented specifically in the Fourth Gospel, and Denney's primary point here is that 'the New Testament is itself the proof that this promise was fulfilled; the New Testament and the new spiritual life to which it bears witness'.[39] In the New Testament we see how the Spirit has led the disciples into the truth embodied in Jesus. It is the witness of the Spirit which has accomplished this and it is that same witness which leads every man who ever comes in true faith to Christ. 'No one', says Denney, 'can understand what Christ is, or what He has done, unless he is led into all the truth by the Spirit, who is the only revealer and interpreter of it.'[40]

The Spirit is also designated as *holy*. Denney commented that in one sense 'this is equivalent to divine, for in truth only God is holy, and the Holy One is an exhaustive description of God'.[41] The Christian life and the character of holiness which flows from it are from beginning to end the work of the Spirit. 'Just as no one can be good without God, nor a Christian without Christ, so, quite definitely, no one can be holy in the New Testament sense without the Holy Spirit.'[42] Denney insists that we should acknowledge in our worship and in our theology this absolute dependence upon the Holy Spirit for the life of God in our souls.

Thirdly, the Spirit throughout the New Testament is recognized as *the Spirit of power*. This is that spiritual characteristic which we have seen underlying everything else which could be said about the Spirit. His work of freedom, His work of illumination, His work of holiness are all made real in the light of His power. In a specific sense, the Spirit's character and work of power are seen in that peculiar reinforcement of the message of the gospel which makes it take effect in the soul of men. Said Denney in this connection,

Only the Spirit can do this. All the essential facts, all the presuppositions of faith, so to speak, may be present, yet faith itself is not born till the touch of God completes the spiritual circuit, and the heart is suddenly thrilled with the atoning and regenerating power of Him who came by water and blood. What was remote, inert and unintelligible flames up under the witness of the Spirit into the present, living, all-powerful love of the Redeemer.[43]

The Spirit of God

In every possible way, Denny's discussion reveals the close relationship between the Spirit and God. But the importance of this relationship should be made explicit. The New Testament, as we have seen, does not give itself to any discussion of the metaphysics of the Spirit. He is clearly regarded as being the Spirit of God; He belongs to the sphere of activity of the divine; yet at the same time, there is something in the Spirit akin to man which enables Him to move into our own experience. He is regarded at one and the same time as being personal and as being a divine impulsion or force. It is certainly clear that there is little ground for abstract distinctions with regard to the relationship between the Spirit and the Father as over against the relations between the Son and the Father. Denney felt that it is important to realize this so that we will not give ourselves to vague speculative constructions concerning the Trinity. At the same time, he maintained that we must recognize in the New Testament the instinctive and spontaneous statements about Father, Son and Spirit which form the beginning of what in the course of centuries was to be elaborated into the doctrine of the Trinity. Denney believes firmly in that doctrine, not on the basis of metaphysics but on the basis of experience.

> It is not a motiveless speculation; it is not the analysis of an arbitrarily chosen idea like knowledge, love, or spirit, as some philosophers and theologians have tried to show; it proceeds from the actual manifestation of God in Christ, and from the actual reception of a divine life through the Holy Spirit. When it departs from this ground it ceases to possess either significance or authority.[44]

Our Christian experience unites with the New Testament in recognizing that the Christian conception of God must include all that is meant by the three Persons. To leave out of our thinking any one of them is to leave the Christian conception unsatisfied. As Denney put it, 'The Father, the Son, and the Spirit in their unity constitute the God whom we know as the God of our Salvation.'[45]

In the light of Denney's interpretation, it is clear that the Spirit held a place of particular importance in his theology. Starting with Christian experience as he does, yet holding firmly to the importance of the objective realities of faith, he has been confronted with the problem of reconciling the two and achieving the wholeness of view which he set himself to seek. The solution to his problem lies in his understanding of the Holy Spirit. Co-ordinate with the totality of Christian experience, it is yet a part of that objective reality in which faith rests, and as such it is the bridge between the objective and the subjective aspects of the wholeness of theology. In thus developing his thought, Denney felt that he was being true to the theology of the New Testament and free to break away from 'orthodoxy' where he found it too rigid. In this he has anticipated some of the most dynamic interpretations of our present age and has revealed once more his ample capacity to stand as a theological prophet for today.

VIII

LISTENING FOR A VOICE
The Holy Scripture

He never reads Scripture as if he had written it: he always reads it as if listening for a Voice.[1]

UNDERGIRDING all of Denney's thought and breaking forth everywhere in his work is the distinctive stamp of the Scripture. We find a constant reference to the Bible throughout his presentation and a continuing appeal to the authority of Scripture in the building of his theology. His was a thoroughly Biblical approach, both to theology and to preaching, and apart from his attitude toward the Scripture and his contributions with regard to the interpretation of it there is no way for us to understand what he had to say. As it drew his interest and his allegiance, it called forth his most profound and comprehensive scholarship. It was in the Scripture that his thought reached its full height and found its most creative and constructive dimensions. He was nothing if not a Biblical theologian.

We realize his Biblical emphasis not so much by what he said about the Scripture itself as by the way in which he used it in dealing with the matters of faith and theology. He actually wrote very little about its place or its nature or its use; he simply used it in the way we have recognized thus far, and in that use it asserted its own nature and assumed its own place. Our approach to Denney's thought in this area, then, must be directly through his use of the Bible rather than through a formal doctrine concerning the Scripture. As we follow this course we shall not be in doubt as to the importance of his conclusions and beliefs about the Bible.

The Inspiration of the Bible

The Bible, Denney asserted, brings us into confrontation with the good news of God.

It is *the* means through which God communicates with man, making him know what is in His heart toward him. It must be known and experienced in this character before we can form a doctrine concerning it. We cannot *first* define its qualities, and *then* use it accordingly; we cannot start with its inspiration, and then discover its use for faith and practice. It is through an experience of its power that words like inspiration come to have any meaning, and when we define them apart from such experience we are only playing with empty sounds.[2]

We know in our experience the meaning of the gospel of reconciliation and, from that experience, the truth of Christianity and the validity of its scriptural foundation. We do not come to this knowledge apart from Scripture; it is the Scripture which, from the very beginning, has led us to this knowledge. It is its power to do this which leads us to acknowledge it as inspired. The Bible holds forth Christ, bearing witness to the good news of who He is and what He has done. Wrote Denney, 'This is the burden of the Bible, the one fundamental omnipresent truth to which the Holy Spirit bears witness by and with the words in our hearts. This, at bottom, is what we mean when we say that Scripture is inspired.'[3]

This is a point on which it is exceedingly important to be clear. There are those who feel that this is an insecure approach to the matter and that what is required is a doctrinal statement concerning inspiration which will serve as the foundation upon which Christian faith can be built. This approach would first of all seek to prove the inspiration of the Scripture and on the basis of that would construct Christian doctrine. This was popular under the patterns of the older orthodoxy and some men still seek to cleave to the appearance of security which it seems to offer. Denney's feeling is that such an approach is exactly opposite to what we know in our Christian experience. Referring to the way in which he used the Scripture in the development of his thought, he said, 'We do not use the Bible because of an antecedent conviction that it is inspired; we are convinced it is inspired because it so asserts its authority over us, as we read, that we cannot but use it in that way.'[4]

This is a vital and lofty view of the inspiration of Scripture, and his emphasis serves to accentuate the importance of the reality of inspiration. Denney did not in any way depreciate the value of inspiration; he simply sought to keep its value in line with the true experience of Christian men. He could be very abrupt with those who indicated that they felt the question of inspiration was a thing of the past. 'The inspiration of the Bible is only another and more formal name for the divine truth, authority, and power of the Gospel, to which the Bible bears witness; and it is so far from being an obscure opinion that it is the very breath of the Church's life.'[5]

The importance of inspiration, then, is not questioned in Denney's mind. What is seriously questioned is the interpretation that would impose that importance upon men, as though their experience of inspiration were inadequate. It is his conviction that the experience of inspiration is sufficient to guide men to the reality of inspiration. It is in this experience alone that the Word of God speaks to us and enables us to recognize the thrilling note of inspiration in the words which we read. This view secures for the Bible a place quite apart from that of any other literature. In fact, Denney felt it an irrelevance to speak of any comparable type of inspiration. 'It is the only book in the world', he observed, 'to which God sets His seal in our hearts when we read in search of an answer to the question, "How shall a sinful man be righteous with God?" ' And then he goes on to add:

> We do not believe in inspiration because we find something in Isaiah which we do not find in Aeschylus—though we do; nor because we find something in St Paul which we do not find in Plato, though again, and more emphatically, we do; we believe in inspiration because in the whole Bible, from Isaiah to St Paul, and earlier and later, there is a unity of mind and spirit and purpose which shines out on us at last in the atoning work of Christ.[6]

The Unity of the Bible

Such a belief in the inspiration of the Scripture is obviously bound up with an understanding and acceptance of the unity of the Bible. Inspiration is dependent upon the realization that within the Bible there is a consistency of mind and spirit and that the Scripture does in fact possess an inherent unity. An emphasis upon the division and disunity of the Bible was at its height during Denney's lifetime, and we can be thankful that we have since moved beyond that point and are concerned in a new way with the unity of the Bible. For Denney this was a primary concern decades ago. He saw that to deny the ultimate unity of the Bible was, in effect, to deny that it is inspired. 'The unity of the Bible and its inspiration are correlative terms,' he maintained. 'If we can discover a real unity in it . . . then that unity and its inspiration are one and the same thing.'[7] From what we have seen of his presentation of the Biblical testimony to the atonement, the incarnation, the resurrection and the experience of the Spirit, it is perfectly evident that the unity of the Scripture was for him an abiding reality. We have found him repeatedly drawing its pages together around the heart of Christian truth. It is God's revelation of His redeeming love in Christ which binds the Scripture into one. On this Denney insisted: 'It is in its testimony to this that the unity of Scripture and its inspiration consists, and whoever believes in this believes in inspiration in the only sense which can be rationally attached to the word.'[8]

This unity goes back through the Old Testament. There Denney finds the same thread of faith and thought which brings the New Testament into one, and he recognizes its force in binding together the whole of the Scripture. 'It is quite fair to say that we do not see Jesus truly unless we see Him in the perspective of the Old Testament, but it is quite fair also to say that we do not see the Old Testament truly unless we see it in the perspective of Jesus.'[9] It is in the light of God's full revelation in Christ that we read His revelation in Scripture, and because of Him we know its unity and its inspiration.

With regard to the New Testament, this same thread of unity was for him both a tested historical fact and a reality of experience. This was an aspect of his theology which we have encountered often enough to assure us that it was as real to him as Christian thinking. He felt its unity of subject, based upon its presentation of the Person and work of Christ. He once wrote with strong feeling to a friend, 'It needs the whole of the New Testament to show what Christ is.'[10] He felt its unity of experience, founded upon faith and the power of the Spirit. As we have seen, on the basis of this unity he brought together the writings of the New Testament and found in them a single focus upon the essentials of Christian faith. There is nothing artificial or imposed about this unity; it is the inherent oneness which is recognized in the faith of believers and which assures the New Testament of its place of primary importance in Christian experience. As Denney expressed it,

> There really is such a thing as the New Testament. There is . . . a real and substantial unity of thought in the books which we call by that name. They were not written with a view to incorporation in a canon; . . . but they have a unity, nevertheless, which is not external or imposed, nor due to the accident of their being approximately contemporary, but which is inward, essential, and spiritual, and which qualifies them to be canonical.[11]

The Creation of the Bible

This leads us to consider the life which stands behind the Bible and out of which it came to be. The Bible was created out of the experience of faith in the life of men. Its books were drawn together on the basis of that living experience. For Denney, the canon of Scripture was not a subject for technical inquiry so much as a testimony to the faith and life of the community of people who produced it. Therefore, he studied the formation of the canon in detail, in order that the unity of the Scripture might be properly understood and accepted. The canon of the Old Testament was determined by the history of Israel and was formed by the time of the New Testament. Its inclusion in the Christian Scripture is to be explained by its relationship to Christ and the use which He made of it. The New Testament canon is not a fortuitous collection of books, but depends for the validity of its limits upon the unity of faith and testimony exhibited in the early Church. The same Gospel which made them into a unity, incorporated them into the canon. Said Denney, 'The books did not come together by chance. They are not held together simply by the art of the bookbinder.' And then he proceeded to state his belief regarding the canon: 'It would be truer to say that they gravitated toward each other in the course of the first century of the Church's life, and imposed their unity on the Christian mind, than that the Church imposed on them by statute a unity to which they were inwardly strange.'[12] One day, in an open lecture to his students, he gave a definition, or description, of the canon and it is still remembered by some of them:

> These books have a unity, and that unity is a unity of faith, being written not *ad narrandum* but *ad probandum*, viz., to prove that Jesus is the Christ. They depend upon first hand, original testimony and therefore are not likely to be added to. They were segregated unconsciously, and therefore all the more originally and scientifically, from the floating mass of first century Christian literature.[13]

What current exponent of source criticism would want to comment on it more adequately than that?

This is to say, then, that the unity and canonicity of the New Testament books are dependent upon the faith and life of the primitive Church out of which they were created. To that creativity which found expression in the New Testament we look for our original norm in theology. Denney's succinct word for it was: 'New Testament theology is the theology of the Church at a time when as yet it had no New Testament.'[14] It is to the primitive Church that we look in order to distinguish the different strains of thought and expression; in order to describe the variety which is contained in the New Testament. But it is likewise to the primitive Church that we go to find the secret of that unity which underlies and binds together all of the variety, and which shows by its very nature that it is the work of inspiration. As Denney commented, 'The New Testament is not simply a document to be examined under the microscope of the scholar; it is the record of an abounding life, which in a hundred varying accents of love and gratitude bears tribute to the Christ Who redeemed it and reconciled it to God.'[15] It is this glowing life of faith which confronts one as he opens the New Testament and which speaks in the books with a word of which one cannot but say, 'This is from God'.

> When we read the New Testament with susceptible minds, we listen to the voice of those who were once themselves estranged from God, but have been reconciled to Him through Christ, and are letting us into the secret of their new life; it is the nearest approach we can make, and therefore the most vital, to the reconciling power which streamed from Christ Himself.[16]

Denney particularly enjoyed pointing out the amazing originality of thought in the early Church and the freedom which they felt in reconstructing the whole world of thought with Christ as its source and center and goal. 'Whatever else the New Testament is', he once said in a sermon, 'it is the most original book in the world.'[17] It was this early faith, with its vitality and originality, which, in the power of the Spirit, created the books of the New Testament which leave in our hearts and minds the imprint of the reality of their inspiration and their authority over our faith and our life.

The Authority of the Bible

When we speak of the authority of the Scripture, we are not speaking of something which stands by itself as a doctrine of the Church, but of something intelligible only in the light of the inspiration, unity and creative life which we recognize in the Bible. There is no authority here which imposes itself upon us against our own wills. As Denney once commented, concerning authority, 'Once the mind has come to know itself, there can be no such thing for it as blank authority. It cannot believe things—the things by which it has to live—simply on the word of Paul or John.'[18] If we are to think of authority at all in connection with the Scripture, then it must be the authority which is inherent within the words themselves. It is as we read these words and feel the force of their inspiration that they assert themselves over us and we find in them an authority which speaks to our minds. 'Truth',

said Denney, 'is the only thing which has authority for the mind, and
the only way in which truth finally evinces its authority is by taking
possession of the mind for itself.'[19] We do not accept the authority of
the gospel on the authority of the Scripture; we experience the authority
of the gospel and therefore gladly acknowledge the authority of the
Scripture which gave us the good news. As Denney put it,

> We find this truth (of the gospel of Christ) in the Christian Scrip-
> tures undoubtedly, and therefore we prize them; but the truth does
> not derive its authority from the Scriptures, or from those who
> penned them. On the contrary, the Scriptures are prized by the
> Church because through them the soul is brought into contact with
> this truth.[20]

This does not put the matter of authority in doubt; rather it binds it
together with the experience of the gospel which the Scripture presents
and with the inspiration which is inherent within. Denney felt that the
authority of the Bible, thus self-attested by its own power, was as real
as Christian experience, and that no one who knew the experience of
faith would have need to question the place of the Scripture. This does
not mean that we find in the Bible authoritative material so outlined
and detailed that we can develop doctrine on the basis of neatly fitted
proof-texts.

> The essential content of faith must certainly be discoverable in
> Scripture if our faith is to answer to historical Christianity; but the
> parts of a dogmatic system neither can be nor need to be demon-
> strated from Scripture in detail. Their true proof is that they are
> integral parts of a whole, the generative principle of which is the
> same faith which the New Testament exhibits.[21]

Denney had great faith in the Bible's power to assert itself in the heart
and mind of one who will consider it with openness and honesty. He
stood firmly in the conviction that 'the Bible way of looking at everything human and divine will win in the long run, because it is the *big*
way'.[22] He used to express himself in no uncertain terms with regard
to those men who sought to belittle the importance of the Scripture,
once writing to a friend,

> I have often been disgusted by men who seem to see nothing in the
> New Testament but things they can take exception to, and who read
> it with a mighty feeling of their superiority to the writers, and often,
> one is tempted to say, to the subject . . . A man who in the presence
> of Christ is delighted to show how far he, a representative of the
> twentieth century, has got before the men of the first century in

manipulating ideas like the divine and the supernatural, I cannot understand.[23]

Men who are devoted to demythologizing should take special note of this early word of warning. One of Denney's most revealing comments on the Scripture came when he was advising his students about reading the Bible in public worship, referring them to the example of his friend, J. P. Struthers: 'He never reads Scripture as if he had written it: he always reads it as if listening for a Voice.'[24] It is as men read and study and preach and teach the Scripture 'listening for a Voice', that they hear and know beyond all doubt its inspiration and its authority.

The Infallibility of the Bible

Denney recognized the dangers which his interpretation of Scripture opened up to him, but the danger which most concerned him was not that of making the inspiration of the Bible less secure, but that of allowing men to take what was actually 'a doctrine of the word of God, or of the divine message to man', and construing it as if it were 'a doctrine of the text of Scripture'.[25] He was living in the day when the battle for the right of Biblical criticism was still being waged, and when questions of infallibility and inerrancy were prominent. As early as 1891 he was involved in the debate concerning the subject on the floor of the General Assembly:

> The Word of God infallibly carries God's power to save men's souls. That is the only kind of infallibility I believe in. Authority is not authorship. God attests what is in this book as His own, but God is not the author of it, in the sense in which a man is the author of the book he writes. To say so is meaningless.[26]

Later he said to the same court, with a frankness which stunned those who held to a doctrine of plenary inspiration and which helped to carry the day for intellectual freedom and integrity: 'For verbal inerrancy I care not one straw, for it would be worth nothing if it were there, and it is not.'[27] It was a position which he was to defend for the rest of his life, for the old interpretations do not die quickly. Some years later he stated his beliefs on the floor of his own Presbytery in Glasgow:

> It is quite possible for me to profess my faith in the infallibility of Scripture. I believe if a man commits his mind and heart humbly and sincerely to the teaching and guidance of the Holy Scripture, it will bring him right with God and give him a knowledge of God and of eternal life. But literal accuracy and inerrancy are totally different things; and we do not believe in that at all.[28]

In his studies of particular passages he pointed out the endless difficulties which face a doctrine of inerrancy. Concerning the mistakes which appear in Scripture and which force those who would secure apostolic infallibility at the cost of making the apostles practice pious deception, he remarked, rather dryly: 'I hope, if we had the choice, we would all choose rather to tell the truth, and be mistaken, than to be infallible, and tell lies.'[29] Denney's belief in the historical beginnings of Christianity and in the place of the vital experience of the first century Church which lay behind the Scripture made it impossible for him to accept any mechanical theory of inspiration or interpretation. Literal inerrancy was, for him, a dead weight which inspiration did not need to carry.

The Critical Study of the Bible

Against this background of the inspiration and authority of the Scripture the critic has his legitimate and necessary field of work and his definite responsibility to search for truth. The gospel is given to us in history, and the books which record the fact were written by men in history and were addressed to particular historical situations, and these have been preserved and transmitted in a process through history. In the light of this the critic finds his place of service, and the Church should welcome his work in search of the truth. As Denney said,

> A Christian who knows that God does speak to the soul through the Scripture ought not to speak of criticism as an alien or hostile power, with which he may be compelled, against his will, to go so far, but which he must ever regard with suspicion . . . True criticism is a science, and will go its own length, and we will all go along with it. Even to speak of 'moderate' and 'extreme' opinions in criticism is out of place. The answers to the critic's questions are not moderate or extreme, but true or false; and of all men a Christian ought to be willing to go any length with truth.[30]

The unity of the Bible which Denney has clearly acknowledged is not such as to destroy the variety which is apparent as well. The description of this variety, in the light of the overruling unity, is a part of the critic's task, according to Denney. 'When he admits that God has spoken, his aim is to distinguish as clearly as possible the many parts and many ways in which He has done so; his interest is set not on what God is saying, but on what, in circumstances which can never be exactly repeated, God long ago said.'[31]

Denney is thought of today, more or less, as a conservative exegete and interpreter. It is not a reputation which fits him altogether, nor is it one which would have altogether pleased him. In his lifetime he was regarded by many as being too liberal, particularly in his handling of the Scripture. He was attacked in the Glasgow Presbytery because of his denial of the Davidic authorship of Psalm 110.[32] Robertson Nicoll, who was far ahead of the body of the Church on this matter, was nevertheless fearful of his friend's advanced positions.[33] When Denney published his major work on Christology, *Jesus and the Gospel*, many were alarmed by his acceptance of the findings of higher criticism, failing to realize that it was his very use of critical results which was the power of his work.

At the same time, he was fully aware of the dangers of criticism, particularly when it became so absorbed in its own special task that it failed to recognize or give proper place to the unity of the gospel presented in the books with which it was dealing. 'The tacit presupposition of much criticism', he once wrote, 'is that Jesus was just another man; and the astonishing thing is that in the circumstances, with this one essential point fixed in advance, people should imagine that there is still anything particular in the New Testament to talk about.'[34] It was the division of thought here that he watched with care; as long as criticism was aware of its relationship to the gospel and to the Church he felt that it was a helpful force, but he was wary of criticism which dissociated itself from any recognition of the gospel or any responsibility to faith. He could be severe with those who dealt lightly in the name of criticism with the faith of the New Testament and of the Church. 'The Church of Christ', he declared trenchantly, 'has not to beg its bread from criticism, nor faith to subsist on the alms of unbelief.'[35] Some of his most devastating remarks were directed against the examples and exponents of the unbalanced higher criticism of his day. A few comments on books and men will give us the flavor of his feeling:

> This is an eminent example of a man so full of his own mind that he sees little in the Gospels but what he brings, and therefore not only misses what is there, but finds a great deal which isn't.[36]

> If the members of the Church read this book and believed it, there would not be two or three left in the world to meet in the name of Jesus.[37]

> I cannot resist the impression that they have baked a huge cake with very little meal.[38]

> I don't think he realizes how much he has thrown away, and how

greatly he deceives himself by verbal association about the worth of what he keeps.[39]

He is . . . a wild man on a monoplane.[40]

He leaves on the mind the impression of a man who has learned to spell, but not to read—or who believes that the life of Christ is in the letters of the dictionary, and that it is merely a matter of putting them properly together to produce the force which has created Christianity.[41]

He once commented to his class, 'It's strange how many uninspiring books have been written on the inspired book.'[42] When he encountered irresponsible criticism he exposed it for what it was, letting it be its own best critic, for, he said, 'The way in which men handle revelation judges them when they do not think of it.'[43] With regard to commentaries he wrote, 'The Gospels were written in the Church and for the Church, and it is a mistake to write commentaries on them in which the Church as such can have no interest.'[44] In similar vein, he wrote of the task of the Biblical scholar, giving his own purpose in words which even the strictest Barthian of today would not wish to refute:

It is certainly a drawback to most recent commentaries that the study of criticism has apparently blinded the commentators to the fact that the books on which they are working are bits of the Bible—that but for that fact they would in all probability never have reached us— and that the chief business of the commentator is to elucidate their significance as vehicles of revelation.[45]

Denney was willing to speak of himself as 'a believing critic',[46] feeling in his faith a complete freedom to ask and answer without fear whatever questions the documents themselves suggest. He regarded criticism as being neither an evil to be avoided nor an end in itself, but rather a means to moving into a better understanding of the Scripture and through it onto a higher ground of faith. He wrote to a friend,

What troubles me is not how to blow the trumpet, or sound an alarm, but how to teach in detail, and persuade people who are alarmed not to close their minds in impatience, but to face the kind of questions which criticism raises, and to meet them with the composure of intelligence, as well as the assurance of faith.[47]

He brought together in his own mind the combined interests of devotion to the truth of God revealed in the Person and work of Christ and commitment to the scientific means of critical and historical study of the record of that revelation. He pointed to the early Church as the pattern for us in our attitude toward the books which they themselves have given us:

> The view the early Christians took of the books they valued was instinctively dogmatic without ceasing to be historical; . . . with a lively sense of their historical relations the Church had an instinctive feeling of the dogmatic import of the books in its New Testament. It is in this attitude, which is not blind to either side of the distinction, yet does not let either annul the other, that we ought to approach the study of New Testament problems.[48]

It is in this union between the historical and the eternal—a union vital to our Christian faith—that Biblical criticism, exegesis and theology have their work to do. In speaking to the Glasgow College at one of its opening sessions, he made this point clear; he then drove it home with a quotation from a distinguished German professor who had said that if he could preach the gospel he would not be lecturing on theology, to which Denney replied,

> If one could be believed to say so humbly, I should rather . . . reverse the words and say that *unless* I could preach the Gospel I should not be lecturing on theology. We have no interest in theology, or in criticism, or in anything else that goes on here, but for the sake of the Gospel, and the Church, and the Lord.[49]

The Study of the Gospels

Denney maintains that the way to vindicate to the mind the claims which are here made for the Bible is to survey the Scripture in its distinctive parts with a view to finding, in each part, the nature of its revelation and the relation to it of critical problems and results. He suggests, further, that the starting point in such an investigation should be the gospels, not because they are earlier, but because here we come most immediately into contact with Christ. Denney's contention is that if anyone will take the gospels in hand and read them sincerely and openly, leaving details aside for a moment and concentrating simply upon the Person depicted, he will find that he comes into contact with reality, that he actually receives revelation through these words.

> Read these books with your eye on Christ, and it will be as certain to you as anything is certain to the mind, heart, and conscience of men, that the character of Christ there exhibited is a real character. It is not a fancy character; it is not a work of imagination; the evangelists did not make it out of their own heads.[50]

The Spirit enables us to understand these words and to appropriate them so that we are assured of the truth and the authority of the revelation of God in Christ. This makes the task of criticism secondary to the understanding of the revelation in the gospels. As Denney commented, 'We do not need to become historical critics before we can believe in Christ and be saved by Him.'[51] These documents bring us into direct contact with God's revelation, and because of this we are assured of their inspiration.

On this general basis, then, criticism is free to give itself to the detailed study of the gospels in an effort to shed new light upon their central spiritual certainty. He felt that the first task of the critical student of the gospels is to understand the purpose for which the evangelists were writing, in order that the methods used could be understood in detail. In defining this for himself, he said,

> The Gospel writers have no independent historical interest, and what they give us is not the representation of Christ as He really was, but Christ as to them He must have been, Christ transfigured in the luminous haze of faith. The task of the historian is to dissipate the haze, to see Jesus as He really was, to reduce Him to the historic proportions in which alone He can have lived and moved among men. To faith it may be an ungrateful task, in performing which it is impossible to avoid wounding the tenderest feelings; yet faith in God can have no interest superior to that of truth, and ought to be confident that whatever it may lose in the process the end can be nothing but gain.[52]

This does not mean that the evangelists' accounts are not historical; it means that they were not writing with historical interest as their primary motive. They were writing gospel, and were quite openly trying to 'make out a case'. But this does not rule out their historicity. As Denney put it, 'It is quite true that it is one thing to tell a story, and another to make out a case; but if a man has a sound case, the simplest way to make it out is to tell his story.'[53] When historical criticism begins with the dogmatic assumption that the evangelists have 'a bad case', it is denying the very principle of scientific inquiry which it pretends to uphold. As we have seen in Denney's theology, he is exceedingly forceful in proving that the evangelists were true to the historical facts and that the Christ of faith was indeed the Jesus of history. In connection with the gospels, a matter of major discussion has been the question of sources. Denney's ability in this area of research is seen in his *Jesus and the Gospel*, where he declines to treat any passages which are not based upon the earliest and most dependable sources. An interesting indication of his modernity is found in his

K

insistence upon the importance of oral tradition lying behind the gospels.

> There must be a far ampler recognition of the fact that the Gospel matter was widely known, and also freely reproduced, apart from documents, even by people like Luke and Matthew, who certainly had documents at command. Oral tradition alone cannot explain some of the phenomena, but there are some which can be naturally explained by nothing else.[54]

His openness to scientific study is revealed in his comment upon the Germans' 'religionsgeschichtliche methode'—the study of religious syncretism within the New Testament itself. He had very little sympathy for its treatment of the gospels, but could say, 'Its right is unquestioned, and though like all new things it is apt to to go to some heads with intoxicating power, it has brought light to a few dark places in the New Testament, and doubtless has more to bring.'[55]

Within the gospels, Denney dealt from time to time with various subdivisions of the material. The teaching of Jesus drew his interest, and he concentrated attention particularly upon the Sermon on the Mount and upon the parables. With regard to the words of the Sermon on the Mount, he wrote,

> Intellectually, they challenge us. Emotionally, they vibrate with passion. Ethically, they suggest if they do not define a new standard the height and range of which make themselves felt through endless imperfections of intelligence . . . His words are only intelligible as partial revelations of Himself: it is through Him we must understand them, as much as through them we understand Him . . . They are not statutory injunctions: they are jets of living flame. They are not meant to save us the trouble of thinking, but to kindle in us the most intense and vivid thought.[56]

To those who sought to bring in the Kingdom by incorporating the Sermon on the Mount in the national legislation, he said tersely, 'It would be a great point gained if people would only consider that it was a sermon, and was preached, not an act which was passed.'[57] Concerning the parables, he once commented, 'They can hardly fail to convey the word of the Lord, but they are not so likely to convey it in His very words.'[58] Or again, he wrote, 'Jesus did not conceive or speak the Parables to provide illustrations for a text-book of rhetoric, nor even to indulge His delight in literary art; He had nothing in view but the practical purpose of making His message more intelligible to men.'[59] To those who were insistent upon pushing back to the *ipsissima verba* of Jesus, and distinguishing in the parables and throughout His teaching the actual and exact words which He spoke, Denney had a word of warning to give:

> The Apostolic reading of the truth, as truth is in Jesus, is perfectly conscious that it goes beyond the *ipsissima verba* which Jesus spoke on earth; but the Apostles would have felt it strangely unreal if they had been asked to cut down their testimony to Jesus to what Jesus Himself had expressly put into words. There were many things which circumstances made it impossible for Him to put into words —many things which it was rather for them to say about Him than for Him to say about Himself; but when they said these things, under the guiding and quickening impulse of His Spirit, they had no doubt that they were declaring the truth of Christ . . . Once they had listened to His voice on earth, now they heard Him in their hearts interpret all He had been, and between the voices they made no distinction.[60]

Within the area of the life and ministry of Jesus, one of the most vexed problems has to do with the matter of His miracles. Denney's feeling was that the miracles were a part of the total picture of Christ's life and were not particularly helpful when isolated and made to yield individual facts and interpretations. Said he, 'To prove the miracles one by one is as impossible as to disprove them in the same way, but they unite with the Person and the words of Jesus into one divine whole through which God reveals His very heart to man.'[61]

It was with this same general emphasis that he treated almost all of the problems connected with the study of the gospels, feeling that through all the questions of detail they do succeed in doing for us what the evangelists intended them to do.

> The Gospels have every quality which they need, to put us in contact with the Gospel; they do put us in contact with it, and the Spirit makes it sure to our faith; why should we ask for more from them? If they truly represent Christ to us, so that we gain the faith in Him which their authors had, is not that all we can desire?[62]

This was the emphasis which he laid upon the gospels themselves, feeling that they are to be trusted, and that men should give the primary place in their study of the gospels to the books themselves rather than to the latest works on critical analysis of them. It was this which lay behind the answer which he gave to a student in one of his classes. He was assigning subjects for individual study and to one man he gave the subject, 'Prophecy in St Matthew's Gospel. The student spoke up and asked what books he should read to help him, to which Denney

replied simply, 'Read St Matthew's Gospel.'[63] This was likewise the
point of his pungent reply to the American student who asked him to
recommend a good 'Life' of Christ. The question shot back from
Denney,'Have you read the one by Luke?'[64]

The Study of the Old Testament

Having thus established a sure starting-point of understanding and
of inquiry into the revelation of Christ found in the Scripture, it is
possible to work out from it so that the area of acceptance of revealed
truth becomes increasingly enlarged. Denney suggests that one can
turn easily from here to the Old Testament. There the basic issue for
the Christian reader is the fact of the importance to Jesus of the older
revelation. The Old Testament was a source of real revelation to Him
and He used it as a means of fellowship with His Father. Said Denney,
'It is quite true that He fulfills it, transcends it, in some sense super-
sedes it; but what was so priceless to Him can surely never lose its
worth for those who call Him Master.'[65] Not only so, but it is particularly significant for the Christian that Christ saw Himself in the Old
Testament, that, apart from any artificial interpretation of the fulfillment of prophecy, Jesus saw Himself as the center of God's revelation
and the key to its unity.

> His calling and career were outlined in the ancient revelation, and
> He came to fulfill it. They were not only outlined, but prepared for.
> All He was had vital roots and points of attachment in that Divinely-
> guided history. It spoke of Him not only in terms, but in purport;
> He was not only predicted, but prefigured in it.[66]

Thus the Old Testament is seen in vital relationship with the New,
and in that connection it has an unquestioned place in the life of the
Christian. It is clear that it held such a place for the writers of the New
Testament. 'The apostles', Denney commented, 'read the Old Testa-
ment as a Christian book, and we do not get into their minds till we
can do the same.'[67] They express New Testament concepts in Old
Testament words; their very use of the words makes them Christian
in meaning. Denney insisted that it is possible to read the whole of the
Old Testament in this sense and, while erring in detail, not be in error
as to the whole. On the other hand, it is likewise clear that the New
Testament is intensely aware not only of its identification with the
Old, but of the fact that it transcends it.

> The New Testament does what the Old failed to do; it brings us to
> victory where the Old only led us to defeat . . . The ministry of the

one ends in condemnation, that of the other in justification . . . The last word which the one wrings from human lips is the despairing cry, 'O wretched man that I am! Who shall deliver me?' The first word which the other inspires is, 'So then there is no condemnation to them that are in Christ Jesus.'[68]

The conclusion which Denney reaches is that even in transcending the Old Testament, the New Testament gives to the Old a place of unique importance and that in stating its own doctrines it depends for its background upon the older revelation. The Old Testament bears witness to the gospel and as such is a necessary means to the full understanding of the New Testament presentation of it.

Upon this basis of the assured place of the Old Testament in the religious life of believers, it is possible for criticism to do its work and to contribute greatly to our understanding of the books themselves. Denney pointed out the areas of the Old Testament in which new and valuable insights have come by way of the work of criticism. One such area has been the writings of the prophets. They have been seen in their historical settings and have been made to come alive as men who spoke God's word to particular situations. The mechanical solutions to the problems of prophecy have been replaced, and for this Denney was glad. 'We do not need to believe that the prophets could write history beforehand. The revelation they have to make to us is not the revelation of this or that incident in the fortunes of men or nations; it is the revelation of God.'[69] Another area of progress in understanding has been the opening chapters of Genesis. Denney felt that we must learn from the critics that the only possible interpretation of these passages which can have any real meaning is that which recognizes them as being mythological in form, of being prescientific and pre-historical answers to questions of science and history. These myths, he suggested, are born out of experience and through them God speaks to the experience of all men. 'It is not the story of the first man, but of every man; and, if the key to its form is to be sought in comparative mythology, the key to its contents can be found only in the soul.'[70] This interpretation makes these early chapters live with meaning for us and that is a contribution to our religious understanding for which we can be thankful. Denney felt this strongly.

I should not hesitate to say that the man who cannot hear God speak to him in the story of creation and the fall will never hear God's voice anywhere. But that does not make the first Chapter of Genesis science, nor the third Chapter history . . . What is of authority in these Chapters is not the quasi-scientific or quasi-historical form, but the message, which through them comes to the heart, of God's creative wisdom and power, of man's native kinship to God, of his calling to rule over nature, of his sin, of God's judgment and mercy.[71]

Denney regarded the Old Testament as a significant part of revelation and urged an interpretation of its passages which is in keeping with its spiritual vitality.

There are high ideal utterances in it in which the eternal truth is revealed—the unchanging will of God in all its height and grace; and he who reads the Old Testament in the spirit in which it is written will not miss them; and it is only for such a reader that the Old Testament never grows old.[72]

The Study of the Apostolic Writings

Passing beyond the Old Testament, we come to the apostolic testimony to the gospel as we find it in their writings in the New Testament. Just as he moved back from the gospels enlarging the area of assured revelation and of critical study to include the Old Testament, so Denney would have us move forward into the apostolic writings and there seek to find the same ground for building faith and theology and the same acceptance of the methods and purposes of Biblical criticism. We do not need to pause on the matter of the authority of the apostles or on the question of the unity of their testimony, for these are subjects with which we have been concerned more than once in our discussion of New Testament theology. Denney's insistence from the first has been that the New Testament represents a basic unity, and that that unity rests in its witness to the gospel of God in Christ. He has also stressed throughout his work the fact that the apostolic testimony is of primary importance for the Church and for individual believers, that it represents the original norm for faith and theology. At no point has the authority of the apostles been forced, but at every point it has asserted its own authority by its ability to lead into a proper and positive understanding of the gospel. 'The very grace of the apostolic Scriptures', Denney asserted, 'is that God by means of them interprets to us His love in Christ, and enables us to grasp it with heart and mind.'[73]

Within this unity there is, of course, a dynamic variety which is descriptive of the life and creativity of the New Testament Church. It is well for us to consider briefly Denney's comments on various sections of apostolic writings in order to appreciate the value of the variety. He began in his thinking about the apostolic testimony with *the primitive kerygma*. On this body of material found in the early sermons in the Book of Acts, as we have seen, Denney built his interpretation of the atonement and of the incarnation, using this primitive proclamation as the bridge between the other elements of New Testament writing, and as the early foundation upon which was developed the New Testament theology. He was anticipating some of today's most helpful contributions when he insisted that 'some source or sources of the highest value underlie the speeches of Peter'. He went on to add, 'They do not represent the nascent catholicism of the beginning of the second century, but the very earliest type of preaching Jesus by men who had kept company with Him.'[74] He outlined the development of thought in this primitive preaching in connection with the original baptismal confessions and creeds.[75]

Coming to *the Epistles of Paul*, we find Denney in his natural element. If he must be identified with some one area of New Testament thinking, we should locate him there. He felt instinctively at home in the apostle's thought and the Pauline influence upon his theology is apparent. No one will assume that he felt Paul possessed a monopoly upon the truth; his concept of the unity of the Scripture would deny that. Denney could readily point out weaknesses in the apostle's presentation,[76] but there was a strong sympathy on his part with almost all of Paul's writing. His commentaries are all devoted to Pauline Epistles, and his works in New Testament theology seem to concentrate, necessarily and quite naturally, upon the Pauline passages. The new appreciation of Paul at the present time, and the reassertion of the importance of his place in theology, have served to give Denney's writings a particular appropriateness of prophectic quality for our day.

He did not simply labor with Pauline thought, he lived with it. He once wrote to a friend, 'It always does me good to see a man enjoying St Paul, and that neither on the surface only, nor with an air of superiority to the subject, which in some people drives one mad.'[77] He viewed the apostle in the light of his environment in the early Church, saying, 'Paul did not live in a vacuum; he lived in the primitive Christian society in which all that was known of Jesus was current, and he could not, by the most determined and obstinate effort, have been as ignorant of Jesus as he is sometimes represented to be.'[78] At the same time, Denney emphasized the bold originality of Paul's mind as reflected in his epistles. After discussing Paul's Christology, he paused to say pointedly, 'No one ever soared so high on borrowed wings.'[79] He frankly admitted that he was not particularly concerned about the historical peculiarities of Paul's life, but that he found his keenest interest caught up in that which gave Paul his spiritual power, that which he expresses in his writings, that which has made Paul 'incomparably the greatest source of spiritual revivals in the Christian Church for nearly two thousand years'.[80] He had little patience with those scholars who pretended a lofty indifference to the apostle's presentation of his gospel, on one occasion writing to his friend, Alexander Whyte, 'The unintelligent and inexperienced books about Paul are dreadful—all done by just men who need no repentance and therefore have no glimmerings of what was vital to the apostle. It is always a marvel to me that the street preacher goes straight to the point in Paul, and finds all his answers where the ninety-and-nine just men find all their difficulties.'[81] He was later to put this same thought in more formal and more forceful words:

> To say that Paul is unintelligible, or that he presents Christianity in a way which does it every kind of injustice and is finally unacceptable to us, is to fly in the face of history and experience. There have always been people who found Paul intelligible and accepted the Gospel as he preached it. There are such people still, if not in theological class rooms, then in mission halls, at street corners, in lonely rooms. It is not historical scholarship that is wanted for the understanding of him, and neither is it the insight of genius; it is despair. Paul did not preach for scholars, nor even for philosophers; he preached for sinners.[82]

Denney tended to regard all of the epistles ordinarily attributed to Paul—including Ephesians—as being genuine products of his hand or influence, with the exception of the Pastoral Epistles—I and II Timothy and Titus. These he was inclined to credit to another mind, as we can see in this typical epigram: 'St Paul was inspired, but the writer of these Epistles is sometimes only orthodox'.[83]

With regard to *the other apostolic writers* Denney had some interesting comments to make. The First Epistle of Peter he felt was quite likely connected in some direct way with the apostle Peter. He recognized in it things which are best explained by reference not to Paul, but to the memory of the life of Jesus or to parts of the Old Testament. 'His antecedents', said Denney, 'properly speaking, are not Pauline, but prophetic and evangelic.[84] The Epistle to the Hebrews he spoke of as 'the most solitary of the primitive Christian books',[85] and pointed out that in it we find the extremes meet: 'The most humanitarian book of the New Testament can also be fairly described as the most theological'.[86] Elsewhere he notes with regard to Hebrews that 'the author was not an evangelist so much as a pastor, and it is not the initiation of Christianity but its conservation with which he deals throughout'.[87] He was not very enthusiastic about the final effect of the Epistle, however; and once commented, 'Many people are attracted and even fascinated by the Epistle to the Hebrews, but few are inspired.'[88] With regard to the Epistle of James, he commented on the apparent difference which exists between Paul's doctrine of faith and James' doctrine of works, saying, 'If the writer is controverting St Paul, it must be admitted that he has not grasped the Pauline point of view, and that Luther's verdict on his work was justified.'[89] This was not his final word on the comparison between the two writers, however, and he concludes by saying, 'To St Paul Christianity is a new religious relation to God which he defines by contrast to legalism; to St James it is rather a new ethical life, which he describes in terms of law, but of law from which legalism has been eliminated.'[90]

When dealing with *the Johannine literature*, we find him insisting on the underlying similarities which can be found in the Fourth Gospel, the First Epistle and the Apocalypse. Recognizing the differences, both in content and in form, between Paul and this writer, he nevertheless argues that they are at one in their presentation of the gospel of Christ. The differences seem to him to lie in the distinction between the two personalities. 'St John's mind is not of a dialectical turn like that of St Paul, but given rather to intuition than to reflection—in other words to the contemplation of results rather than of processes, of ends rather than of means or conditions'.[91] He sums up the differences which are evident between them, urging that the distinction not be overstated: 'In Paul Jesus mediates revelation through redemption, whereas in John He mediates redemption through revelation. But the distinction is true only when it is not pressed. In both writers it is the specifically Christian sense of mediation that is vital: Jesus is mediator between God and men.'[92] Concerning the Fourth Gospel, Denney observes that it is best understood as the fulfillment of one of its own words: 'I have yet many things to say unto you, but ye cannot bear them now. Howbeit when he, the Spirit of truth, is come, he will guide you into all the truth . . . He shall glorify me: for He shall receive of mine, and shall show it unto you.'[93] Denney's feeling is that the author made no differentiation between the words of the historical Jesus and the words of the risen Jesus speaking through His Spirit, for they were for him one and the same reality and therefore no distinction was necessary.

His words are the expression of the eternal truth which was revealed in Jesus, and which for the writer is identical with Him. They are the word, rather than the words of the Lord. They are the authentic revelation of what He is and was, as His Spirit has interpreted Him to the evangelist, rather than the *ipsissima verba* of Jesus of Nazareth.[94]

Denney depends upon the Fourth Gospel in historical detail, particularly when it seems clear that the author was trying to correct the Synoptic tradition, but feels that we must depend upon the Synoptics for the historical form of Jesus' teaching. He is willing to take a firm stand upon the question of the similar authorship of the Epistle and of the Gospel: 'If these two books cannot be ascribed to the same pen, literary criticism is bankrupt.'[95] He goes on to offer the conjecture that 'the Epistle is a sort of covering letter accompanying and recommending the Gospel.'[96] In writing about the Book of Revelation, he employs the graphic comparison between the Apocalypse and a tunnel:

> There is light at the one end as you enter—everyone can make something of the Epistles to the Seven Churches; and there is light at the other end as you come out—everyone can make something of the New Jerusalem. But between the two there is a long stretch of darkness, through which lurid objects thunder past, bewildering and stunning the reader.[97]

Such was Denney's approach to the Scripture—its inspiration and unity, the creative life out of which it came to be, its authority and infallibility, and the critical and constructive study of its details and of its major sweep. It is immediately apparent that his basic approach is in line with much that has been done in the field of Biblical interpretation in recent decades and that his conclusions often ring with that contemporaneous note which causes him to speak with astonishing force to the mind of our own day. If there is a certain want of thoroughness in his treatment, it is to be explained by the fact that he seldom dealt with the Bible as an objective area of study, and that we have had to gather his contributions from his books and articles, his lectures and letters, in which he makes constant use of the Bible with reference to the major themes with which he is dealing. There will be some who feel that his whole approach to the inspiration and authority of Scripture is too subjective, based as it is upon experience. This is a criticism which Denney anticipated, and in reply he has said, 'It is like urging that a man does not see at all, or does not see truly, because he only sees with his own eyes. This is the only authentic kind of seeing yet known to mankind.'[98]

IX

THE PREACHING CHURCH
The Church and the Kingdom

*The kind of testimony to Christ which wins men to
commit themselves to God's redeeming love in Him . . .
is the Church's chief end.*[1]

In recent years the world of theology has come into a deeper understanding of the meaning of the Church and to a more dynamic conception of the Kingdom. In Denney's time, it was popular to castigate
the Church in the name of the Kingdom. Men with motives differing
from those of the strict dogmatists—who held that the Church was not
a proper study for theology—to those of the socialist thinkers—who
felt that the Church was a great obstacle in the way of total progress—
delighted in sniping at the Church or in thrusting hard at its heart. A
new understanding of the Church in the New Testament and a new
experience of its wider fellowship in our own age have combined to
lead us beyond that barren position.

Denney's relationship to this development is interesting and intriguing. The Church came increasingly to hold an important place in
his life and thought, and this is reflected in the expanding emphasis he
gives to it in his theology. The explanation for the growing importance
to him of the Church came from two concerns in his life: his study of
the New Testament and his own personal experience of the wider
fellowship of the Church. These have been the same concerns which
have led to the modern reaffirmation of the meaning and importance
of the Church. Denney has anticipated us in yet another area of thought.

The Importance of the Church

'If we want something effective done, there are two things we have
to revive', declared Denney, speaking on the floor of the General
Assembly of 1912,

> We want a revival of spiritual life in the Church, and along with that
> a revival in the minds of Christian people of the sense of the value
> of the Christian Church. Many have disparaged the Church in the

past. But I am sure of this, that the Church is the great witness to Christ and spiritual things in the world, and that the witness of the Church as an institution, bearing its continuous testimony, is the thing on which the permanence of the Christian faith in the world depends. We have to plead the importance of the Church in maintaining the great tradition of faith through the generations of men.[2]

He felt that a great deal of the Church's problem in confronting society was its own responsibility, that its members and its ministers had derogated the Church to such an extent that it was suffering from its own abuse. Its great need was a reassertion in the minds of Christians of its inherent importance. 'We have run down the Church', he wrote to a friend, 'as if it had no real relation to living Christianity, and the lesson has been only too well learned.'[3] In seeking to provide leadership in the reclaiming of the importance of the Church, he directed attention to the place of the Church in the New Testament.

The Church in the New Testament

In turning to the New Testament, we find that the idea of the community of believers is expressed primarily in two different words: the Church and the Kingdom. It was being pointed out on all sides around Denney, that Jesus said a great deal about the Kingdom and very little about the Church. Therefore men drew a clear distinction between them, arguing that the Church is simply a human institution while the Kingdom is a divine ideal for society. This sort of contrast can be found in forms of varying elaborateness in the books on theology of a half-century ago. Said Denney wryly, 'This must be an attractive distinction, for it has attracted many.'[4]

Denney contended that, while these people clearly had in their minds an idea of what the Kingdom meant, they could not appeal to Christ for that idea. When we look to Christ, what do we find? 'The Kingdom is so central and comprehensive in His teaching', observed Denney, 'that it is difficult to speak of it without introducing the whole contents of the Gospel. Jesus spoke of it as present, and also as future; as in process of development, and as yet to be revealed in power; as among men, and yet as transcendent.'[5] In seeking to find the heart of such a crucial conception in Jesus' teaching, Denney pointed to two particular aspects of the subject.

The first of these is the King. Denney feels that a great deal of the confusion in men's minds is based on their concentration upon the Kingdom, rather than the King.

It is from the idea of sovereignty, or reign, rather than from that of kingdom that we must start in attempting to grasp the teaching of Jesus. The exercise of royal power by God is primary, not the sphere within which it is exercised, nor the community subject to it, nor the blessings attendant on its establishment. All these are involved, but the main thing is that God takes to Himself His great power and reigns.[6]

Thus as men see God at work in Christ and are drawn within the sway of His reign, they find a new understanding of the Kingdom and know themselves to be involved in it. Said Denney, 'The various ideas of the Kingdom have the unity which belongs to the personality and life of Jesus, in whom God is revealed. Jesus did not preach a new God, but He embodied a new revelation of God, and the Kingdom which He preached is specifically the Kingdom of the Father.'[7] As He reveals the Father, and brings men into reconciliation with Him, Jesus is building the Kingdom. It is characterized by the same qualities—the divine and the human, transcendence and incarnation—which we have recognized in the Person of the King.

The second point of emphasis which Denney makes concerns the Kingdom itself, the reality of the society thus created in the world by faith in the King. The reign of God does not take place in a vacuum, but implies a people who live under that reign, and Jesus acted in such a way as to establish that people as a new Israel. While there is nothing formal or institutional about its creation, Denney feels that it is beyond question that Jesus called men into the Kingdom by associating them with Himself, and in so doing brought them together binding them into a unity in Him. This community accomplishes its work, not by legislation nor by force, but by individual loyalty to the King which serves to transform and transfigure the whole of society with all of its institutions.

The Kingdom of God becomes a conquering and transfiguring power in proportion as the citizens of the Kingdom are intensely conscious of their new relation to God, and of the new obligations it imposes . . . It is not by corporate, legislative, compulsory action of the Christian community; it is by free spontaneous, spiritual action of Christian individuals, each in his own sphere, each in the calling in which his life is to be given to God, that God's Kingdom comes.[8]

When we pass from the teaching of Jesus in the gospels to the thought of the other books of the New Testament, there is a noticeable difference in language with regard to the Christian community. The

'Kingdom' does not disappear, but it is not nearly so prominent as it was in the gospels. The word which is taken by the apostles and used to refer to the fellowship in Christ is the word ἐκκλησία—'church'. Denney sees the forceful meaning which the word received from Greek usage in the market-place—where it referred to the people assembled—and from the Septuagint translation of the Hebraic reference to God's people. But it seems to him that these are not adequate to explain the use which the apostles made of the word. For them it had all of the points of reference which we have seen concerning the Kingdom: the Church is divine and yet realized in human terms; it is present and yet is to come; it is temporal and yet is transcendent. Denney feels that the reason they came to use the word rather than the term Kingdom lies not in dogmatic but in practical considerations. They moved out of the environment of the Jewish mind in which Jesus had taught and, finding the image of the Kingdom less effective under these circumstances, they took up in its stead a word which was lying at hand and was ready to be filled with the same content. As Denney observed,

> It means whatever the apostles use it to mean, and it will be very hard, if justice is done to their use of it, to put it in any subordinate place . . . They did not lapse from His idea of the Kingdom, and discard it for an inferior one, because they could not carry all its contents; they practically exchanged it for another idea, when they found that through another the grace of God could find easier access into the minds of men.[9]

In their use of the term Church, we find the same two basic emphases: the crucial importance of Christ, the Head of the Church; and the concentration upon the unity of the members of the body. Therefore for Denney, the reply to those who would stress the distinction between the Church and the Kingdom rests in the fact that there is no real distinction in the New Testament's use of the terms. The Church is the Kingdom as we know it in experience, just as the apostles took the reality of the Kingdom concept and transferred it to the living fellowship of the Church which they knew in their experience. That is why all of the suggested definitions of the one as over against the other are always unsatisfactory. Said Denney sharply, 'They are arbitrary answers to an unreal question.'[10]

The frequent references which the apostles make to the Church indicate that the term covered a broad expanse of the experience of the early Christians. In its simplest form, it was the local fellowship which they knew. As Denney commented,

The Church is at first a local community. It is the totality of those who have accepted the salvation which is in Christ, and who are living in mutual love as children of God. It is filled with the Holy Spirit, which is the Spirit of Jesus; and it is this which is the bond of union among its members.[11]

There was no compulsory form of life and no prescribed type of organization, and the authority of the apostles in the local community was the natural recognition of their familiar knowledge of the Lord, not an authority which was forced upon the Church. The authority was in Christ and in His Spirit felt in the Church.

These local communities, each independent, were nevertheless united as one. They formed together the Church. The Church, then, is seen as the total fellowship of those who in every place call upon Christ as Lord and Saviour. Said Denney, 'I do not think the New Testament contemplates the existence of unattached Christians—persons who have accepted the Christian salvation and embraced the Christian ideal and vocation—but who are not members of a Church.'[12] The unity of this universal Church does not rely upon organization nor officials, but upon the basic reality of the Spirit, who unites all the members into one.

What the brethren have is indispensable to us; what we have is indispensable to them. In this sense the dogma is true—*extra ecclesiam, nulla salus*. It is the recognition of this truth on which the vital unity of the Church depends . . . It is not in the fellowship of a priestly or episcopal order—much less in the fellowship of a Pope —that it is one; it is one in the fellowship of the Holy Ghost.[13]

Over this concept of the Church, local and universal, stands the figure of the ideal Church. This has for the apostles all of the implications of the eschatological image of the Kingdom. It is this which calls forth from them their most exalted statements about the Church, exhausting their imagery in seeking to picture the ultimate significance of this the goal of all God's works.

The Church in History

Against this background of New Testament thought we are able to look with clearer vision at the Church as it has moved through history up to the present. Denney's feeling is that we must constantly recall the Church to its original significance as seen in the New Testament, and that against that standard the Church can and must be judged.

The note of allegiance to the King and Head of the Church is found throughout Denney's theology. It is valuable to notice as well that he came increasingly to emphasize the other note in the New Testament's presentation of the Church: the reality of the Kingdom in the unity of the body of believers. The movement toward unity has become the historic ecumenical force of our modern time, and for most of us today it is not difficult to think in ecumenical terms. For Denney, the commitment to the unity of the Church grew out of the dear-bought discipline of prayer and study and experience. He had been reared in one of Scotland's smallest and most conservative Churches and he admitted an early prejudice in favor of small denominations. But as he studied the New Testament he could not avoid its demand for unity; and as he took his responsible place in meeting the widening call for service he moved forward and began to take an active part in the cause of union. And with him moved his Church. Men trusted him as one of integrity who could, with care for their own distinctive principles, lead the Churches of his nation out into a broader field of union. A leader of another Church commented, 'If Dr Denney advocates union, there will be union; if Dr Denney is opposed to union, there will be none.'[14] The result of his early work was felt in the formation in 1929, twelve years after his death, of the reunited Church of Scotland.

It seemed to him that the history of the Church since the time of the New Testament reveals two developments which have militated against the fellowship and unity of the Church, though in their inception they were thought to be protecting that unity. The first of these is the phenomenon of the erection of formal creeds within the life of the Church. These creeds were initially seen as the Church's self-defence against attacks on its faith from without and from within. As definitions of true faith, they became increasingly complex and increasingly binding upon the members of the Church. This would appear on the whole to have been an inevitable process, and Denney does not deny this. But his point is that we must understand the effect which this has had upon the Church. 'It was well meant', he observed, 'and it was well done, but it shifted the emphasis in the conception of the Church, and we have had to pay for that ever since.'[15] It pushed into the background the essentially spiritual character of the fellowship and brought into prominence a dogmatic conception of the Church.

It is no longer the fellowship of the saints, the community of those who possess salvation in Jesus Christ; it is the community which confesses certain historical facts, and recognizes certain interpretations of them . . . It is always dangerous when we call in the law, no matter in what shape, to defend the Gospel.[16]

Denney maintained that men must free themselves from encumbering statements of what is 'orthodox' and move back to the spirit and the truth of the New Testament. On the basis of the New Testament's insistence upon faith in Christ and in Him alone, Denney suggested a confession or creed which might draw the Church together. The creed which he offered was this: 'I believe in God through Jesus Christ His only Son, our Lord and Saviour.'[17] All that has preceded in our study of Denney's theology will have served toward making the elements of this suggested creed intelligible. It was his thought that such a statement would bind the Church to all that is fundamental to Christian faith and only that which is fundamental, and he offered it as early as 1910 in the interest of Christian unity and Christian freedom. As one thinks of the modern ecumenical movement, united in its confession of 'Our Lord Jesus Christ as God and Saviour', we can appreciate the insight of Denney's early suggestion. Even as he offered it, he recognized the inadequacy of any creedal statement. 'It is not the signing of a creed which keeps men true to their religion, but something quite different. The men who drew up the confessions which we sign could not themselves sign them before they were drawn up.'[18] On the same subject he once commented,

> It is not open or unanswered questions that paralyze; it is ambiguous or evasive answers, or answers of which we can make no use, because we cannot make them our own. And it is not the acceptance of any theology or Christology, however penetrating or profound, which keeps us Christian; we remain loyal to our Lord and Saviour only because He has apprehended us, and His hand is strong.[19]

Elsewhere, he said succinctly, 'The Church's confession of faith should be sung, not signed.'[20]

The second phenomenon of Church history which seemed to him to have become dangerous and divisive was the creation of the conception of the Church based upon the order of the clergy. This was again a development of defence on the part of the Church in an effort to assure itself of a spiritual heritage by means of a tangible guarantee. Denney felt that it was doomed to failure from the beginning, as far as the Church's spiritual goal is concerned, but in that doom lay the loss of the original conception of what the Church actually is. Having started upon this road—by the middle of the third century—it had to follow it on to the end, and we see that end in the ecclesiastical hierarchy

L

of the Roman Church. As he studied this historical phenomenon, he observed,

> There are two things to be said. The first is, that there is not a Christian minister in the world, from the Bishop of Rome up or down, who can prove that he himself stands in any unbroken succession. And the second is, that even if it could be proved, it would be quite irrelevant as a mark of the true Church. Such an external, legal, formal continuity, even if it existed, could guarantee nothing spiritual, and it is on spiritual consanguinity with the apostles and their testimony to Jesus that everything depends.[21]

The results of this development of hierarchy he did not like. It seemed to him to close off the area of genuine inquiry on the part of Roman scholars. He read them, but came away with this feeling: 'The total impression left in one's mind is that of dealing with a man whose one principle is, "Heads I win, tails you lose".'[22] And as for the Roman priesthood's claim of 'evangelical poverty', he commented, 'It is not evangelical poverty when a man buys even with all his money the power to enslave his fellow-men and to lord it over their faith. I had just as soon be Dives in the parable: the misrepresentation of Christianity and defamation of Jesus are not a whit worse or better in the one than in the other.'[23] One of his impatient words on the whole matter of 'apostolic succession' was, 'It is a dead weight which some Churches carry, and which, though sometimes imposing to the imagination, is never in the truest Christian sense inspiring.'[24]

The answer to both of these historical predicaments of the Church is a return to the conception and to the life of the Church as we see it in the New Testament. Upon this Denney was insistent, and toward it he gave guidance.

The Church Today

In the light of the heritage of the Church, Denney would call our attention to the life and work of the Church in the present day, as he speaks to us in terms of what the Church should be and do.

His first point of emphasis is a call to the Church to worship.

> The primary function of the Church is to assert its origin; it is to bear witness to Christ as the author of all the blessings it enjoys. Its first duty, as its primal impulse, is worship; and worship is the adoring confession of the God revealed in Christ and possessed in the Spirit as the Redeemer of sinful men. There is nothing so characteristic of the Church's life as doxology.[25]

The tendency to disparage the value of worship has had its effect upon the Church's program and life, and Denney maintains that we see clear indications of this in the casual attendance at worship services, in the perfunctory fashion in which services frequently are carried out, in the absence of awe and real solemnity. In place of an experience in which the souls of men are subdued and exalted by God, we too often see the sort of situation in which 'a clever man exerts all his cleverness to keep a congregation from wearying as they observe a decorous convention'.[26]

The Church has an essential call to be at work in the world, but its task does not begin there. Says Denney, 'The Church is concerned in the first instance not with what it has to do, but with what God has done for it.'[27] On the other hand, men have sought to elevate the place of worship by elevating the means of worship, which Denney regards as an indication of the same basic sickness lying at the heart of the worshipping community, for 'the elaboration of ritual and symbol . . . overpowers the spirit and defeats its own original purpose'.[28] From Italy he wrote his observations of the high liturgy of the Roman Church's worship:

> There is nothing in it that is not artificial. They have not even fresh air, but an atmosphere so pulluted with incense that I positively shrink from entering a church, and a worship in a dead language which no explanation can make anything else than a piece of mere mummery. It is pitiful to see to what the New Testament religion can come.[29]

The answer to men's need in worship lies in the renewal in their hearts of the experience of that which makes man worship. For Denney, it is as we know the experience of the gospel of Christ and know the fellowship of those who share with us that experience that we come naturally into the deeper meaning of worship.

> Just as in the ancient tabernacle every object used in worship had to be sprinkled with atoning blood, so all the parts of Christian worship, all our approaches to God, should consciously rest on the atonement. They should be felt to be a privilege beyond price; they should be penetrated with the sense of Christ's Passion, and of the love with which He loved us when He suffered for sins once for all, the just for the unjust, that He might conduct us to God.[30]

It is this which makes worship the breath which is native to the believing community, and as long as men respond to the gospel of Christ they will recognize the adoration of the Lord as the concern which is first and dearest to their souls.

Preaching

Denney would next direct our attention to the Church's task and privilege of preaching. 'If the spontaneous expression of the Church's life is worship, its first duty is to evangelize.'[31] In moving into this area of the Church's responsibility, he feels that we have not changed our ground, but are simply regarding it with a different emphasis. The common contrast between preaching and worship did not impress him.

> If the sermon in Church is what it ought to be—if it is not an exhibition of the preacher but of Jesus—there should be nothing in it even conceivably in contrast with worship, but the very reverse. What can be more truly described as worship than hearing the word of God as it ought to be heard, hearing it with penitence, with contrition, with faith, with self-consecration, with vows of new obedience? If this is not worship in spirit and in truth, what is ?[32]

It is as men bear testimony to Jesus, and do it in such a way that the gospel can speak to people's hearts with its own power, that real worship becomes possible and the forms of worship become meaningful.

Denney could scarcely conceive of preaching which was anything other than a presentation of the gospel. We have seen his passion for the preaching of the truth as his theology has unfolded before us. The conclusion to each area of his theological endeavor is a challenge to himself and to the Church to preach the insights which have been received with the power and authority of the New Testament. This is, in part, the reason for his concentration upon the theme of the atonement. It is the doctrine which provides a gospel for men in need, and only as that doctrine is put to the discipline of preaching does its final reality become apparent.

> I do not hesitate to say that a doctrine of atonement which cannot be preached is not true. If it cannot be told out, lucidly, unreservedly, passionately, tremblingly, by any simple man, to gentle and simple alike, it is not that word of the Cross which Paul describes as the power of God unto salvation to every one who believes.[33]

Thus theology and preaching are bound up into one. We have seen that his doctrine has the stern quality of reality about it, and it is just this which seems to him to make it so apposite for preaching. Discussing his view of the depth of sin and of God's condemnation which rests upon it, he argues that the preaching of this note alone binds men ultimately to Christ. He uses in this connection one of his rare illustrations, telling of a fishing incident in which a man lost his bait without catching anything, with the explanation that by some accident the barb had been broken from the hook. Said Denney, that is just what happens when men try to present the love of God apart from His terrible righteousness.

> The condemnation of our sins in Christ upon His Cross is the barb on the hook. If you leave that out of your Gospel, I do not deny that your bait will be taken; men are pleased rather than not to think that God regards them with goodwill; your bait will be taken, but you will not catch men. You will not create in sinful human hearts that attitude to Christ which created the New Testament. You will not annihilate pride, and make Christ the Alpha and the Omega in man's redemption.[34]

It is not just popular preaching which he commends to the Church, but the preaching of the gospel with its irrepressible calls to repentance and to faith.

Upon this he was insistent, as the first responsibility of preaching, that men should preach the gospel with all its inherent power. 'The preacher's business is not to be original, but to be true. If he has Gospel to preach, truth with saving virtue in it, he cannot repeat it too often.'[35] He recognized that this was a difficult task to fulfill, and was in fact willing to speak of evangelistic preaching as the highest and hardest work to which a man could be called. He recognized in a great deal of the ethical preaching which he heard about him the voice of men who were willing in preaching simply to take the line of least resistance. Said he,

> It is far easier to preach ethics than religion. It is far easier to preach the law than to preach the Gospel. It is infinitely easier to tell men what they ought to do, and to tell them impressively, with penetration, good sense, and moral earnestness, than to tell them what God has done, and to do it with the awe, the tenderness, the profound sense of obligation, the consciousness of Christ's constraining love, the pledging of the heart to God and man, which so great a task requires.[36]

He found particular distaste for the type of sermon which sought to startle and win attention by the clever use of sensational ideas or by the discussion of current controversial subjects from the newspapers.

> To shoot at folly as it flies, to preach on the sensation of the hour, and to do it with the over-emphasis of a generation fed on excitement, to fall back on economic and political questions as though they had a reality which could not be claimed for God and the soul, sin and atonement, death and immortality, is not the way.[37]

He has given us examples of what he feels to be the way in his own sermons. They ring with the intensity of his passion behind them and the force of the gospel within them.

The spirit in which men preach is an important matter to him as well. 'When we preach the Gospel,' he said, 'it must be in the spirit of the Gospel.'[38] Our preaching must have about it the gospel's sympathy and certainty, and must be directed to the spiritual needs of individual people. 'In the first instance the Gospel has nothing to do with society. It has to do with the soul.'[39] The criticism which calls this attitude selfish, Denney regards as being 'extraordinarily blind'. Said he, 'It forgets that what is in question is the soul's relation to God, and that where God is there can be no selfishness.'[40] The appeal in preaching is to be made to the individual conscience. All other aspects of man's nature are brought into the orbit of the preacher's interest, but direct appeal must be made to the conscience, for the gospel is a revelation of sin and of redemption from sin and it is the conscience which translates that into the conviction of sin and of the hope and assurance of deliverance from it. Men must preach for conviction, for there is that in the gospel of Christ which demands a conscious decision and an unconditional surrender. As Denney put it, 'You cannot drift into eternal life.'[41] To preach in the spirit of the gospel means to preach with the note of the absolute seriousness of the issues. 'To receive the reconciliation, or not to receive it—to be a Christian, or not to be a Christian—is not a matter of comparative indifference; it is not the case of being a somewhat better man, or a man, perhaps, not quite so good; it is a case of life or death.'[42] To minimize the awful aspect of the gospel is to lose the New Testament sense on which the power to preach depends. At the same time, in the light of the ultimate significance of the salvation offered in the gospel, it is imperative that we preach with the New Testament note of assurance. Denney observes that the Roman Church regards assurance as a presumption, while Protestants regard it as a privilege or a duty. And then he continues,

> But in the New Testament it is simply a fact. This explains the joy which, side by side with the sense of infinite obligation, is the characteristic note of apostolic Christianity . . . The New Testament spirit is not meant for our despair, but for our inspiration; that assurance of sin-bearing love, that sanctifying strength and gladness, are the type of genuine Christian life.[43]

It is difficult to preach in the fulness of that spirit, with a sense of both the freedom and the cost of salvation, a sense both of infinite love and of infinite responsibility, but it is not a difficulty which men can possibly evade if they are to preach the gospel.

He was insistent that preaching should be Biblical. This is not at all surprising in the light of the significant place which the Scripture holds in all of his writing. Biblical preaching seemed to him to be the logical course of commitment when one understands the nature of the Scripture records, the apostolic and prophetic preaching which lay behind them and the authoritative quality which they possess. He urged his students, with sarcasm, not only to take a text, but 'to treat their texts with proper respect, and to give them an inning in their sermons somewhere.'[44] He once commented in this connection that 'it is disrespectful to Scripture when the text contributes nothing to the sermon except the subject—when it jogs the mind, but does not feed it'.[45] Biblical preaching, to his mind, involved the life-long study of the Scripture and was never to be cheaply or lightly undertaken. Some of the men in the Glasgow College will never forget the day when a noted evangelist addressed the students and included as a piece of solemn advice the recommendation that men should sometimes go into the pulpit, find a text on the spur of the moment and preach, trusting in inspiration for the message. Denney was in the chair, and rose with his face white. Turning to the speaker and wagging his finger, he said, 'We are here in this College, set aside by the Church, to tell these men that there is no preparation too sacred or solemn for the ministry of Jesus Christ, and you come now and try to undo our work with these students. I think, sir, you confuse inspiration with desperation!'[46] Admitting the difficulty of the task of preaching, he pointed to the Bible as the solution, saying, 'A man need never go gravelled for lack of matter with the New Testament in his hand and the world round about him.'[47]

In the nature of his vocation of training ministers he concentrated also upon the techniques which are requisite to good preaching, and advised his men, 'Write one sermon a week at least, and write it as if for the compositor.'[48] But he counselled against simply reading from the manuscript, for as he said, 'You never know until you look a congregation in the face whether what you have prepared is fit to preach or not.'[49] He advised against the use of illustrations unless they 'fit like a glove',[50] and discouraged dependence upon quotations. One student recalls how 'he stopped in his class one day and said, "Gentlemen, have you ever noticed that the apostles seldom quote, except from the sole source of their authority?" '[51] 'Don't preach above people's heads'; he told his students, 'the man who shoots above the target does not prove thereby that he has superior ammunition. He just proves that he can't shoot!'[52] He could be a severe critic of the type of sermon which he described as 'heat without light'.[53] But he was delighted when he heard one 'with the rare quality of getting better and better as it went on; the fire burnt up in it instead of, as is usually the case, burning out'.[54] And as for the conclusion of the sermon, he had this succinct word of counsel: 'Keep something of a gallop for the avenue.'[55]

Denney viewed the work of the ministry as a total commitment of a man, feeling that his whole personality was involved in his preaching. As he prepared his students for the task of preaching he urged them to let their total life be expressive of their call and of their gospel. He held before them the example of a pastor in a small Scottish community for whom he had great respect:

> He honored his calling; he never disparaged the office of the work of a minister. He never spoke unworthily or slightingly of it, or lapsed even for a moment into anything out of keeping with it. Yet no one ever found it difficult to get past the minister to the man. The man in short was the minister. What a happening too rare, the person and the calling are one.[56]

This understanding of the total commitment of a man standing behind his preaching was vitally important for him. He would counsel his men, 'Beware of making the holy ministry the stage for a career.'[57] There were those who came to him seeking not so much advice as advancement, like the young man who tried to suggest that the professor should use his influence in order to help him get a desirable appointment in 'a larger sphere of influence'. One who overheard the conversation recalls how Denney listened patiently and then shot back the reply, 'Mr——, the only way to secure a larger sphere is to make yourself indispensable in the sphere in which you are.'[58] He was constantly reminding his students of the need for combining within their interests the preacher's zeal with the pastor's heart. 'Gentlemen', he was accustomed to say, 'I beseech you to remember that there are in every congregation—even the humblest—men and women of ripe Christian experience whose shoe latchet you are not worthy to unloose.'[59] Yet even as he emphasized the pastoral role he never diminished the importance of preaching, for as he said, 'Only good preaching makes the minister's visit a thing prized; nobody wants an idle, inefficient minister perpetually dropping in.'[60] James Moffatt recalled that he used to say, 'Gentlemen, don't be the pet lamb of your flock; be their shepherd!'[61]

It scarcely needs to be added that there is no way to preach the gospel in the spirit and with the spontaneity and force which Denney sought, apart from the personal experience of the gospel on the part of the preacher himself. 'It is only faith that preaches', he said. 'Preaching is faith's testimony to Christ.'[62] His feeling was that the preacher is bearing witness to his own personal experience of the grace of God in Christ and that apart from that experience there can be no such thing as real proclamation. 'No preaching is of any value unless it has the character of testimony, unless the preacher is delivering *himself* through it, and setting the seal of his personal faith to a divine truth, with the intention of evoking the same faith in others.'[63] In doing so, the preacher is not putting himself forward as a person to be admired or a pattern to be copied. On the contrary, it is as he bears witness to Christ that he himself is able to stand aside and let Christ speak from the experience of one heart to the hearts of others. Denney had little or no patience with self-important preachers. He once wrote to a friend, 'To preach as a paragon would have struck an apostle as a most extraordinary kind of presumption.'[64] He recognized the danger which this sort of presumption holds for the Church and saw that in asserting his own importance the preacher was blocking Christ's way into the hearts of men. It was this which called forth from him one of his most characteristic and familiar sayings. Its closing words may be seen in some of the pulpits and vestries of churches in Scotland; they are words which should be written into men's hearts: 'No man can bear witness to Christ and to himself at the same time. *Esprit* is fatal to unction; no man can give at once the impression that he himself is clever and that Christ is mighty to save.'[65] When a man does rise to the full vocation of being a preacher of the gospel, there is a force within him and a power felt through him which cannot but be from God. As Denney put it, 'A reconciled man, preaching Christ as the way of reconciliation, and preaching Him in the temper and spirit which the experience of reconciliation creates, is the most effective mediator of Christ's reconciling power.'[66]

The Sacraments

For Denney, the place of preaching in the life of the Church is coupled with the place which the sacraments hold in its worship. He has emphasized in his theology the fact that the sacraments spring from the early and authoritative origin of the first Christians' experience of Christ. We can recognize the validity of his conclusion as he holds to the primary place of the sacraments in the New Testament:

> The New Testament nowhere gives us the idea of an unbaptized Christian—by one Spirit we were all baptized into one body (I Cor. 12.13)—and Paul, in regulating the observance of the Supper at Corinth, regulates it as part of the Christian tradition which goes back for its authority, through the primitive Church, to Christ Himself.[67]

The meaning of this is that 'there is nothing in Christianity more primitive than the Sacraments'.[68] In the light of their central place in the life of the Church from the beginning, we can see more clearly their rightful place in our worship today.

In addition to their primitive origin, Denney emphasized the relation of the sacraments to the facts of the gospel. Both sacraments stand as memorials to the atoning death of Christ, and as such they are the Church's continuing witnesses to the gospel of reconciliation. As he put it, 'From the New Testament point of view, the sacraments contain the Gospel in brief; they contain it in inseparable connection with the death of Jesus; and as long as they hold their place in the Church the saving significance of that death has a witness which it will not be easy to dispute.'[69] To Denney it seems possible to fill them with as much meaning as the gospel itself involves.

> Both the sacraments are forms into which we may put as much of the Gospel as they will carry; and St Paul, for his part, practically puts the whole of his Gospel into each. If Baptism is relative to forgiveness of sins, so is the Supper. If Baptism is relative to the unity of the Church, so is the Supper. We are not only baptized into one body, but because there is one bread, we, many as we are who partake of it, are one body. If Baptism is relative to a new life in Christ, in the Supper Christ Himself is the meat and drink by which the new life is sustained. And in both the sacraments, the Christ to Whom we enter into relation is Christ Who died; we are baptized into His death in the one, we proclaim His death till the end of time in the other.[70]

These are Pauline phrases, deep in their content and strong in their spiritual force, and they are characteristic of the conception of the sacraments which Denney held and frequently expressed.

A third point which we should note is the connection which Denney made between the sacraments and the Spirit. From Jesus' baptism with the Spirit the Church has caught a new understanding of that ancient symbol. Said Denney, 'For others baptism with water and baptism with the Spirit were contrasted, for Him they coincided. Their normal coincidence was to be the rule in the Church, and in this sense the baptism of Jesus is the type of Christian baptism.'[71] The same intimate relationship with the Spirit is seen in the sacrament of the Supper, and the presence of the Spirit there makes the whole of the symbolic experience meaningful. It is the Spirit, known in the sacraments, which keeps them from becoming merely material on the one hand, or merely magical on the other. It is the Spirit which enables them to speak with continuing significance and power through the centuries of the Church. One of Denney's most telling statements concerning the power of the gospel of the cross was given in connection with his discussion of the Roman sacrament of the mass. Concluding a session with his class, in which he had described the Roman Catholic accretions to the cross and yet had held that even through them human souls could find its virtue and power, he said, 'Gentlemen, the Cross is such a thing that even when you bury it, you bury it *alive!*'[72] His students still recall the feeling of awe which the words carried with them. It is in their intimate connection with the Spirit that the sacraments hold this power.

A final consideration which we should notice is Denney's insistence that, in the Spirit, Christ is actually present in the sacraments. The elements do carry a value, and one which is all the more meaningful because it is spiritual. The New Testament suggests, and Christian experience confirms, that in the baptism Christ is present, not in the water, but in the sense signified by it; that in the Supper He is also present, not in the sacramental elements, but in their significance. This means that they are symbols, but it does not mean that they are to be depreciated thereby. 'They are Christ's pledge of His real presence in the sense of the symbols, and it is this which gives the sacraments their place of honor in the Church.' And Denney goes on to say, 'They are not explanations, or theories, but facts; they remind us that faith rests not on any doctrine or wisdom of men, but on the presence and the action of a redeeming God.'[73]

The older Protestant theologians gave three marks by which the true Church could be distinguished: the Church was the community of faith in which the gospels was truly preached, the sacraments rightly administered and discipline duly exercised. Denney's thought concerning the continuing life of the Church seemed to follow this same pattern and he has something to say concerning this third mark of the Church.

In effect, his emphasis here is that the Church must give itself to the task of guiding its members into the full realization in their lives of the meaning of reconciliation. The Church must seek to enable men to live lives worthy of their calling as Christians. This leads us into the whole matter of Christian ethics; but ethics, for Denney, can never be properly seen apart from an intimate relationship with the eschatological elements of theology. Therefore, it is to this interconnection of eschatology and ethics that we must now turn our attention.

X

THE DAWN IS PART OF THE MORNING
Ethics and Eschatology

It is because the Bible is so intensely ethical that it is so rich in eschatological elements.[1]

THE emphasis which Denney placed upon experience in the creation of theology caused him by instinct to stress Christian life as essential and integral to the holding of Christian truth. No amount of dogmatic theology can take the place of Christian conduct. For Denney true dogmatics will be declared in deeds. Theology which is separated from life and which fails to find its fulfillment in experience is unworthy of the gospel, and because unworthy it is unreal and untrue.

When we have acknowledged the intimate relationship between faith and ethics, however, we have entered also upon an interpretation of history's climax and the field of eschatology. Denney was insistent that ethics and eschatology must be understood as being intertwined. The life which now is is a part of the life which is to come. 'If we take an ethical view of the world and of history', he said, 'we must have an eschatology: we must have the moral order exhibited, vindicated, brought out in perfect clearness as what it is.'[2]

It is important to listen to what Denney had to say in the field of Christian ethics in the light of all that has gone before and in the face of the final fulfillment which stands in the future.

Ethics and the Cross

Denney rooted his conception of Christian ethics in the reality of the cross. The truth of Christ's atonement must be reflected in the life of the man who has given himself to Him in faith. This is not simply a matter of following the maxim that a man's beliefs will be expressed in his life. That would be true for the Moslem and Buddhist and humanist, just as much as for the Christian. Denney's emphatic point is that what the Christian believes in is the regenerating truth of the atonement through the cross of Christ. If the Christian has been re-deemed and reconciled to God through Christ—and that is what being

a Christian means—then the remainder of his life will be marked by
the glad responsibility of realizing that reconciliation in daily experience. It is the sure knowledge of atonement and reconciliation
which probes the depths of human nature and casts it into a new
mold. It is the experience of the cross which makes Christian life
possible and which gives meaning and motive to Christian ethics. 'It
is the pierced side,' Denney observed, 'the thorn-crowned brow, the
rent hands and feet, that make us Christians—these, and not our profoundest thoughts about the ethical constitution of the universe.'[3] It
is by the grace of God in Christ that we are saved, and, declared Denney,
'The correlative of grace is gratitude.'[4] Upon this response of gratitude
the Christian ethic is grounded.

Denney could become surgical when he encountered the kind of
hypocrisy which separates Christian truth from Christian life. Concerning one group of rigidly theological minds who held a lofty doctrine
of the atonement but who were seeking to cripple and divide the
Church and the nation, he said, 'It looks as if they thought the highness
of their creed could cover any depth of lowness in their conduct.'[5]
Faith is not something for men to hide behind; it is something by
which men must live. Denney recognized the difficulty which this
places upon us, but it is not a difficulty which men may avoid. It was
with deep understanding that he once remarked, 'It is easier to profess
the true creed or to come to the Lord's table than to live the life to
which they pledge us.'[6]

Denney's aim in this area of Christian ethics was to show that far
more important than seeing the distinction between what we call
justification and sanctification is the recognition that they are inseparably related. Both are made possible for us by faith. Denney is
Pauline in his conception of the total significance of faith and, like the
apostle, he is willing to comprehend in it the whole of Christianity on
its personal or subjective side, and the whole of the meaning of Christian
life. 'Essentially', he wrote, 'there is nothing in the Gospel but Christ
and faith; and faith . . . is the unreserved abandonment of the sinful
soul to Christ, its unreserved identification of itself with Him in trust
and love.'[7]

This response of faith in gratitude for the grace of God provides the
basis for Christian morality. No one who has committed himself to
the truth in the cross can take lightly the moral quality of daily life and
his own ethical responsibility to do that which is right. As Denney used
to tell his young ministers, 'The difference between right and wrong

is real and ultimate: Christ died for the difference between right and wrong.'[8] Because this is the nature of the universe which is revealed in the atonement, and because this is the cost of reconciliation which is the ground of our faith, therefore we can never avoid the moral obligations which in His love are laid upon us.

Ethics and the Resurrection

The Christian faith, of course, concerns itself not only with what God has done, but also with what God is doing. It is in the light of the past that we see the present and the outlines of the future. The Christian life is a life of hope, and the Christian ethic has reference to what lies ahead. The resurrection, which was so closely bound up with the cross in Denney's thought, provides the key which opens up this theme of hope and of victory.

> The resurrection of Christ . . . was the resurrection of One Who had known the Father's love and died to fulfill the Father's will; and when it took possession of men's hearts, it took possession of them as a power in which divine love, and martyr faithfulness, and the victory over death, were inseparable elements of one whole . . . He makes us immovably sure of God's love, and He enables us to become conformed to His own death. It is in this sense that Christ in us is the hope of glory.[9]

The victory of Christ revealed in the resurrection initiates the new age of God's power and conquest within which the Christian life is realized.

It is in the light of the resurrection that we can turn and face the future without being overcome by fear. God's victory is already in process of being won. Denney felt that to miss this note, and simply to recognize that God is struggling against evil, is not far removed from simple atheism. In face of the hope which stands before us because of the resurrection, he wrote, 'It is essential to believe not only that good is in conflict with evil, but that it is essentially and eternally superior to evil, and destined to be manifestly "all in all".'[10] This points us to the day when all that is implicit in the victory of the resurrection will be explicit in the coming consummation of history.

The resurrection, with its implication in the eschatological hope, provides the note of triumph in the Christian life, and makes that triumphant life worth living even unto death. The Christian faith in immortality is not a vague speculation. It is bound up with the understanding of the Christian life which begins in the power of Christ's resurrection and culminates in the great Day of the Lord. For Denney, then, ethics and immortality and eschatology are all intimately related to the resurrection. It is out of the experiential knowledge of God—as Creator and Redeemer and Risen King—that Christian faith in life and immortality arises. 'Reduced to its simplest terms', commented Denney, 'the question of immortality is the question of how much God will give, and how much man is able and willing to receive.'[11] Thus we see God giving all in Christ, and through Christ calling men to give themselves to Him and to be willing, if need be, to die in their allegiance to Him. As Denney put it, 'Martyrs . . . do not die because they believe in immortality; . . . immortality is revealed and becomes sure to them because they find it in their hearts to lay down life itself for God.'[12] This is the temper of mind which we find in the New Testament. God gives in such degree and man responds in like degree. The Christian, in the New Testament sense, knows 'an overpowering experience of the redeeming love of God, and a response to that love so absolute and unreserved that it does not count life itself dear to be true to it'.[13]

The Christian life with all of its ethical significance is rooted in this commitment to Christ which does not even recognize the limitation of death. It rings, both in time and in eternity, with the note of victory which has been won by God in the resurrection of Christ.

Ethics and Eschatology

This leads us to consider what Denney had to say in the field of eschatology. This is the field of theology which focuses upon the future and which deals with the doctrine of the Christian hope. It finds the ultimate vindication of God's purpose in the Day of the Lord, which marks the end of the world, the consummation of history, and is signalled by the return of Christ. For Denney, the whole field of eschatology is ethical in its origin and nature, and this correlation of eschatology and ethics he finds declared in the Scripture. 'It is because the Bible is so intensely ethical that it is so rich in eschatological elements.'[14]

The area of eschatology has had a history more varied than that of almost any other in the range of theology. In the early Church it was a theological topic of primary importance. For centuries following it was a subject which was treated quite dogmatically and quite abstractly, and men spoke as though they had been initiated into all the secrets of the unknown. The pendulum swung in the opposite direction, and in more recent generations eschatology became something of an embarrassment, and men expressed a complete willingness to confess ignorance which left a distinct silence on the subject. Within the past century of theology, the silence bore its natural fruit as liberalism reached its crest of influence and the theological positivists came to deny that eschatology had a place in theology at all. Since that time, theology has been marked by the revival of interest in eschatology and there is nothing more typical of the vitality of theological thought in our day than the move to interpret the sweep of revelation and of history in eschatological terms.

Denney would have enjoyed the eschatological tenor of our present-day discussions and would have appreciated the dynamic interpretation of theology which has come from our emphasis upon eschatology. He was out of step with his contemporary patterns of thought in this area, being neither conservative nor liberal enough to satisfy either faction, and in searching for a solution to the problems here encountered he was able to anticipate aspects of our present emphasis. He sought to go back of the history of the Church's interpretation of the subject to the Biblical eschatology itself, and there he was not satisfied simply to give an exegetical statement, but sought to speak in terms of 'what is of faith in the matter, what is made sure to the heart by the witness of the Spirit, what is the religious conviction in the strength of which we face the unknown future'.[15]

The close relationship existing between eschatology and ethics is one important point which he held to be 'of faith in the matter', and this emphasis he holds in common with the characteristic thought of present-day theology. Denney insisted that an understanding of the final denouement rests with our realization of the ethical nature of the world in which we live under God. To deny that the world culminates in the full expression of His moral authority seems to Denney to embark on a perilous course which denies the moral quality of life itself.

> Man's life is not a natural, but a moral concern; it is subject not only to physical, but to divine laws. The meaning and worth of it may be obscure here, but a day is coming when they will be made plain; and on that day Jesus Christ will be the Revealer and the Judge.[16]

If we take an ethical view of history, then we must have an eschatology which includes this strong fiber of revelation and judgment.

This ethical understanding of eschatology provides Denney with an approach to the field of study which is at once vital and consistent with the ethical nature of reality as we know it now. To put it in Denney's strong words,

M

It is not ethical to suppose that the moral condition of the world is that of an endless suspense, in which the good and the evil permanently balance each other, and contest with each other the right to inherit the earth. Such a dualistic conception is virtually atheistic, and the whole Bible could be read as a protest against it . . . The Christian doctrine of a final judgment is not the putting of an arbitrary term to the course of history; it is a doctrine without which history ceases to be capable of moral construction.[17]

The future is thus intimately connected with the present and the Christian doctrine of the last things, so far from being a matter of wish fulfillment, is derived from the moral nature of life under God and from His self-disclosure in Christ. In the light of His revelation history has upon it the seal of moral quality and moves on to the consummation about which Christ spoke and toward the understanding of which we give ourselves in the study of eschatology.

Such a final focal point of morality is related to all of life. Denney observed, 'In the light of that great coming event the moral significance of things stands out even now, and when it does come, it is not to determine, but only to declare, what they are.'[18] Denney pointed out that the vitality of the early Christians' eschatological expectations was what kept the ethical quality of the New Testament at its level of purity and faithfulness. They lived their lives in clear understanding of the facts of Christ's revelation and in the promise of His return. 'The Cross of Christ and his Judgment-seat are the powers which make saints, and it is the solemn acceptance of responsibility as fixed for us by these divine realities, and not the preaching of ideals, which will evoke in human souls a life correspondingly Christian and real.'[19]

Until that final event, the discipline and the conflict of life go on. But they go on for the Christian under the challenging reality of that conclusion. Eschatology and ethics are essentially united in Denney's understanding of the Christian faith and in his interpretation of the Christian life.

Freedom and Self-discipline

Conceiving of life and of the future as having this dynamic quality, Denney interprets Christian conduct in terms of eschatological vitality and value. Our life is lived in the context of what Christ has done and is yet to do. Here he has an interesting division and balancing of the twin emphases of freedom and self-discipline in the conduct of the Christian life.

On the one hand, the complete adequacy of the Christian experience of faith assures us that all is freedom in the Christian life. Denney is insistent upon this, commenting that 'without freedom there is no Christianity'.[20] The Christian is not under law in this eschatological age, not even the law of Christ's words; he is under grace. Denney wrote, 'Jesus, Who came to abolish one literalism, did not come to institute another.'[21] Christ's life is not even to serve as a form of legalism over the Christian's life. He is to serve as our inspiration, not primarily as an object for our imitation. It was in this connection that he spoke of the *Imitatio Christi* of Thomas a Kempis, saying, 'There is not a Christian book so utterly unlike the gospels. It is a book of the cloister from beginning to end; not a word of it could have been conceived or written in the open air. Not a word of the gospels could have been conceived or written anywhere else.'[22] It was in this same line of thought that he once commented, 'It is not restraint, but inspiration, which liberates from sin; not Mount Sinai but Mount Calvary which makes saints.'[23] It is this freedom in faith which places responsibility upon the Christian for the conduct of his life in this eschatological age, and it is this responsibility which develops the Christian conscience.

On the other hand, there is in Denney a strong emphasis upon the place of discipline—self-imposed—in the Christian life, and this too he subsumes under the total response of the personality in faith. There is a stern, almost puritanical, element in Denney's thought as there was in his life. He insisted that for the Christian life to be a reality, there must not only be great consecration but there must be great renunciation as well.

> All things are not lawful for us if we wish to remain in the Lord's company and to share in His life. If a man holds the principle that nature is entitled to assert itself through all the impulses implanted in it, and holds it so absolutely that he will go wherever his feet can carry him—that he will handle whatever his fingers itch to touch— that he *will* glut his eyes with gazing on whatever they crave to see —the result will not be that that man will have an ampler and a richer character; it will be that he has no character at all. It will not be an abundant entrance into life, it will be the sinking of an exhausted nature into hell.[24]

When James Moffatt asked him what the definition of a 'heretic' is, he replied, 'An obstinate, self-willed creature with fads, in doctrine and in morals.'[25] He had an uncanny way of cutting through the subterfuges which men erect around their conduct and of inserting in conversation, sermon and lecture the note of conscience and integrity. On one occasion he observed, 'A great deal might be done in the world if nobody cared who got the credit of it.'[26] On another occasion he said, 'The natural man loves to find fault; it gives him at the cheapest rate the comfortable feeling of superiority.'[27] Once he wrote to a friend, 'Honesty is the best policy only when it is not a policy.'[28] His keen insights are not just clever sayings, they are the expressions of a moral zeal and commitment which was impatient with looseness and laziness in the practical and ethical affairs of men. Christian discipline was never regarded by him as a legalism, but as the natural expression of repentant faith, the identification of the soul with God's attitude toward sin. 'For the Christian', he said, 'law is abolished, and yet in the Christian, and in him only, the just demand of the law is fulfilled.'[29]

Ethics in the Eschatological Age

Within this age between the resurrection and the great denouement the Christian ethic is expressed in terms of service, and thus is reconciliation realized in the Christian's encounter with the lives of others about him. Loving service, he asserts, is the law of Christian life. 'The law of the Kingdom', he wrote, 'is illustrated supremely in the person of the King: it is in Him we see what greatness is and how it is attained. It is attained by service; at its greatest height it is attained by a service which for lowliness and sacrifice can never be outdone.'[30] It is this continuing reference back to the Servant Lord and to His great and ultimate love which is the inspiration of all Christian service. 'Christ Himself was a martyr, and the typical Christian is a martyr too. To be a martyr is to furnish the decisive proof that the abiding power of Christ's blood is being exercised over one's life.'[31] This limitless love which springs from faith in Him is the final interpretation of the Christian life. 'The Christian is a man with something to die for; and to bear his cross daily signifies that he is ready to die for it all the time. The man who has nothing he would die for has nothing to live for; he does not know what life is.'[32]

The point at which the Church has come under most severe criticism in recent decades has been with regard to its understanding and implementation in the field of social ethics. Men have felt that the Church has not been sufficiently concerned with the needs of society, and it was in this connection that the distinction between Church and Kingdom was most frequently employed in Denney's time, in an effort to turn men from worship—in the Church, to work—in the Kingdom. The fallacy of the distinction has already been made clear, and it is not surprising to find Denney, in the light of his identification of the Church with the Kingdom, urging the Church to perform its best service to society precisely by being the Church. Denney had a deep social concern which expressed itself both in his work and in his writings. During his later years he was caught up in the fight over the dramatic social issues of his time. In the early years of the First World War he rose to a position of national importance in the moral life of his people. Convinced of the nation's cause in the struggle, he was deeply concerned about the moral degradation which had accompanied the war, particularly as it expressed itself in a more loose sexual code and in the liquor traffic. From more than one national platform he pointed to the moral inconsistency and tragedy, crying out, 'We open our veins to bleed ourselves white, and pray for strength!'[33] It was within this period that he became in many ways the embodiment of the moral intentions and purposes of his nation, and when he died there were many people who used the same phrase to describe him: 'The conscience of Scotland.'[34]

He was keenly conscious of the nation's needs, and was particularly helpful in his treatment of such problems as the breakdown in home life, the illicit liquor trade, the needs and nature of public education, and the honest conduct of the affairs of government. He held that Thomas Chalmers' greatness lay in part in the fact that, 'He had the greatness of the nation in him as well as that of the Church.' And he added that 'it is an immense gain to a Churchman when he has such an interest in the State as keeps his ethics from becoming ecclesiastically narrow in range.'[35]

With this social concern, however, he felt that the Church could best fulfill its task of witness through shared personal service.

All life has to be Christianized; but the process is to be accomplished, not by dragging everything under the scrutiny and sentence of the Church as it exists among us, but by sending out into all the departments of life men to live and work there in the Spirit of Christ . . . Christian ethics is not casuistry, still less is it the doing of other people's duties for them. There were things Christ refused to do; there are things that the Church should refuse in His name. We shall speak often of money, if we speak as He spoke; but we shall not divide the inheritance.[36]

He felt particularly the fallacy of the Church's move toward securing its social ends by means of legislation. 'The multiplication of laws', he observed, 'and the deterioration of character to a large extent keep pace with each other, and I believe it is one of the lessons the Church needs to learn that it can help society best by minding its own business.'[37] Elsewhere he put it even more succinctly: 'We should hardly, with our minds full of the Gospels, anticipate the coming of the Kingdom through the House of Commons.'[38] It was his continuing interest that the Church be conscious of its place within this eschatological age and that it concern itself with the deepest needs in men's lives. It has the unique task of presenting men with the ultimate reality in Christ, of bringing them into a living relationship with Him, of enabling them to realize in their own lives the power of reconciliation in Him. It is to this task that the Church must give itself with all its purpose and power, and as it does so it will find that all else moves forward toward the final consummation in Christ.

Realized Eschatology

How are we to interpret the great coming consummation of history? What is the Day of the Lord? What does it mean that Christ is coming again? Denney insists that we must understand that to some extent Jesus' words of prophecy about this climactic event have already been fulfilled. In a very real sense, Christ has already returned, and with Him the Kingdom has come and is in process of coming. While Denney does not use the term 'realized eschatology', his eschatology is none the less strongly influenced by the insight that eschatological fulfillment is already in process. It was this, in part, which made more conservative minds wonder about him. On this point Robertson Nicoll, his close friend, expressed serious doubts and wrote to another concerning him, 'There is a singular vein of scepticism in him, for all his apparent orthodoxy. For instance, he does not... believe in the Second Advent.'[39] Others failed to see the dynamic quality of Denney's insight into eschatology. It is only after many decades in which the doctrine of the last things has come in part to be understood through the approach of realized eschatology that we can actually appreciate the value of what Denney was saying a half-century ago.

His understanding of this implication of eschatology came out of his study of the Scripture. He simply came to feel that unless we accept, to some extent at least, the fact that many of the Scriptural promises have been fulfilled, there are passages which will remain forever unintelligible for us. He indicated this particularly in the eschatological passages in the synoptic gospels. One passage which he discusses rather fully and helpfully is Mark 14.62 (with parallels in Matt. 26.64

and Luke 22.69), in which Jesus makes final confession of Himself
before the Sanhedrin, promising that they shall see 'the Son of Man
sitting on the right hand of power, and coming in the clouds of heaven'.
Denney commented,

> It is no remote future to which Jesus appeals; the fulfillment of His
> words begins with the moment at which they are spoken. His enemies
> think they have expelled Him from the world, but from the very
> moment of their triumph His victory sets in. He filled Jerusalem
> from His death onward as He had never done in His life; it was
> impossible to escape His Presence or His Power; the Council had
> more to do with Him, was made more sensible of His predominance,
> found His challenge more inevitable, in the early days of Acts than
> in the period of the Gospel history.[40]

Jesus came again in His appearance to the disciples after the resurrection. He clearly came again when His Spirit was given to them in
the experience of Pentecost. Denney goes on to insist that He came
again in the destruction of Jerusalem and that 'He comes still . . . in
the great crises of history, when the old order changes yielding place to
new; when God brings a whole age, as it were, into judgment, and
gives the world a fresh start.'[41]

In speaking in terms of realized eschatology, Denney did not think
that he was exhausting the truth of the second coming of Christ. He
felt that it was a part of the truth and that as such it should be understood and accepted. At the same time, he recognized that all such
interpretations are but anticipation of the personal return of Christ at
the end of the world which is certainly stated beyond all doubts in the
New Testament and which absorbed so much of the thought of the
first Christians. It is in the tension between that which has already
been fulfilled and that which has yet to take place that Denney's vital
doctrine of eschatology exists. The present is part of the future.

At times the expectations of the eschatological event are stated in
the gospels in rather crude terms, and Denney feels that we need not
be dependent upon the imagery here any more than we are dependent
upon some of the earlier imagery of the Old Testament. They were
seeking to express what could not be limited to expression. The truth
which they saw was dear to their hearts, and their communication of
it—even through faltering imagery—finds its place in our understanding so that it becomes important for us in the same way in which
it was crucial for them. Said Denney, 'We need lay no stress on the
scenery of New Testament prophecy, . . . but if we are to retain any

relation to the New Testament at all, we must assert the personal
return of Christ.'[42] The balance of these two conceptions, realized and
futuristic eschatology, Denney reconciled in the larger reality of Christ
Himself and what it means for Him to have come and for Him to come
again. He wrote,

> The question whether the Kingdom is present or future is another
> form of the question whether it is spiritual or eschatological. The
> answer is that it is both, and that in the perspective of Jesus the
> difference tends to disappear. The end is near, the dawn is part of
> the morning, the present time is part of the last time.[43]

The End of the Age

When all has been said about the fulfillment of Christ's promises in
his continuing to come among men and in the quality of life lived in
Him, there is still that strong and dramatic note of eschatology which
is as yet unfulfilled. Christ points men beyond their own experience to
the final triumph of His cause. Said Denney, 'Whatever the course of
history may be, Jesus always contemplates a consummation of it.
There *is* an end. There *is* a final separation. There is an expulsion for
the Kingdom of all scandals and of all that do iniquity, and a glorious
perfecting of the righteous.'[44] This is the Day of the Lord to which all
of the New Testament writers look and which still lies before us as the
culmination of life and the world.

Denney feels that the dominant theme of the references to the Day
of the Lord is that of judgment. This is its note in the teachings of
Jesus, and it is this which marks it with an ethical quality. There are
three factors which he stresses with regard to the theme of judgment.

The first of these is *the Judge*. The paramount truth about the judgment is the personality of the One who judges. Christ Himself is the
Judge and that determines the nature and the effect of the consummation. He judged men when He was on earth and He will judge in the
Day which is to come. Said Denney,

> Until He came, inspired men had always looked onward to something
> that was to come, something that was not yet there. The future was
> filled for them by a Coming One. Jesus also looked into the future,
> but what He saw there was not the coming of another, but His own
> coming again. In other words, He was no prophet, but the subject
> of all prophecy. To His own consciousness, He was the last as well
> as the first. In His own consciousness, the revelation which He
> brought had the character of finality; there was no more grace to
> come than was there already in Him; no more perfect knowledge of

God to come than that which He was there to impart; what the future would disclose would only be the relation which men had assumed to Him, and this He Himself would declare when He came in glory as Judge.[45]

His life and work form the principle of judgment. The same righteousness of God which we have seen revealed in the life and death of Jesus is declared with finality in the judgment. The whole of Jesus' life— from incarnation to judgment—is of a piece, and He stands as the only basis on which we can be declared righteous. It is not surprising to find Denney at this point binding the cross and the judgment closely together. 'If any one thinks that in Christianity he comes into a non-moral region, or one in which morality can in any way be discounted, the Cross and the Judgment-Seat are there to correct him.'[46] Within these two focal points we find in Him the ultimate expression of morality and thus the one who is able to give ultimate judgment. For Denney, we have not seen the Christ clearly unless we have encountered in Him this eschatological note of judgment.

> Wherever Christ is, men are judged by Him; they gather to His side or are repelled from Him, and a day is coming in which it will be apparent that this is so, and that it is final. All the most solemn and inexorable words about judgment and its finality are from the lips of Jesus; it is almost as though no lips but those of love incarnate were at liberty to say things so tremendous.[47]

As the Christian stands before the Biblical view of the future he finds his hope is secured not by the fact that judgment will take place, but by the revelation that the Judge is no other than the Christ whose love has redeemed us.

The second point of reference in Denney's view of unfulfilled eschatology has to do with *the Judged*. Denney does not believe in a limited judgment; all men stand judged before God in Christ. It is possible to become involved in intricate problems of distinction at this point and to narrow one's interest to fine divisions in judgment, but Denney feels that it is unrealistic to press such distinctions. His underlying thought here is that judgment comes upon all men on the positive basis of their relation to the purpose of God, as that purpose has been revealed in Christ. Even in the Old Testament men approached the idea of immortality and judgment in a belief in God. As such, the idea of judgment originates on the basis of a positive religious motive. God is bringing His own purpose to fulfillment, and He shall judge. This concept has by its own quality of breadth expanded so that judgment was seen to include those who were outside of the community, which came as a logical necessity in the interest of an impartial understanding of divine action. All men are judged.

It is the glory of God declared in His faithful community, however, which is of primary importance for eschatology, and our thought of the judgment must be based on that if it is to be spiritually significant. As Denney put it,

> I believe it is necessary, if we are to reflect in our minds the true proportion and balance of Scriptural teaching, to escape from the pre-occupation with individuals and exceptions, and to get into the center and foreground of our thought God's purpose to perfect His Kingdom and glorify His people. That is the main thing, and an interest in that is accessible to all.[48]

Thus, concentration upon eschatological woes; the concept of 'the millennium', which Denney does not count essential to faith; the state of probation, which he does not consider realistic; the matter of prayer for the dead, which he maintains depraves the very idea of prayer; the idea of conditional immortality, which seems to him an unsatisfactory 'half-way house'; the ultimate perfecting of all nature, which he interprets as having all the force of poetry and only that force—all these he regards as beside the essential point. God's action toward all men, as seen particularly in His relation to His own people, is central. The nature of this action is already known in the love revealed in Christ. It is this positive value for all men which Denney emphasizes whenever he speaks of man under judgment, and he counsels the preacher to do the same. 'It is the love of Christ which constrains the true evangelist, and not the apprehension of an awful future.'[49] The future, for all, lies in the hand of One who has revealed Himself as righteous love.

This leads us to consider the third point of reference, *the Judgment*. The judgment given, with its issues and outcome, can only be understood aright against the background of relationship between the Judge and the judged. The positive and negative aspects of the judgment can now be understood and accepted. The positive side is that which is the motive for faith, but the negative side is there as well. Denney feels that dogmatic universalism is unscriptural and unethical. The very fact of human freedom demands the possibility of choosing that which is sin. But the negative side of judgment is only relevant for us in the light of the positive movement within it. Denney quoted Ruskin's statement, 'I do not wonder at what men suffer; I often wonder at what they lose.' He then went on to comment,

God has set before us a great future, a great hope, in His perfected Kingdom; as far as it has positive contents, Christian eschatology deals with that, and with that alone. Those who do not share it lose it, and when the time comes the exclusion will be found awful enough. The last judgment is the decisive event through which the Kingdom of God is consummated, and the state of eternal perfection begins.[50]

The concentration upon the condition of those who do not share in that state of perfection is futile. The images which are used to depict either issue of judgment are the projections from conscience and faith; they are symbolic and are to be interpreted as poetry and not as prose.

The ideas which seem to me to comprehend all that is of faith on the subject are those of separation and finality. There is such a thing as being excluded from fellowship with God and with good spirits; there is such a thing as final exclusion. It is not for us to say on whom this awful sentence falls, or whether they are many or few; we can trust the God and Father of our Lord Jesus Christ that it will not fall on any who do not freely and deliberately pronounce it themselves.[51]

Throughout his work, Denney sought to lay his emphasis upon the positive thrust of eschatology which stands in close association with the needs of men here and now, and which depends upon the experience of faith rather than upon dogmatic assumptions. Said he, 'There are real relations between what now is, and what is to be . . . If we are only humble enough, we may depend on being shown our way.'[52] This approach to eschatology caused him to speak of the future in the exciting and exalting language of the Christian hope. To approach the matter in any other way seemed to him to be focusing in the wrong direction. It is upon Christ and the Christian faith in Him that true theology stands as it turns to face the future under God. And in that faith there need be no fear.

EPILOGUE

Denney of Glasgow—here is one who lived and wrote before Barth or Niebuhr, before Dodd or Bultmann and the host of others with whom we associate the dramatic steps now being made in the resurgence of Biblical theology. Yet he wrestled then with many of the more important emphases which are current in the world of thought today. This is a remarkable fact, and a good commentary both upon the man and upon our own contemporary theological climate.

However, there is something more than surprise in this fact; there is stability as well, and assurance. His work sounds consistently the basic chords of the Christian faith. His deep and passionate commitment to these enabled him to range far beyond into new areas of exploration and discovery and to sound notes of deep and profound interpretation which were blended into a harmonious whole within his own experience. He teaches us that where faith is there is freedom, and where both are present in intense degree—wedded to a disciplined understanding of God's disclosure of Himself—there is prophetic vision and penetration into what is enduring and real. His work then is of genuine interest to us not simply because it is modern—which it is, nor simply because it intrigues—which it does, but because we recognize within the dialogue of his words and our lives the force of that which is true.

He did not, of course, anticipate all of the dynamic aspects of the present day. He did not put so much emphasis as do we in this post-Barthian age upon the revelation of the Word within the lives of men. Even on his chosen theme of the cross, he did not stress the important insight of the atonement as the scene of cosmic struggle and of victory, which Gustav Aulén and others have brought back into focus. Even with his strong accent upon the experience of the Spirit, some will feel that he has not done full justice to the concept of the Trinity. He did not reorient all of life around its relationship to the Kingdom, nor press the demands of social need upon the corporate body of the Church. In some areas—notably eschatology—his thought is somewhat sketchy. Many will take issue with him at one or another of the points of his theology, and this he would have loved and encouraged.

When his work is viewed as a whole, however, these distinctions tend to lose their importance in the face of the full power of the presentation he makes of theological truth. Perhaps the greatest lesson which he has bequeathed us is the lesson of his own person. In all that he says he is sharing a theology which has been wrought out in experience and lived out in life. His life and work stand as a challenge to men and women of this day to commit ourselves as courageously to the search for the truth which is timeless. He calls us in our own time to the serious study of theology as the adventure of our lives.

In the Chapel of the Glasgow College, now Trinity College of the reunited Church of Scotland, there is an impressive memorial window in his honor. Beside the window is a brass plaque on which are inscribed words which are not only his memorial but also his call to all who follow in the field of study of the Christian faith: 'Principal James Denney—supreme alike as scholar, teacher, administrator, and man of God, to whom many owed their souls.' And then, from Bunyan, words which sound as though they came from the man himself:

My sword I leave to him that shall come after me in pilgrimage, and my courage and skill to him that can get it.

THE WORKS OF JAMES DENNEY

BOOKS

On 'Natural Law in the Spiritual World', by a Brother of the Natural Man. 1885.

The Epistles to the Thessalonians. The Expositor's Bible. 1892.

The Second Epistle to the Corinthians. The Expositor's Bible. 1894.

Studies in Theology. 1894.

Gospel Questions and Answers. 1896.

St Paul's Epistle to the Romans. The Expositor's Greek Testament. 1900.

The Death of Christ. 1902.

The Atonement and the Modern Mind. 1903.

The Literal Interpretation of the Sermon on the Mount (with Marcus Dods and James Moffatt). 1906.

Jesus and the Gospel. 1908.

The Church and the Kingdom. 1910.

Factors of Faith in Immortality. 1911.

The Way Everlasting. 1911.

War and the Fear of God. 1916.

The Christian Doctrine of Reconciliation. 1917.

Letters of Principal James Denney to W. Robertson Nicoll, 1893-1917. 1920.

Letters of Principal James Denney to his Family and Friends. 1921.

DICTIONARY AND ENCYCLOPEDIA ARTICLES

A Dictionary of the Bible. ed. Hastings. 1898-1902.

A Dictionary of Christ and the Gospels. ed. James Hastings. 1906-1908.
   Vol. I: 'Anger', pp. 60-62.
            'Authority of Christ', pp. 146-53.
            'Holy Spirit', pp. 731-44.
            'Jealousy', pp. 847-8.
   Vol. II: 'Offence', pp. 259-62.
            'Preaching Christ', pp. 393-403.
            'Regeneration', pp. 485-9.
A Standard Bible Dictionary. ed. M. W. Jacobus. 1909.
   'Church Life and Organization', pp. 129-36.
   'Jesus Christ', pp. 406-23.
   'Paul', pp. 645-51.
Encyclopaedia of Religion and Ethics. ed. James Hastings. 1908-1926.
   Vol. V (1912):   'Fall (Biblical)', pp. 701-705.
   Vol. VIII (1915): 'Mediation', pp. 515-20.
   Vol. X (1918).   'Righteousness (in St Paul's teaching)', pp. 786-90.

MAGAZINE ARTICLES

'Three Motives to Repentance', *The Expositor.* March, 1893, pp. 232-7.
'The Sadducees and Immortality', *The Expositor*, Series IV, Vol. X, December, 1894, pp. 401-409.
'Caesar and God', *The Expositor*, Series V, Vol. III, January, 1896, pp. 61-69.
'The Great Commandment', *The Expositor*, Series V, Vol. III, April, 1896, pp. 312-20.
'David's Son and David's Lord', *The Expositor*, Series V, Vol. III, June, 1896, pp. 445-6.
'The Dissolution of Religion', *The Expositor*, Series V, Vol. IV, October, 1896, pp. 263-76.
'Dogmatic Theology', *The Expositor*, Series V, Vol. VI, December, 1897, pp. 422-40.
'The Apostolic Age: Its Life, doctrine, worship and polity', *The Critical Review*, Vol. X, No. 3, May, 1900, pp. 253-9.
'Ritschl's "Justification and Reconciliation" ', *The Expository Times*, Vol. XII, December, 1900, pp. 135-9.
'The Theology of the Epistle to the Romans' 'Introductory', *The Expositor*, Series VI, Vol. III, January, 1901, pp. 1-14.
'The Doctrine of Sin', *The Expositor*, Series VI, Vol. III, March, 1901, pp. 172-81.
'The Doctrine of Sin', *The Expositor*, Series VI, Vol. III, April, 1901, pp. 283-95.

'The Gospel a Divine Righteousness', *The Expositor*, Series VI, Vol. III, June, 1901, pp. 433-50.

'Faith and the Righteousness of God', *The Expositor*, Series VI, Vol. IV, August, 1901, pp. 81-85.

'The Righteousness of God and the New Life', *The Expositor*, Series VI, Vol. IV, October, 1901, pp. 299-311.

'The New Life and the Spirit', *The Expositor*, Series VI, Vol. IV, December, 1901, pp. 422-36.

'The Letters of John Richard Green', *The Union Magazine*, Vol. II, January, 1902, pp. 20-23.

'The Letters of a Man of Taste', *The Union Magazine*, Vol. II, June, 1902, pp. 259-63.

'The Place of Christianity in Education', *The Union Magazine*, Vol. II, July, 1902, pp. 292-6; August, 1902, pp. 341-4.

'The Varieties of Religious Experience', *The Union Magazine*, Vol. II, September, 1902, pp. 417-20.

'The Questions of Jesus—I. "Have Ye Never Read?" ', *The Union Magazine*, Vol. III, January, 1903, pp. 34-37.

'The Life of Bishop Westcott', *The Union Magazine*, Vol. III, June, 1903, pp. 261-4.

'The Atonement and the Modern Mind', *The Expositor*, Series VI, Vol. VIII, August, 1903, pp. 81-105; September, 1903, pp. 161-82; October, 1903, pp. 241-66.

'Is the Church Losing Her Hold on the Working classes, especially the Poor?', *The Union Magazine*, Vol. III, September, 1903, pp. 389-91.

'Hard Sayings of Jesus', *The Union Magazine*, Vol. IV, January, 1904, pp. 31-33.

'Adam and Christ in St Paul', *The Expositor*, Series VI, Vol. IX, February, 1904, pp. 147-60.

'The Education of a Minister', *The London Quarterly Review*, Vol. CII, July, 1904, pp. 1-16.

'Thomas Chalmers', *The British Monthly*, September, 1904.

'Mark Rutherford', *The United Free Church Magazine*, November, 1904, pp. 20-23.

'New Light on the Apocalypse', *The United Free Church Magazine*, January, 1905, pp. 13-16.

'Harnack and Loisy on the Essence of Christianity', *The Expositor*, Series VI, Vol. XI, February, 1905, pp. 103-23.

'The Wittiest Englishman of his Generation', *The United Free Church Magazine*, April, 1905, pp. 27-30.

'John Wesley on Books', *The United Free Church Magazine*, February, 1906, pp. 24-28.

'The Doctrine of the New Birth', *The Expository Times*, Vol. XVIII, No. 4, January, 1907, pp. 182-3.

'Speaking Against the Son of Man and Blaspheming the Spirit', *The Expositor*, Series VII, Vol. IV, December, 1907, pp. 521-32.

'The Cup of the Lord and the Cup of Demons', *The Expositor*, Series VII, Vol. V, April, 1908, pp. 289-304.

'He that Came by Water and Blood', *The Expositor*, Series VII, Vol. V, May, 1908, pp. 416-28.

'Jesus' Estimate of John the Baptist', *The Expositor*, Series VII, Vol. V, May, 1908, pp. 416-28.

'Hate', *The Expository Times*, Vol. XXI, No. 1, October, 1909, pp. 41-42.

'Love', *The Expository Times*, Vol. XXI, No. 2, November, 1909, pp. 72-76.

'Factors of Faith in Immortality', *The Expositor*, Series VIII, Vol. I, January, 1911, pp. 1-20; February, 1911, pp. 118-28.

'Criticism and the Parables'

    I. 'The Transmission of the Parables', *The Expositor*, Series VIII, Vol. II, August, 1911, pp. 117-36.

    II. 'The Interpretation of the Parables', *The Expositor*, Series VIII, Vol. II, September, 1911, pp. 219-39.

'Christianity and the Historical Christ', *The Expositor*, Series VIII, Vol. V, January, 1913, pp. 12-28.

'A Commentary on St Matthew', *The Expositor*, Series VIII, Vol. IX, March, 1915, pp. 285-8.

NEWSPAPER ARTICLES

'The Everlasting Gospel', *The British Weekly*, February, 3, 1898.

'Dr Dale's Life', *The British Weekly*, November 17, 1898.

'Dr Dale as a Churchman', *The British Weekly*, December 1, 1898.

'The Historical New Testament', *The British Weekly*, February 21, 1901.

'Principal Fairbairn's New Book', *The British Weekly*, June 12, 1902.

'Offended in Christ', *The British Weekly*, September 4, 1902.

'The Gospels and the Gospel', *The British Weekly*, November 6 and 13, 1902.

'We Would See Jesus', *The British Weekly*, April 7, 1904.

'A State Church Theologian', *The British Weekly*, August 25, 1904.

'Jesus Christ the Righteous', *The British Weekly*, November 2, 1905.

'The Latest Word on the Atonement', *The British Weekly*, November 16, 1905.

'Faith and Freedom', *The British Weekly*, December 13, 1906.

'Principal Rainy', *The British Weekly*, December 27, 1906.

'The New Theology', *The British Weekly*, March 23, 1907.
'Faith and Science', *The British Weekly*, April 11, 1907.
'The Literal Interpretation of the Sermon on the Mount', *The British Weekly*, August 23, 1906.
'The New Theology', *The British Weekly*, March 21, 1907.
'God, Sin and the Atonement', *The British Weekly*, March 28, 1907.
'The Gospel According to St Matthew', *The British Weekly*, April 18, 1907.
'Christian Theology in Outline', *The British Weekly*, July 18, 1907.
'Positive Preaching and the Modern Mind', *The British Weekly*, October 24, 1907.
'The Historical Evidence for the Resurrection of Jesus Christ', *The British Weekly*, November 21, 1907.
'Taking Away the Lord', *The British Weekly*, April 9, 1908.
'Jerusalem', *The British Weekly*, May 28, 1908.
'Principal Hutton', *The British Weekly*, June 4, 1908.
'Criticising the Church', *The British Weekly*, February 4, 1909.
'The Church and Worship', *The British Weekly*, February 11, 1909.
'The Church and the Gospel', *The British Weekly*, February 25, 1909.
'The Church and Christian Character', *The British Weekly*, April 8, 1909.
'The Church and the Kingdom of God', *The British Weekly*, May 20, 1909.
'The Tests of Life', *The British Weekly*, May 20, 1909.
'The Church and Legislation', *The British Weekly*, August 19, 1909.
'Jesus and Christ', *The British Weekly*, December 9, 1909.
'A Jewish View of Christ', *The British Weekly*, January 27, 1910.
'Modern Substitutes for Christianity', *The British Weekly*, February 24, 1910.
'The Quest of the Historical Jesus', *The British Weekly*, April 7, 1910.
'Dividing Lines', *The British Weekly*, June 2, 1910.
'Our Lord's Last Words on Prayer', *The British Weekly*, July 28, 1910.
'The Christian's Cross', *The British Weekly*, August 18, 1910.
'The Eschatology of the Gospels', *The British Weekly*, October 13, 1910.
'The Expositor's Greek Testament', *The British Weekly*, October 27, 1910.
'The Work of Christ', *The British Weekly*, November 10, 1910.
'Why was Jesus Sent to the Cross ?', *The British Weekly*, December 29, 1910.
'Discipleship and the Church', *The British Weekly*, February 16, 1911.
'Studies in the Synoptic Problem', *The British Weekly*, March 23, 1911.
'The Missionary Motive', *The British Weekly*, April 27, 1911.

N *

'Introduction to the Literature of the New Testament', *The British Weekly*, May 18, 1911.

'St Paul and Woman', *The British Weekly*, August 24, 1911.

'The Christian Doctrine of Man', *The British Weekly*, August 31, 1911.

'Principal Wm. Patrick', *The British Weekly*, October 5, 1911.

'First Corinthians', *The British Weekly*, October 12, 1911.

'The Living God', *The British Weekly*, November 2, 1911.

'Principal Fairbairn', *The British Weekly*, February 15, 1912.

'Professor Denney at Regent Square Church', *The British Weekly*, June 6, 1912.

'God's Forgiveness and Ours', *The British Weekly*, June 13, 1912.

'Christian Faith in God', *The British Weekly*, September 12, 1912.

'Foundations', *The British Weekly*, December 24, 1912.

'There He Spake with Us', *The British Weekly*, August 14, 1913.

'Religions and the True Religion', *The British Weekly*, August 21, 1913.

'Professor James Orr', *The British Weekly*, September 11, 1913.

'The New Testament and the English Tongue', *The British Weekly*, December 4, 1913.

'St Paul and the Mystery Religions', *The British Weekly*, January 29, 1914.

'The Late Rev. A. D. Grant', *The Greenock Telegraph and Clyde Shipping Gazette*, Monday, February 2, 1914.

'Can Faith Dispense with Facts?' *The British Weekly*, May 21, 1914.

'The Christian Community and the War', *The British Weekly*, August 13, 1914.

'The War and the National Conscience', *The British Weekly*, August 20, 1914.

'A Unique Book on St Paul', *The British Weekly*, December 24, 1914.

'War and the Fear of God', *The British Weekly*, January 21, 1915.

'Men and Money', *The British Weekly*, February 4, 1915.

'The Darkness and the Light', *The British Weekly*, August 12, 1915.

'Victory over Death', *The British Weekly*, August 26, 1915.

'Mr Balfour's Gifford Lectures', *The British Weekly*, October 7, 1915.

'The Constraint of the Cross', *The British Weekly*, March 30, 1916.

'Shall He Find Faith?', *The British Weekly*, April 6, 1916.

'Conscience', *The British Weekly*, July 13, 1916.

'After the War', *The British Weekly*, August 17, 1916.

'State Purchase', *The British Weekly*, January 18, 1917.

'Burns and Present Distress', *The Glasgow Herald*, January 25, 1917.

'Prohibition', *The British Weekly*, February 15, 1917.

NOTES

I

1. Mackintosh, H. R., 'Principal James Denney as a Theologian', *The Expository Times*, Vol. XXVIII, No. 11—Aug. 1917, p. 493.
2. Quoted by Macgregor, W. M., *Persona and Ideals*, p. 22.
3. Op. cit., pp. 493-4.
4. Op. cit., pp. 13-14.
5. It was during this time, in 1885, that he published his first work, a searching and trenchant review of Henry Drummond's *Natural Law in the Spiritual World* bearing the title *On 'Natural Law in the Spiritual World' by a Brother of the Natural Man*.
6. *What is the Faith ?*, pp. 11-12.
7. The original edition in German, entitled *Das Wesen des Christentums*, was published in 1900. The first English translation was in 1901.
8. Op. cit., p. 489.
9. *The Union Magazine* was published from January, 1901 through February, 1904. In July of that year Hodder and Stoughton took over its publication under the new title *The United Free Church Magazine*, which continued until August, 1906.
10. 'Appreciation', *Letters of Principal James Denney to W. Robertson Nicoll, 1893-1917*, pp. xxiii-xxiv, xxvi.
11. In a personal letter to Wm. Robertson Nicoll dated November 25, 1920, made available through the courtesy of Lady C. Robertson Nicoll.
12. Thurneysen, Edward, *Zwischen den Zeiten*, 1927, p. 513.

II

1. Quoted by James Moffatt, 'Introduction', *Letters of Principal James Denney to His Family and Friends*, pp. xii-xiii.
2. *The Death of Christ*, p. viii.
3. See Footnote no. 1.
4. *The Expositor*, June 1901, pp. 440.
5. Quoted by George Jackson, *Reasonable Religion*, p. 211.
6. *Letters to Family and Friends*, pp. 69-70.
7. *Recollections*, p. 47.
8. Quoted by Alexander Gammie, *Preachers I Have Heard*, p. 163.
9. *The Death of Christ*, p. 283.
10. Robertson, J. A., 'Memories of a Student', *Letters of Principal James Denney to W. Robertson Nicoll*, p. xxxiii.
11. Quoted by T. H. Walker, *Principal James Denney, D.D.—A Memoir and a Tribute*, p. 25.
12. *Reasonable Religion*, p. 211.
13. *The Death of Christ*, p. 314.
14. *The Expositor*, December 1897, pp. 429, 432.

15. *The Christian Doctrine of Reconciliation*, pp. 26-27.
16. *Jesus and the Gospel*, pp. 375-6.
17. *The Expositor*, January 1913, p. 28.
18. Ibid., December 1897, p. 424.
19. Robertson, op. cit., p. xxxii.
20. *The Expositor*, December 1897, p. 426.
21. *Studies in Theology*, p. 17.
22. *Letters to Family and Friends*, p. 109.
23. *The Expositor*, December 1897, p. 427.
24. *The Atonement and the Modern Mind*, p. 38.
25. *The Way Everlasting*, pp. 2, 4.
26. *Letters to W. Robertson Nicoll*, p. 80.
27. *The Expositor*, December 1897, p. 430.
28. *The Way Everlasting*, pp. 274, 275.
29. *The United Free Church Magazine*, November 1904, p. 22.
30. Walker, op. cit., p. 87.
31. *Letters to Family and Friends*, pp. 53-54.
32. Op. cit., p. 14.
33. Quoted by Robertson, op. cit., p. xxxvi.
34. *The Way Everlasting*, p. 271.
35. Ibid., p. 273.
36. *The Union Magazine*, August 1902, p. 343.
37. Op. cit., 489.
38. Smith, D. B., in a personal letter to the writer.
39. Jeffrey, George Johnstone, 'In Praise of James Denney', *The Evening Citizen*, Glasgow, October 8, 1938.
40. Quoted by Walker, op. cit., p. 63.
41. Quoted by Philip W. Lilley, in a personal letter to the writer.
42. Recalled by W. H. Hamilton, in a conference with the writer.
43. Jeffrey, op. cit.
44. Reith, George M., *Reminiscences of the United Free Church General Assembly*, p. 195.
45. *Proceedings and Debates of the General Assembly of the United Free Church of Scotland*, 1913, p. 267.
46. Quoted by Alexander Borland, in a personal letter to the writer.
47. Quoted by Reinhold Niebuhr, *The Nature and Destiny of Man*, Vol. II, *Human Destiny*, p. 117.
48. Peake, A. S., *Recollections and Appreciations*, p. 145.
49. *Studies in Theology*, p. 1.
50. Ibid., p. 2.
51. Ibid., p. 10.
52. Ibid., p. 16-17.
53. *The Way Everlasting*, p. 28.
54. Quoted by Moffatt, op. cit., p. 153.
55. See Mackintosh, op. cit., p. 490.
56. *Letters to Family and Friends*, p. 80.
57. Ibid., p. 73.
58. Ibid., p. 81,

59. *The Union Magazine,* June 1903, p. 261.
60. The reviewer was Bruce M. Metzger, Professor of New Testament Language and Literature in Princeton Theological Seminary, and the review appears in the *Princeton Seminary Bulletin,* Vol. XLVIII, May 1955, pp. 56-57.
61. In a personal letter to William Robertson Nicoll, dated November 16, 1920, made available by the courtesy of Lady C. Robertson Nicoll.
62. *The Union Magazine,* January 1902, p. 23.
63. *The Expositor,* December 1897, p. 438.
64. Quoted by Adam W. Burnet, *Pleading with Men,* p. 162.
65. Quoted by Macgregor, op. cit., p. 17.
66. *The Union Magazine,* June 1903, p. 261.
67. Quoted by Alexander Borland, in a personal letter to the writer.
68. *The Christian Doctrine of Reconciliation,* p. 84.
69. Quoted by Moffatt, op. cit., p. xii.
70. *Letters to W. Robertson Nicoll,* p. 6.
71. *Letters to Family and Friends,* p. 144.
72. *The Union Magazine,* September 1902, p. 417.
73. Quoted by Macgregor, op. cit., p. 15.
74. For some examples of this grouping together of Denney and Forsyth, see Wilhelm Vollrath, *Theologie de Gegenwart in Grossbritannien,* pp. 273, 284-85; John Dickie, *Fifty Years of British Theology,* pp. 97, 99, 100; J. K. Mozley, *Some Tendencies in British Theology,* pp. 34, 45, 131; A. M. Hunter, *Interpreting the New Testament,* p. 125.
75. *Letters to W. Robertson Nicoll,* p. 97.
76. Ibid., p. 165. The book was *Missions in State and Church.*
77. *The Expository Times,* June 1949, p. 240.
78. Ferguson, A. W., *The Dundee Advertiser,* November 23, 1920.

III

1. *Studies in Theology,* p. 109.
2. *The Atonement and the Modern Mind,* pp. 1-2.
3. *Studies in Theology,* p. 109.
4. *The Death of Christ,* pp. 15-16.
5. Ibid., p. 20.
6. Ibid., p. 21.
7. e.g. Mark 2.19 f.; 3.6, 20-30; 9.12-13.
8. *The Death of Christ,* p. 31.
9. Ibid., p. 32.
10. Ibid., p. 43.
11. Ibid., p. 45.
12. Ibid., p. 55.
13. Ibid., p. 56.
14. *Studies in Theology,* p. 123.
15. *The Death of Christ,* p. 75.
16. There are similar expressions of the divine necessity in 3.18, 4.1, 4.28.
17. *The Death of Christ,* pp. 80, 81.

18. cf. 3.13, 4.27, 5.35.
19. *The Death of Christ*, pp. 35-36.
20. cf. 2.38, 3.19, 5.31, 10.43.
21. *The Way Everlasting*, p. 147.
22. *The Death of Christ*, p. 97.
23. Ibid., p. 99.
24. Ibid., p. 90.
25. Ibid., p. 100.
26. Ibid., p. 111.
27. Ibid., p. 109.
28. Ibid., p. 123.
29. *Studies in Theology*, p. 132.
30. *Expositor's Greek Testament* (Rom. 3.21); *The Death of Christ* pp. 164f.
31. *The Death of Christ*, p. 166.
32. In Romans 1.17-18.
33. *The Christian Doctrine of Reconciliation*, p. 142.
34. Ibid., p. 148.
35. *The Death of Christ*, p. 128.
36. Gal. 2.20.
37. *The Death of Christ*, p. 126.
38. *Ibid.*, p. 133.
39. *The Second Epistle to the Corinthians*, p. 195.
40. *The Christian Doctrine of Reconciliation*, pp. 157, 158.
41. *The Death of Christ*, pp. 146-7.
42. *The Christian Doctrine of Reconciliation*, p. 163.
43. *The Death of Christ*, p. 187.
44. Ibid., p. 137.
45. Ibid., p. 213.
46. Ibid., p. 215.
47. Ibid., p. 208.
48. Ibid., p. 227.
49. Ibid., p. 234.
50. *The Christian Doctrine of Reconciliation*, p. 173.
51. *The Death of Christ*, p. 239.
52. Ibid., p. 244.
53. Ibid., p. 259.
54. Ibid., p. 276.
55. *Studies in Theology*, p. 124.

IV

1. *The Christian Doctrine of Reconciliation*, p. 162.
2. Mackintosh, op. cit., p. 491.
3. *The British Weekly*, June 21, 1917.
4. *Studies in Theology*, p. 19.
5. *The Christian Doctrine of Reconciliation*, p. 6.
6. *The Death of Christ*, p. 280.

7. *The Atonement and the Modern Mind*, p. 11.
8. *Studies in Theology*, pp. 106, 108.
9. *The Death of Christ*, p. 248.
10. *Studies in Theology*, p. 102.
11. Ibid., p. 74.
12. Ibid., p. 79.
13. *The Atonement and the Modern Mind*, p. 45.
14. Ibid., p. 47.
15. Ibid., p. 49.
16. *The Christian Doctrine of Reconciliation*, p. 185.
17. Ibid.
18. *Studies in Theology*, pp. 83-84.
19. *The Christian Doctrine of Reconciliation*, p. 190.
20. Rom. 1.28.
21. *The Atonement and the Modern Mind*, p. 58.
22. *The Christian Doctrine of Reconciliation*, p. 191.
23. *Studies in Theology*, p. 86.
24. Ibid., p. 91.
25. *The Christian Doctrine of Reconciliation*, p. 195.
26. *The Atonement and the Modern Mind*, p. 60.
27. *Letters to Family and Friends*, p. 147.
28. *Studies in Theology*, p. 85.
29. *The Christian Doctrine of Reconciliation*, p. 199.
30. *Studies in Theology*, p. 99.
31. *The Atonement and the Modern Mind*, p. 66.
32. Ibid., p. 68.
33. *Studies in Theology*, p. 103.
34. Psalm 5.4.
35. *The Epistle to the Thessalonians*, p. 62.
36. *The Christian Doctrine of Reconciliation*, p. 233.
37. *The Atonement and the Modern Mind*, p. 15.
38. *The Christian Doctrine of Reconciliation*, p. 17.
39. Ibid.
40. *The Atonement and the Modern Mind*, p. 94.
41. *The Christian Doctrine of Reconciliation*, p. 162.
42. *Studies in Theology*, p. 103-104.
43. *The Atonement and the Modern Mind*, p. 94.
44. *The Christian Doctrine of Reconciliation*, p. 278.
45. Quoted by W. H. Hamilton in a conference with the writer.
46. *The Death of Christ*, p. 103.
47. *The Christian Doctrine of Reconciliation*, p. 160.
48. *The Death of Christ*, pp. 177-8.
49. *The Expositor's Greek Testament*, p. 613a.
50. *Studies in Theology*, p. 116.
51. *The Epistles to the Thessalonians*, pp. 15-16.
52. *The Way Everlasting*, pp. 303-304.
53. Ibid.
54. Ibid., pp. 24, 25.

55. *The Second Epistle to the Corinthians*, p. 221.
56. Recalled by many, among them, Robert McKinlay in Walker, op. cit., p. 71.
57. Ibid.
58. *The Christian Doctrine of Reconciliation*, p. 236.
59. Ibid., p. 237.
60. Ibid., p. 239.
61. Ibid., p. 235.
62. Ibid., pp. 289-90.
63. *The Way Everlasting*, pp. 266, 267.
64. *The Christian Doctrine of Reconciliation*, p. 291.
65. *The Way Everlasting*, p. 267.
66. Ibid., p. 266.
67. *The Atonement and the Modern Mind*, pp. 88-89.
68. *The Way Everlasting*, p. 226.
69. *The Christian Doctrine of Reconciliation*, p. 164.
70. Op. cit., p. 493.

V

1. *Jesus and the Gospel*, p. ix.
2. *Studies in Theology*, p. 24.
3. Ibid., p. 17.
4. *The Death of Christ*, p. 317.
5. Ibid., pp. 319, 320.
6. Ibid., pp. 324, 325.
7. Ibid., p. 327.
8. Ibid., p. 295.
9. *The Atonement and the Modern Mind*, pp. 108, 109.
10. *The Death of Christ*, p. 320.
11. *Jesus and the Gospel*, p. 15.
12. Ibid.
13. Ibid., p. 20.
14. Ibid., p. 24.
15. Cf. I Cor. 15.28.
16. *Jesus and the Gospel*, p. 30.
17. Ibid., p. 37.
18. Ibid., p. 43.
19. Ibid., p. 49.
20. Ibid., p. 52.
21. Ibid., p. 57.
22. Ibid., p. 58.
23. Ibid., p. 60.
24. Ibid., p. 62.
25. Ibid., p. 79.
26. Ibid., p. 82.
27. Ibid., p. 86.
28. Ibid., p. 89.
29. Ibid., p. 91.

30. Ibid., p. 100.
31. *Studies in Theology*, pp. 17-18.
32. *Dictionary of Christ and the Gospels*, Vol. II, p. 393.
33. *Studies in Theology*, pp. 48-49.
34. *Jesus and the Gospel*, p. 101.
35. *Studies in Theology*, pp. 50-51.
36. *The Encyclopaedia of Religion and Ethics*, Vol. VIII, p. 517.
37. *Dictionary of Christ and the Gospels*, Vol. II, p. 402.
38. *Studies in Theology*, pp. 69-70.
39. Quoted by Robertson, op. cit., pp. xxxvi-xxxvii.
40. *Studies in Theology*, p. 68.
41. *Standard Bible Dictionary*, p. 423.
42. See Chapter 2, pp. 32f.
43. *Jesus and the Gospel*, p. 103.
44. The primary treatment of the theme is to be found in *Jesus and the Gospel*, Book II, pp. 159-371, and it is sketched in shorter form in his two articles 'Authority of Christ' and 'Preaching Christ' in the *Dictionary of Christ and the Gospels*; it is touched upon in *The Atonement and the Modern Mind*, pp. 30 ff., and in the *Standard Bible Dictionary*, pp. 415 ff.
45. *Jesus and the Gospel*, p. 203.
46. Ibid., p. 206.
47. Ibid., p. 213.
48. Ibid., p. 219.
49. Mark 6.7-13.
50. *Jesus and the Gospel*, p. 228.
51. Ibid., p. 231.
52. Ibid., pp. 238-9.
53. Ibid., pp. 243-4.
54. *Dictionary of Christ and the Gospels*, Vol. I, p. 146.
55. *Studies in Theology*, p. 28.
56. *Standard Bible Dictionary*, p. 415.
57. *Jesus and the Gospel*, p. 292.
58. Ibid., p. 298.
59. Ibid.
60. Ibid., p. 307.
61. *Standard Bible Dictionary*, p. 412.
62. *Jesus and the Gospel*, p. 323.
63. Ibid.
64. Ibid., p. 330.
65. Ibid., p. 358.
66. Ibid., p. 365-6.
67. Ibid., p. ix.
68. Ibid., p. 382.
69. Ibid.
70. Ibid., p. 383.
71. Ibid., p. 380.
72. *The Expositor*, December 1897, p. 425.
73. *Studies in Theology*, pp. 45, 46.

VI

1. See note no. 3.
2. *Studies in Theology*, p. 154.
3. Ibid.
4. *Jesus and the Gospel*, p. 107.
5. *Studies in Theology*, p. 154.
6. Ibid., p. 153.
7. *Jesus and the Gospel*, pp. 107-108.
8. Cf. *What Is Christianity ?*, pp. 101 f.
9. *Jesus and the Gospel*, pp. 111-12.
10. Ibid., p. 113.
11. Ibid.
12. Ibid., pp. 117-18.
13. Ibid., p. 120.
14. Ibid., p. 121.
15. Ibid., pp. 122-3.
16. Ibid., p. 125.
17. Ibid.
18. Ibid., 131.
19. Ibid., 133.
20. I Cor. 15.14.
21. I Cor. 15.18.
22. I Cor. 15.19.
23. *Jesus and the Gospel*, pp. 135-6.
24. Ibid., pp. 137-8.
25. Ibid., p. 146.
26. Ibid., p. 153.
27. Ibid., p. 156.
28. Ibid., p. 158.
29. *The Death of Christ*, p. 67.
30. *The Atonement and the Modern Mind*, p. 112.
31. *The Christian Doctrine of Reconciliation*, p. 287.
32. *The Death of Christ*, p. 272.
33. *Studies in Theology*, p. 169.
34. *Dictionary of the Bible* (ed. J. Hastings), Vol. I, p. 161.
35. *Studies in Theology*, p. 170.
36. Ibid.
37. Ibid., p. 171.
38. Ibid., p. 172.
39. Ibid., p. 162. Cf. Rom. 8.29 f., Heb. 7.25, I John 2.1.
40. Ibid., p. 168.

VII

1. *The Expositor*, May 1908, p. 422.
2. *Studies in Theology*, p. 162.
3. *Dictionary of Christ and the Gospels*, Vol. I, p. 731.
4. *Studies in Theology*, p. 156.
5. *Standard Bible Dictionary*, p. 409.

6. *Dictionary of Christ and the Gospels*, Vol. I, p. 732.
7. Ibid.
8. Ibid.
9. Ibid.
10. Mark 3.30-35; Mat. 12.22-32.
11. *Dictionary of Christ and the Gospels*, Vol. I, p. 733.
12. Ibid., p. 734.
13. Ibid., p. 736.
14. Ibid., p. 737.
15. Ibid.
16. Ibid.
17. Ibid., p. 738.
18. Ibid.
19. *The Christian Doctrine of Reconciliation*, pp. 166, 169.
20. *Dictionary of Christ and the Gospels*, Vol. I, p. 738.
21. Ibid., p. 739.
22. *The Expositor*, December 1901, p. 432.
23. *Dictionary of Christ and the Gospels*, Vol. I, p. 740.
24. Ibid.
25. Ibid., p. 741.
26. Ibid., p. 742.
27. Ibid.
28. Ibid., p. 743.
29. Ibid.
30. Ibid.
31. *Studies in Theology*, p. 157.
32. *The Death of Christ*, p. 193.
33. *Dictionary of Christ and the Gospels*, Vol. I, p. 744.
34. *Jesus and the Gospel*, pp. 400-401.
35. See *Jesus and the Gospel*, pp. 398-401.
36. *Dictionary of Christ and the Gospels*, Vol. I, p. 738.
37. *Encyclopaedia of Religion and Ethics*, Vol. X, p. 789.
38. Ibid.
39. *Studies in Theology*, p. 159.
40. Ibid.
41. Ibid.
42. Ibid., p. 160.
43. *The Expositor*, May 1908, p. 422.
44. *Studies in Theology*, p. 71.
45. *Dictionary of Christ and the Gospels*, Vol. I, p. 744.

VIII

1. Quoted by Adam Burnet, op. cit., p. 102. The reference was to J. P. Struthers.
2. *Studies in Theology*, pp. 202-203.
3. *The Death of Christ*, pp. 313-14.
4. *Studies in Theology*, p. 204.
5. *The London Quarterly Review*, July 1904, p. 8.

6. *The Death of Christ*, pp. 314-15.
7. Ibid., p. 314.
8. Ibid., p. 317.
9. *The Christian Doctrine of Reconciliation*, pp. 123-4.
10. *Letters to W. Robertson Nicoll*, p. 20.
11. *The Death of Christ*, p. 282.
12. Ibid., p. 3.
13. Quoted by Graham Park, from notes taken in class, to the writer.
14. *The Death of Christ*, p. 282.
15. Quoted by Walker, op. cit., p. 73.
16. *The Christian Doctrine of Reconciliation*, p. 9.
17. *The Way Everlasting*, p. 271.
18. *The Atonement and the Modern Mind*, pp. 7-8.
19. Ibid., p. 8.
20. Ibid., p. 9.
21. *The Expositor*, December 1897, p. 429.
22. *Letters to W. Robertson Nicoll*, p. 86.
23. *Letters to Family and Friends*, pp. 150-1.
24. Quoted by Adam Burnet, op. cit., p. 102.
25. *Studies in Theology*, p. 205.
26. Quoted by Moffatt, in *Letters to Family and Friends*, p. 23.
27. Quoted by P. C. Simpson, *The Life of Principal Rainy*, II, p. 115.
28. Reported by Walker, op. cit., p. 91.
29. *The Epistle to the Thessalonians*, p. 177.
30. *Studies in Theology*, p. 213.
31. *The British Weekly*, August 14, 1913.
32. See Walker, op. cit., pp. 89 ff., for an account of the debate.
33. Cf. *Wm. Robertson Nicoll—Life and Letters*, pp. 348-50.
34. *Letters to W. R. Nicoll*, p. 44.
35. *The British Weekly*, December 3, 1908.
36. *Letters to W. R. Nicoll*, p. 220. The reference is to Charles Foster Kent.
37. Ibid., p. 111. The reference is to Alfred F. Coivy's work on the Synoptic Gospels.
38. Ibid., p. 150. The reference is to the book *The Thousand and One Churches*, by Sir William Ramsay and Miss Gertrude Bell, 1909.
39. Ibid., p. 120. The reference is to J. Warschauer, *Jesus: Seven Questions*, 1908.
40. Ibid., p, 183. The reference is to Benjamin W. Bacon.
41. Ibid., p. 22-23. The reference is to P. W. Schmiedel.
42. Quoted by Moffatt, 'Principal Denney', *The British Weekly*, June 21, 1917.
43. *Studies in Theology*, p. 213.
44. *The British Weekly*, April 18, 1907.
45. *Letters to W. R. Nicoll*, p. 171.
46. *The British Weekly*, November 13, 1902.
47. *Letters to W. R. Nicoll*, pp. 23-24.
48. *The Death of Christ*, p. 8.

49. *The British Weekly*, November 13, 1902.
50. *Studies in Theology*, p. 206.
51. Ibid., p. 207.
52. *Jesus and the Gospel*, pp. 56-57.
53. Ibid., p. 163.
54. *Letters to W. R. Nicoll*, p. 174.
55. *Jesus and the Gospel*, p. 11.
56. *The Sermon on the Mount*, pp. 27-28, 30-31.
57. *Letters to W. R. Nicoll*, p. 71.
58. *The Expositor*, August 1911, p. 120.
59. *The Expositor*, September 1911, p. 227.
60. *Dictionary of Christ and the Gospels*, Vol. I, p. 744.
61. *Studies in Theology*, p. 208.
62. Ibid.
63. Recalled by D. B. Smith, in a personal letter to the writer.
64. Quoted by Hunter, op. cit.
65. *The Union Magazine*, January 1903, p. 34.
66. Ibid., p. 36.
67. *The Christian Doctrine of Reconciliation*, pp. 122-3.
68. Ibid., p. 124.
69. *Studies in Theology*, p. 215.
70. *Encyclopaedia of Religion and Ethics*, Vol. V, p. 702.
71. *Studies in Theology*, p. 219.
72. *The Union Magazine*, January 1903, p. 35.
73. *Studies in Theology*, p. 224.
74. *The Death of Christ*, pp. 75-76.
75. Cf. *Dictionary of the Bible* (Hastings), Vol. I, pp. 516-17; *Dictionary of Christ and the Gospel*, Vol. II, pp. 399-400.
76. Cf. e.g., *Dictionary of the Bible* (Hastings), Vol. I, p. 37.
77. *Letters to Family and Friends*, p. 15.
78. *Jesus and the Gospel*, p. 21.
79. Ibid., p. 42.
80. *The Christian Doctrine of Reconciliation*, p. 179.
81. Quoted by F. F. Barbour, *The Life of Alexander Whyte*, pp. 508-509.
82. *The Christian Doctrine of Reconciliation*, pp. 179-80.
83. *The Death of Christ*, p. 203.
84. Ibid., p. 86.
85. *Jesus and the Gospel*, p. 43.
86. Ibid., pp. 43-44.
87. *The Death of Christ*, p. 235.
88. *The British Weekly*, January 5, 1911.
89. *Dictionary of the Bible* (Hastings), Vol. III, p. 82. Luther called the work 'an epistle of straw'.
90. Ibid.
91. *The Death of Christ*, p. 264.
92. *Encyclopaedia of Religion and Ethics*, Vol. VIII, p. 518.
93. John 16.12-15.

94. *Jesus and the Gospel*, p. 88.
95. *The Death of Christ*, p. 242.
96. *Jesus and the Gospel*, p. 89.
97. *The Union Magazine*, January 1905, p. 13.
98. *The Atonement and the Modern Mind*, p. 10.

IX

1. *The Church and the Kingdom*, pp. 51-52.
2. *Proceedings and Debates of the G.A., U.F. Church of Scotland*, 1912, p. 165.
3. *Letters to W. R. Nicoll*, p. 127.
4. *Studies in Theology*, p. 181.
5. Ibid., p. 175.
6. *Standard Bible Dictionary*, p. 413.
7. Ibid.
8. *Studies in Theology*, pp. 176-7.
9. Ibid., p. 185.
10. Ibid., p. 186.
11. Ibid., pp. 186-7.
12. Ibid., p. 188.
13. Ibid., pp. 188, 189.
14. Quoted by Walker, op. cit., p. 137. The minister is identified by several as Dr John White.
15. *Studies in Theology*, p. 195.
16. Ibid., pp. 194, 195.
17. *Jesus and the Gospel*, p. 398.
18. Ibid., p. 409.
19. Ibid., p. 410-11.
20. Quoted by Moffatt, op. cit., p. ix.
21. *The Way Everlasting*, p. 102.
22. *Letters to W. R. Nicoll*, p. 207.
23. Ibid., p. 157.
24. *Studies in Theology*, p. 198.
25. *The Church and the Kingdom*, p. 7.
26. Ibid., pp. 10-11.
27. Ibid., p. 8.
28. Ibid., p. 11.
29. *Letters to Family and Friends*, p. 102.
30. *The Death of Christ*, pp. 103-104.
31. *The Church and the Kingdom*, p. 27.
32. *The Way Everlasting*, pp. 104-105.
33. *Studies in Theology*, p. 127.
34. Ibid., p. 128.
35. *The Death of Christ*, p. 283.
36. *The Church and the Kingdom*, pp. 15-16.
37. Ibid., pp. 19-20.
38. *The Way Everlasting*, pp. 60-61.
39. *The Church and the Kingdom*, p. 29.

40. Ibid., p. 31.
41. *Gospel Questions and Answers*, p. 128.
42. *The Death of Christ*, pp. 310-11.
43. Ibid., p. 289.
44. *Letters to W. R. Nicoll*, p. 173.
45. *The British Weekly*, December 9, 1909.
46. Quoted by James Black, *The Mystery of Preaching*, p. 80.
47. *Letters to Family and Friends*, pp. 97-98.
48. Quoted by Burnet, op. cit., p. 152.
49. Quoted in the article, 'A Character Sketch of Rev. Professor James Denney, D.D.', *The British Weekly*, Vol. XLII, April 11, 1907, p. 14.
50. Quoted by Burnet, op. cit., p. 148.
51. Black, op. cit., pp. 116-17.
52. Quoted by Gammie, Alexander, op. cit., p. 162.
53. Quoted by Black, op. cit., p. 122.
54. *Letters to Family and Friends*, p. 202.
55. Quoted by Burnet, op. cit., p. 143.
56. Sermon at the funeral of A. D. Grant, quoted in *The Greenock Telegraph and Clyde Shipping Gazette*, February 2, 1914.
57. Quoted by Alexander Borland, in a personal letter to the writer.
58. Quoted by J. Christian Brown, in conference with the writer.
59. Quoted by Walker, op. cit., p. 149.
60. *Letters to Family and Friends*, p. 132.
61. Quoted by Moffatt, op. cit., p. viii.
62. *Dictionary of Christ and the Gospels*, Vol. II, p. 402.
63. *The London Quarterly Review*, July 1904, p. 11.
64. *Letters to Family and Friends*, p. 66.
65. *Studies in Theology*, p. 161.
66. *The Christian Doctrine of Reconciliation*, p. 8.
67. *The Death of Christ*, p. 84.
68. Ibid.
69. Ibid., p. 85.
70. *The Death of Christ*, p. 137.
71. *Standard Bible Dictionary*, p. 409.
72. Quoted by Robert McKinlay, in Walker, op. cit., pp. 71-72.
73. *The Way Everlasting*, p. 110.

X

1. *Studies in Theology*, p. 240.
2. Ibid., pp. 239-40.
3. *The Way Everlasting*, p. 145.
4. *The Expositor*, February 1904, p. 160.
5. *Letters to W. R. Nicoll*, p. 41.
6. *The Church and the Kingdom*, p. 61.
7. *The Christian Doctrine of Reconciliation*, p. 316.
8. Quoted by Robertson, op. cit., p. xxxv.
9. *Factors of Faith in Immortality*, pp. 88-89, 90

10. *Letters to Family and Friends*, p. 187.

11. *Factors of Faith in Immortality*, pp. 69-70.

12. Ibid., pp. 74-75.

13. Ibid., p. 76.

14. *Studies in Theology*, p. 240.

15. Ibid., p. 229.

16. Ibid., p. 42.

17. Ibid., p. 240.

18. Ibid.

19. *The Church and the Kingdom*, p. 78.

20. *The Sermon on the Mount*, p. 51.

21. *The Dictionary of Christ and the Gospels*, Vol. I, p. 62.

22. *The Church and the Kingdom*, p. 70.

23. *The Expositor's Greek Testament*, Vol. II, p. 635.

24. *The Way Everlasting*, pp. 239-40.

25. Quoted by Moffatt, *Letters to Family and Friends*, p. ix.

26. Sermon at the funeral of A. D. Grant, quoted in *The Greenock Telegraph and Clyde Shipping Gazette*, February 2, 1914.

27. *The Epistles to the Thessalonians*, p. 280.

28. *Letters to Family and Friends*, p. 140.

29. *The Christian Doctrine of Reconciliation*, p. 171.

30. *Jesus and the Gospel*, p. 341.

31. *The Death of Christ*, p. 250.

32. *The British Weekly*, August 18, 1910.

33. Quoted by Walker, op. cit., p. 131.

34. Cf. Robertson, op. cit., p. xlii; Walker, op. cit., p. 149.

35. *Letters to W. R. Nicoll*, p. 123.

36. *Studies in Theology*, pp. 200-201.

37. *Letters to W. R. Nicoll*, p. 137.

38. *The Church and the Kingdom*, p. 105.

39. *William Robertson Nicoll, Life and Letters*, p. 364.

40. *Jesus and the Gospel*, p. 370.

41. *Studies in Theology*, p. 239.

42. Ibid.

43. *Standard Bible Dictionary*, p. 414.

44. *Studies in Theology*, p. 238.

45. Ibid., pp. 42-43.

46. *Encyclopaedia of Religion and Ethics*, Vol. X, p. 790.

47. *Standard Bible Dictionary*, p. 420.

48. *Studies in Theology*, p. 246.

49. Ibid.

50. Ibid., pp. 246-7.

51. Ibid., pp. 255-6.

52. Ibid., p. 21.